D1195998

Reading Shakespeare
in Performance: *King Lear*

Reading Shakespeare in Performance: *King Lear*

James P. Lusardi and June Schlueter

Rutherford ● Madison ● Teaneck
Fairleigh Dickinson University Press
London and Toronto: Associated University Presses

Associated University Presses
440 Forsgate Drive
Cranbury, NJ 08512

Associated University Presses
25 Sicilian Avenue
London WC1A 2QH, England

Associated University Presses
P.O. Box 39, Clarkson Pstl. Stn.
Mississauga, Ontario,
L5J 3X9   Canada

The paper used in this publication meets the requirements
of the American National Standard for Permanence of Paper
for Printed Library Materials Z39.48-1984.

Library of Congress Cataloging-in-Publication Data

Lusardi, James P.
    Reading Shakespeare in performance : King Lear / James P. Lusardi,
June Schlueter.
        p.   cm.
    Includes bibliographical references.
    ISBN 0-8386-3394-3 (alk. paper)
    1. Shakespeare, William, 1564–1616. King Lear. 2. Shakespeare,
William, 1564–1616—Dramatic production. 3. Lear, King (Legendary
character), in literature. I. Schlueter, June. II. Title.
PR2819.L8   1991
822.3'3—dc20
                                                              89-46412
                                                              CIP

PRINTED IN THE UNITED STATES OF AMERICA

To William W. Watt

PROFESSOR OF ENGLISH EMERITUS

LAFAYETTE COLLEGE

Contents

A Note about Texts   9
Acknowledgments   11
Introduction   15

1. Cordelia's Plight: 1.1   23
2. The Wicked Sisters: 1.4 and 2.4   61
3. The Mock Trial: 3.6   91
4. Dover Cliff: 4.6   105
5. The Anonymous Captain: 5.3   122
6. The Promised End: 5.3   135
Conclusion   158

Notes   160
Cast and Production Teams   167
Works Cited   169
Appendix on the BBC and Granada Productions
    of *King Lear*: Production Commentary and a Select
    Bibliography of Reviews   172
Index   241

A Note about Texts

All references to Shakespeare's plays are taken from David Bevington, ed., *The Complete Works of Shakespeare*, 3d ed. (Glenview, Ill.: Scott, Foresman, 1980). Bevington uses the Folio (1623) for his copy text of *King Lear*, introducing Quarto (1608) only readings in brackets; in citing Bevington's edition, we ignore the brackets but frequently take notice of variations between Folio and Quarto.

References to the Quarto text are taken from Michael J. B. Allen and Kenneth Muir, eds., *Shakespeare's Plays in Quarto: A Facsimile Edition of Copies Primarily from the Henry E. Huntington Library* (Berkeley: University of California Press, 1981). References to the Folio are taken from Charlton Hinman, ed., *The Norton Facsimile: The First Folio of Shakespeare* (London: Paul Hamlyn; New York: W.W. Norton, 1968).

Acknowledgments

Our conversation on Shakespeare in performance has, over the years, involved a host of colleagues. Among the many academics with whom we have had ongoing exchanges are Harry Keyishian, Alan C. Dessen, Maurice Charney, Michael Goldman, Bernice W. Kliman, Margaret Loftus Ranald, Cary Mazer, and Elaine and Charles Hallett. We had the opportunity to test a number of our assumptions in an NEH Summer Seminar we directed at Lafayette College, in an "Activating Shakespeare" workshop at Fairleigh Dickinson University, in an NEH Seminar at Nassau County Community College, at the annual meetings of the Shakespeare Association of America and the international congress in Berlin, and at the Columbia University Seminar on Shakespeare. Moreover, as co-editors of *Shakespeare Bulletin*, a journal of performance criticism and scholarship, we have been part of the community of scholars who recognize Shakespeare as a man of the theater.

Over the years, our interest in theater has put us in touch with actors and other theater professionals who have also contributed to the discourse. Chief among these are Si Isenberg, John Kane, Jenny Stoller, David Rintoul, John Burgess, Chris Ravenscroft, and Patrick Stewart. Several of these, whom we originally met through the ACTER program, have participated in a January London Theater course we regularly mount for Lafayette students. Seeing close to a hundred plays a year has provided us with a production vocabulary for most of Shakespeare's plays; we draw upon that vocabulary in this study and in our forthcoming companion volume on *Hamlet*.

As we worked on this book, we had the continuing support of the reference librarians at Skillman Library, Lafayette College. Lafayette College provided us both with sabbatical leaves, during which we accomplished much of our writing; with funds for research and publications costs; and with a faculty development stipend that permitted us to mount and team-teach a course at Lafayette College on Shakespeare in performance.

As director of Fairleigh Dickinson University Press, Harry

Keyishian deserves special thanks, not only for his encourage-
ment and insights but for his continuing commitment to developing a line of high quality drama books. Sidney Homan, who
read the manuscript and offered valuable comments, also has
our thanks, as does Paul Schlueter, who prepared the index
and offered support throughout.

For permission to reprint production photos, we acknowledge
the British Broadcasting Corporation and Granada Television
Limited. Special thanks go to Margaret Kirby, photo librarian
at the BBC, and Kathryn de Belle of Granada TV. For permission
to reprint the essays in the appendix, we acknowledge Henry
Fenwick; *Theatre Crafts*, Theatre Crafts Associates; Peter Cowie,
Sight and Sound, British Film Institute; *The New York Times*;
Shakespeare Bulletin (formerly *Bulletin of the New York Shake-
speare Society*); Bernice W. Kliman and Kenneth Rothwell,
editors of *Shakespeare on Film Newsletter*; *Literature/Film
Quarterly*; *CEA Critic*; and University Press of New England.
The chapter on the mock trial previously appeared in *Shake-
speare on Television: An Anthology of Essays and Reviews*, ed.
J. C. Bulman and H. R. Coursen (Hanover: University Press of
New England, 1988).

Reading Shakespeare
in Performance: *King Lear*

Introduction

Mingling among playgoers at the Stratford, Ontario, Shakespeare Festival a few years ago, we heard a would-be director ask, "But does it read?" The director (if he was one), listening to a proposal from a colleague on staging the storm scene in *King Lear,* was applying the visual test that for him was a touchstone. It is the same test that Maurice Charney, approaching *Hamlet* from the perspective of one trained to analyze text, speaks of in "*Hamlet* without Words." Charney, prominent among literary scholars who write about Shakespeare's plays as they might appear on stage, states the principle that our work has urged us to see as essential to any analysis of Shakespeare's plays: that we should think of the "written text and its realization in performance at one and the same time."[1]

We propose a methodology that does just that, preserving the close attention to text that the academic community prizes and exploring the range of interpretations that performance provides. We mean to bring together the too-long divided commitments of academics and theater people, in the conviction that either bias can offer only partial access to the plays. Michael Goldman, who well understands the activity in which we are engaged, puts it this way: "It is a mistake to speak as if we have a choice between a literary Shakespeare and a theatrical Shakespeare. The choice is rather between some of Shakespeare and more of him."[2]

Our approach to "more" of Shakespeare encourages mining the texts of the plays for the cues and clues that represent guideposts of meaning and directives for the stage. Though spare in stage directions, Shakespeare's plays are richly laced with prescriptions and suggestions that give insight into how Elizabethans and Jacobeans saw the plays and how modern productions might take form. At the same time, our approach acknowledges the multiple stagings a single text allows. In doing so, it discards the concept of inevitability in staging expressed by the apocryphal professor who, leaving the theater following a production of *Hamlet,* grumbled, "Four hundred years of trying, and they

15

still haven't gotten it right." Naive playgoers contribute another sense of inevitability to this unproductive discourse: seeing a production of *King Lear* for the first time, they lock themselves into that reading, unable to imagine the play any other way. If they have read the text, the production becomes a corrective to an earlier "misreading"; if they have seen the production first, that production becomes the authority informing the text and any subsequent productions they might see. Regular playgoers who understand the nature of the interpretive process, however, know that, while there will be resemblances between one production and the next, no two productions will be the same. Alan C. Dessen reports on how new the promised end of *King Lear* became when, at the 1985 Oregon Shakespearean Festival, the distraught monarch directed his final line, "Look there, look there!", not to the assembled witnesses but, through casting his eyes upward, to the heavens, in defiance.[3] And we still marvel at the new emphasis that Derek Jacobi brought to a line in the nunnery scene of the BBC *Hamlet*: shaking Ophelia with more violence than he intended, Hamlet recoils to utter in astonishment, "it *hath* made me mad." Such readings send us back to the text to rediscover that "reading" Shakespeare in the limited sense of the term, reading "words, words, words" on the page, may not reveal the multiple possibilities inscribed in the text.

As academics educated in the gospel of "fidelity" to the text, we are, of course, sympathetic to the curmudgeon professor; yet, as beneficiaries of poststructuralist revisionings of the interpretive process, we can hardly endorse such a fundamentalist approach to Shakespeare. Neither can we take the position of the deconstructionists, for whom, finally, even contingent textual meaning must disappear. More contemporary theoretical approaches that are subversive to textual meaning, while valuable in encouraging us to understand the multiple perspectives that collaborate in the production of meaning, have not succeeded in erasing the empirical evidence of the text. Language remains cultural and relational. Whatever the claimed or proclaimed political or pedagogical agenda of a text, writer and reader have access to that text by virtue of their common participation in linguistic and cultural codes. Even as we acknowledge the force of interpretive negotiation, therefore, we insist on resident textual meaning signified by verbal clues.

Language, of course, has inherent ambiguities, which may or may not have been created by an unrecoverable authorial

intention and which are surely complicated by cultural and
linguistic change. Such ambiguity confronts the reader of any
literary genre, indeed any written text. The dramatic text further
complicates reading, for—particularly with Shakespeare—the
dramatic text stands as a blueprint for production. No doubt,
production may be said to simplify text, choosing as it must
among the possibilities of meaning and making manifest only
one. In giving theatrical form to the language of the play, however, production also enriches. Finally, production creates yet
another text, a series of readings involving a dynamic between
and among author, text, director, designers, actors, and audience.
The audience, of course, while it shares linguistic and cultural
master codes, is a heterogeneous gathering of individuals, which
changes from night to night. Indeed, "audience," whether in
Shakespeare's time or ours, remains the most elusive component
in the shaping of a performance text—just as the reader does
in the shaping of a written text.

Our purpose here is not to confront reception aesthetics in
any formal sense, only to acknowledge the interactive process
that generates meaning. Like earlier critics, both formalist and
structuralist, who have adopted the strategy of assuming an
"ideal reader" despite the deficiency of the concept and their
own skepticism about it,[4] we in effect assume an "ideal audience": one capable of recognizing and responding to the visual
and aural signals that production provides. This "ideal audience" includes, on one hand, those who are intimate with the
material, who have read and perhaps taught the plays dozens
of times and seen them performed in a variety of ways; it includes, on the other, those who are "naive," who have never
read the text or seen a production of the play in question but
who nonetheless prove responsive to theatrical signs.

Finally, it is "theatrical signs," whether in the production
or the written text, that interest us. What interests us most
is the relationship between signals in the text and their translation into representation on the stage—which brings us back
to our original question. "Does it read?" Does the business on
stage—the singular and the patterned translation of written text
into performance—provide a series of coherent signals that an
"ideal audience" can read?

Our emphasis throughout this study is on contemporary production. Unlike Dessen and David Bevington, whose insights
about the relationships between text and performance are offered
mainly in service of reconstructing the Elizabethan or Jacobean

production,[5] we are concerned to treat Shakespeare as our contemporary in the sense that a "classic" playwright is always contemporary and the plays are scripts in which directors and actors may find images that speak to an audience of our time. Occasionally, we notice how an Elizabethan or Jacobean audience might have read a particular theatrical sign, and occasionally we distinguish between the reactions that members of a contemporary audience, according to their knowledge of the material, could reasonably be expected to register. But, generally, our interest is in the audience as a community of heterogeneous spectators who, within the context of Western cultural assumptions, individually and collectively participate in the process of reading theatrical signs.

Our method of reading Shakespeare in performance is essentially threefold. Like other readers, we are preoccupied with patterns and problems of meaning, but we pursue these by scrutinizing the text for the signals that may guide production. When we identify moments that represent textual and performance cruces, we analyze those moments and the sequences[6] of which they are a part to suggest possible ways of realizing them on the stage and thus of shaping and sometimes fixing meaning. We then turn to actual productions for a close look at ways in which performance has in fact staged and interpreted text.

For the purpose of this study, we concentrate on one of Shakespeare's richest plays, *King Lear*, which represents a significant challenge to readers of all kinds—in the study, on the stage, and in the theater audience. We make no claim, of course, to having said all that needs to be said about the play, nor all that we ourselves have to say. As it is, we have been painfully selective in our choice of sequences to analyze. Yet those we have selected represent paradigms for performance-oriented study, and collectively our analyses amount to a substantial exploration of the play.

We begin our discussion of *King Lear* with the enigmatic opening scene. A somewhat indulgent consideration of the problems associated with Lear's intention to set his rest on Cordelia's "kind nursery" leads us to a look at the "full agenda" of the scene, the relationship among the division of the kingdom, the love test, and Cordelia's betrothal. We then turn to two stage properties, the map and the coronet, to see how this relationship might be represented in visual form. We move on to Lear's elder daughters, exploring Peter Brook's concern with staging character when preconceptions have been established by stage tradition. The possibility that the text might not require Goneril and Regan to be wicked from the outset but might permit them to grow into evil, in their own discrete ways, takes us through a close consideration of the scenes in which Goneril (1.4) and Regan (2.4) rebuff Lear and in effect abandon their father.

The mock trial (3.6) and Dover Cliff (4.6) present special challenges to the reader, for, in the context of the interplay between Lear's fiction and Shakespeare's (the mock trial) and Edgar's fiction and Shakespeare's (Dover Cliff), implied stage directions no longer guide and realized stage images deceive. If a mad king sees his daughter in a "joint-stool," should the stool appear on stage? If Edgar labors as he and Gloucester climb the hill, should the stage represent the incline? The permutations of these two dramatic fictions, one orchestrated by a madman, the other by a man pretending to be mad and leading the blind, speak with force to the process of reading theatrical signs.

In the Anonymous Captain sequence (5.3), in which Edmund gives an attending officer the warrant for Cordelia's and Lear's deaths, we turn to the verse line, noting the pauses generated by short lines and considering opportunities for stage business, especially with Edmund's passing of the note and the Captain's receiving—and reading?—it. Decisions involving such business, though seemingly of little consequence, determine the sequence's contribution to what the play has to say about "man's work" and bestiality.

In the final sequence of King Lear, "seeing" becomes our focus, as we look at the interplay between language and stage image, at Lear's attempts to secure ocular proof that his daughter lives (a looking glass, a feather, Cordelia's lips), at verbal frames and shared verse lines, and at the audiences, both onstage and off, who witness the promised end.

As if the cruces we have mentioned were not sufficiently intriguing and daunting in themselves, the analysis of King Lear in performance involves yet another complicating circumstance. Though we have for convenience referred to the text of the play, the text (as the new Oxford edition makes manifest) does not exist in a single authoritative version.[7] As Shakespeareans know, the received text of King Lear is an artificial construction—a conflation of two originals, Quarto 1 (1608) and the Folio (1623). Even if a contemporary production purports to be uncut, therefore, unless it follows the Quarto or the Folio, which is not common practice, it is yet unlike any production that Shakespeare's audience would have seen, and it is not the play as Shakespeare wrote or rewrote it. Adopting the currently viable position that neither of the texts is to be dismissed as merely spurious and that each is likely to represent the play at stages of Shakespeare's writing, we refer to differences between the editions, noting how knowledge of these might contribute to theatrical meaning.

For the performance portion of our analysis, we have selected two productions to examine in detail: the BBC-TV production (1982), with Jonathan Miller directing and Michael Hordern in the title role, and the Granada made-for-television film (1983), directed by Michael Elliott and featuring Laurence Olivier. There are a number of other productions we might have chosen, some of which are referred to in our discussions of specific textual cruces, but we selected these two, first because they are both significant productions, second because they offer provocatively different interpretations, and third because videos and/or films of each are readily available for individual or classroom use. Admittedly, both film and television introduce conventions that differ from those of the live theater and hence from those of Shakespeare's own stage, but we see the camera and the frame as integral parts of the contemporary discussion of Shakespeare's plays and the media themselves as a boon to teaching.

We do urge our approach not only on readers of Shakespeare in performance but on teachers as well. Technology has provided us with an opportunity that could not have been dreamed of in the teaching philosophy of previous generations of Shakespeareans. With the love test in the BBC *King Lear* not only available but available for repeated viewings and for consecutive screenings, we no longer need to accept vague recollections from our students about Lear's reactions to each of his daughters' replies but can insist that the precise details of the scene be recorded, analyzed, and compared. Our own experience with teaching Shakespeare in Performance has taught us that such close reading of production is a valuable and illuminating corollary to close reading of text.

In considering the relationship between text and performance, then, we are, in effect, providing models that enable readers of Shakespeare to take their place within an audience equipped to discover the signifying details of production. As Autolycus, speaking of the profession of cutpurse, explains in *The Winter's Tale*, "To have an open ear, a quick eye, and a nimble hand is necessary for a cutpurse; a good nose is requisite also, to smell out work for the other senses" (4.4.778–801). So also are these prerequisites for the reader of Shakespeare (the nimble hand to take production notes!). Our book, in effect, provides models of discourse: how to hear, how to see, how to "smell," how to read Shakespeare in performance.

1

Cordelia's Plight: 1.1

In his still respected lectures on Shakespearean tragedy, A. C. Bradley reviews a common misconception concerning act 1, scene 1 of *King Lear*: that Lear divided his kingdom on the basis of the love test. The division of the kingdom, he points out (as Coleridge had before him), is "already settled in all its details, so that only the public announcement of it remains."[1] Bradley is relying on the opening conversation between Kent and Gloucester, in which the two express surprise at the king's not preferring Albany over Cornwall, as they thought he would. But that conversation does not mention Cordelia, for whom Lear has set aside the most opulent share. Might it be, as John Roland Dove and Peter Gamble argue, that Kent and Gloucester, with others at court, expected the kingdom to be divided not in three but in two, thinking that Cordelia's impending marriage to France or Burgundy would remove her from rule and residence in Britain?[2]

The possibility that Cordelia's inclusion in the apportionment comes as a surprise to the members of Lear's court becomes more intriguing when it is viewed in conjunction with the retiring king's living arrangements. Lear's plan to alternate residencies between Goneril and Regan is well known, for it becomes the cause shortly of his elder daughters' discontent and at length of their unkind behavior. What might have happened had Cordelia cooperated is never made clear. Bradley contends that Lear's scheme of living by months with Goneril and Regan is "forced on him at the moment by what he thinks the undutifulness of his favourite child." He points to Lear's comment to Kent as an expression of the king's original plan: "I lov'd her most, and thought to set my rest / On her kind nursery." Bradley confidently concludes, "he meant to live with Cordelia, and with her alone."[3]

Yet Cordelia is about to marry one of the two suitors at court

23

and become either Duchess of Burgundy or Queen of France. Although Lear's decision to "retain / The name, and all th' addition to a king" may not preclude his removal to the conti- nent, there is no hint in the play to suggest that such was his intent. If he did plan on remaining in Britain, the line is a puzzling one, for he could only have set his rest on Cordelia's kind nursery if Cordelia lived in Britain as well. Three sugges- tive readings of the opening scene emerge if we assume British residence, each involving a closer look at the connection be- tween Lear's division of the kingdom and Cordelia's impending marriage.

Lynda E. Boose's essay "The Father and the Bride in Shake- speare"[4] examines the tensions in the relationship between Lear and Cordelia. Approaching the scene from the perspective of ritual, Boose identifies in act 1, scene 1 an inverted marriage ritual presided over by a father who does not wish to be sepa- rated from his daughter. France and Burgundy "Long in our court have made their amorous sojourn, / And here are to be answer'd." Lear has delayed Cordelia's marriage as long as he can; now, finally, he must relinquish his youngest daughter. Or so it seems. As Boose remarks, in dividing the kingdom, Lear attaches "to Cordelia's share a stipulation designed to thwart her separation."[5] Cordelia must purchase her dowry "with pledges that would nullify those required by the wedding ceremony."[6] On the occasion in which she is to be bound to a husband, she can hardly say she "loves [her] father all." Yet that is what Lear demands, and when Cordelia does not deliver, he disinherits her. As Boose puts it, "The circularity of Lear's proposition frustrates the ritual phase of separation. . . ."[7]

The ceremony with the prospective husbands sustains the pattern. Though Lear disclaims in Cordelia "all my paternal care, / Propinquity and property of blood," yet he does not encourage her marriage. Offering her first to Burgundy, the lesser in rank of the two suitors, he not only reneges on his promise of a dowry but makes it clear that this "little seeming substance" is "new adopted to our hate, / Dower'd with our curse, and stranger'd with our oath." With France, he tries to unsell his daughter not because she is diminished in economic value but, knowing France the worthier of the two, because his love for France would not permit him to thrust this shameful wretch upon him. The astonished France refuses to reject Cordelia, however, marveling at how quickly she has fallen from her fa- ther's favor. His hope is encouraged by the intervention of Cordelia, who beseeches Lear not to represent her fault as "a vicious blot" but to identify it as merely the want of "A still-soliciting eye, and such a tongue / That I am glad I have not." After offering her once more to Burgundy, who again refuses the dowerless woman, France claims her for himself. If Lear had hoped to retain his hold on Cordelia, in spite of publicly declaring her "a stranger to my heart and me," France has thwarted his intention. Lear again disowns his daughter, as Cordelia and her intended husband prepare to leave Britain.

Viewed as "the basal structure underlying [Lear's] divestiture of his kingdom,"[8] this perversion of betrothal is profoundly subversive. Since his attempt to avoid separation from Cordelia is the impetus for his division of the kingdom, according to Boose, the division becomes the public corollary of the divestiture he cannot bear to make privately:

> In substituting his public paternity for his private one, the inherently indivisible entity for the one that biologically must divide and recombine, Lear violates both his kingly role in the hierarchical universe and his domestic one in the family.[9]

In seeking to substitute state for daughter, Lear fuses "incompatible rituals," fails as both king and father, and fosters the "explosion of chaos" that ensues. Nor does he moderate his wish to keep Cordelia for himself. Boose's comments on the reunion of father and daughter much later in the play suggest that Lear's covert desire to marry his daughter still prevails:

> And for all the poignancy of this reunion, the father's intransigence . . . remains unchanged: it is still writ large in his fantasy that he and his daughter will be forever imprisoned together like birds in a cage. At the end of the play, excluding any thought of Cordelia's new life with France, Lear focuses solely on the father-daughter merger . . .[10]

In this analysis, Lear's division of the kingdom is indeed part of a "darker purpose." Boose's argument, which refers frequently to aspects of the marriage ritual, brings a new and convincing reading to this opening scene that accommodates Lear's thought to set his rest on Cordelia's kind nursery.

There is another reading that might also accommodate Lear's intention to live with his youngest daughter. This reading does not subvert Cordelia's marriage but does prevent her from going

off to the continent with her husband. Boose's suggestion that
Lear's division of the kingdom is not the central occasion of
the scene but rather an occasion attendant upon the selection
of a husband for Cordelia is a thoughtful one. After all, Lear's
first order of business when he arrives on stage is to send
Gloucester to fetch France and Burgundy. "Meantime," he continues, "we shall express our darker purpose." Immediately
prior to the public choice of a husband for his youngest daughter,
Lear announces that he will relinquish to his children and their
husbands his responsibilities as king and divide the kingdom
in three. Once the first two shares are granted, he invites Cordelia to earn "A third more opulent than [her] sisters'." Might
such a gesture have meant that he expected Cordelia to preside
in person over her new kingdom? The text does not resolve
the issue, nor does it project in any precise way an outcome
that, given the unexpected turn of events, remains hypothetical.
But Shakespeare's other plays do not offer examples of absentee
rulers, except temporarily to wage foreign wars or carry out
diplomatic missions (we omit the special cases of Antony and
Pericles). Nor do historical parallels suggest the likelihood of
absentee rule. Surely had Elizabeth I married royalty, no one
would have expected her to leave Britain, any more than Mary
Tudor was expected to leave when she married Philip of Spain.
Lear's intent to grant Cordelia the most opulent share of the
kingdom upon her profession of the fullness of her love may
have been a contrivance, designed by the aging monarch to
obstruct Cordelia's departure. With Cordelia in Britain, he can
retain the addition of king and set his rest on her kind nursery.

In an essay published some years prior to the Boose piece,
Dove and Gamble offer a reading that combines the two suggestions, arguing that Lear intends to grant Cordelia the most opulent share of the kingdom to prevent her marriage and keep
her at home. Their argument introduces another variable: They
see the granting of territory not as Cordelia's marriage dowry
but as a bribe designed to seduce her into not marrying either
Burgundy or France. In Dove and Gamble's reading, Lear surprises everyone with the announcement of a *threefold* division.
The love test is hardly a formality, at least with respect to Lear's
youngest daughter. Prepared to make his handsome offer in return for a profession of love that will bind her to him, Lear
is stymied and outraged by Cordelia's public refusal to earn
more than her sisters have. Even though he loves her most,
he cannot bestow his gift upon her if she says nothing; yet

not granting her a third of the kingdom will abort his scheme. Lest one object that the terms of Cordelia's dowry have been agreed to in advance and are well known to her suitors, Dove and Gamble note that the proposed marriage settlement need not consist of land. It is more likely, as the exchanges with Burgundy (190–209, 243–51) suggest and as cogent political considerations would dictate, to be a financial settlement rather than a territorial one.[11] In a sense, offering Cordelia a share of the kingdom is Lear's way of competing with his daughter's suitors, of putting her in the position of having to choose between abandoning father and kingdom for marriage and reigning as Lear's unmarried daughter over the most opulent third of the realm. Lear is confident she will reject his "rivals" and choose to remain at home.

In all three provisional readings, Cordelia's asides acquire richness and subtlety, expressing not only Cordelia's reluctance to match her sisters' flattery but her awareness of her father's "darker purpose." France and Burgundy are indeed to be answered but not necessarily with Cordelia's hand. Dove and Gamble cite Cordelia's speech to her father as evidence of "how completely she has understood the underlying intention behind the opulent third. The question of marriage has been implicit; she makes it explicit":[12]

> Why have my sisters husbands, if they say
> They love you all? Happily, when I shall wed,
> That lord whose hand must take my plight shall carry
> Half my love with him, half my care and duty.
> Sure I shall never marry like my sisters,
> To love my father all.[13]

(99–104)

At the risk of overloading our readers with ingenious scenarios, we would like to refer to one more reading, which approaches Lear's "darker purpose" from a political rather than a psychological perspective. Harry V. Jaffa, writing for the *American Political Science Review*, proposes that Lear, a clever elder statesman rather than a foolish old man (or a possessive father), intended Cordelia to have the central portion of the kingdom and to marry Burgundy. In Lear's plan for the succession, which began with his marrying Goneril to Albany, from the north, and Regan to Cornwall, from the south, this step would assure that his best loved daughter succeeded to the crown and that the kingdom remained, in the future, secure. As Jaffa puts it,

"Lear was certainly using the dowries, and the marriages, as instruments of policy . . ."[14] Jaffa finds textual evidence that Lear's choice of a husband for Cordelia was Burgundy in his offer of Cordelia to Burgundy first and in the Duke's knowledge of Cordelia's dowry. Politically, he contends, Lear would never allow the King of France to inherit the throne of Britain, since such a move could mean the annexation of Britain to France. But marriage to Burgundy would, in effect, add Burgundy to Cordelia's share, giving Cordelia greater strength in a potential power play by her sisters and assisting the balance of power on the continent as well.[15]

Pointing to parallels in England's history, Jaffa notes that

> The ascent of a foreign duke, William of Normandy, to the throne of England gave English kings claims upon the French throne, but not the reverse. Also, the marriage of Mary Tudor to Philip II was a "Burgundian" marriage. . . . Mary, although married to a foreign prince who was nominally king of England, alone exercised the powers of the sovereign.[16]

In short, "Lear's scheme of marrying Cordelia to Burgundy gave good promise of leading to a stable international system, and a peaceful acceptance of Lear's will and testament at home."[17] Cordelia's refusal to participate in the love test, therefore, seriously flawed Lear's carefully conceived succession design, occasioning an anger that accomplished precisely the opposite of what Lear had planned. Now not only will Cordelia not inherit the kingdom, but she will be allied with France. Things could not have gone worse for Lear or for Britain.

Of all the versions of the King Lear story collected by Geoffrey Bullough, none but Shakespeare's contains any suggestion that Lear intended to live with Cordelia. And in all but one of Shakespeare's probable or possible sources, the division of the kingdom, as well as the selection of husbands for all three daughters, is connected with the love test.[18] For pleasing their father, Goneril and Regan are married to Albany and Cornwall, or their equivalents, who receive equal shares of the kingdom. For not pleasing her father, Cordelia is disinherited. In all of the sources, Cordelia marries France, or his equivalent—someone outside the kingdom who claims the dowerless maid. In none of the sources is her marriage to France by prearrangement. In fact, in Geoffrey of Monmouth's *Historia Anglicana* (ca. 1135), the angry Lear, disappointed by Cordelia's response in the love test, retaliates by announcing he will marry her "to some Foreigner

. . . but will never, I do assure you, make it my Business to procure so honourable a Match for you as for your Sisters."[19]

In the anonymous *The True Chronicle Historie of King Leir* (1605), which Bullough identifies as Shakespeare's major source,[20] there are some interesting variants. Again, the three daughters are unmarried, and Leir means to secure husbands for them all, even as he divides his kingdom equally. In this play, Leir has recently buried his wife, and it is grief, old age, and a desire to think on otherworldly things that occasion his abdication. Notably, the love test, as he confides to his two counselors, is only apparently the deciding factor in the apportionment of shares and selection of husbands. In fact, he has already decided to give each daughter an equal third and to marry Gonorill and Ragan to Cornwall and Cambria, but he wants "To try which of my daughters loves me best: / Which till I know, I cannot be in rest."[21] Skalliger, the less honorable of the king's counselors, reveals Leir's plan to the elder daughters, giving them the time to prepare and the knowledge to shape their flattering answers. But the unsuspecting Cordella does not play the game.

What is most intriguing in *The True Chronicle Historie* is that the love test is not only a formality, as it also is in Shakespeare (at least with respect to Goneril and Regan); it is also a device to trap Cordella into compliance with her father's wishes. In the Gonorill and Ragan marriages, Leir assures that the shares of his kingdom allotted to the two elder daughters will be ruled by "neer neyghbouring Kings."[22] If he has his way, his youngest daughter will marry the King of Hibernia, a match that will, with the others, protect Albion "'gainst all forrayne hate."[23] As Leir confides to his lords, "if my policy may her beguyle, / Ile match her to some King within this Ile."[24] Knowing that Cordella does not wish to marry the Irish king, he expects to use her profession of love to extort her promise to do whatever he desires. In response, he will apply the real test: "Then, daughter, graunt me one request, / To shew thou lovest me as thy sisters doe, / Accept a husband, whom my selfe will woo."[25]

There is precedent, then, in Shakespeare's major source for the love test as stratagem, and the presence of France and Burgundy at court, a situation unique to Shakespeare, may suggest this is implicit in *King Lear* as well. In Shakespeare's version of the opening scene, there are not *one* but *two* love tests. In the first, the elder daughters are the pragmatists, offering Lear the protestation of love he wants to hear, while Cordelia defends the integrity of her love. In the second, Burgundy is the pragmatist, refusing the penniless Cordelia, while France recognizes that Lear's youngest daughter is "herself a dowry." As a consequence of the first love test, Lear embraces his practical daughters and disowns Cordelia; as a consequence of the second, he bids the "noble Burgundy" join him in his exit and permits France (by Gloucester's report in 1.2) to depart "in choler." As the play progresses, the audience measures Lear's experience in terms of his earlier failure to recognize Cordelia's love, a failure that acquires an even sharper outline in the second test, in which France, unlike Burgundy and unlike Lear, recognizes Cordelia's worth.

But the presence of France and Burgundy at court does not simply introduce a parallel episode; it also prompts reevaluation of the purpose of the first test. Manifestly, events in act 1, scene 1 take an unexpected turn for Lear. In the traditional reading, the king is unprepared for his youngest daughter's refusal to compete with her sisters. Though he had intended to marry Cordelia either to Burgundy or to France, he is so angered by her qualified profession of love that he disinherits her on the spot. In Dove and Gamble's reading likewise, where the challenge is a ruse that Lear deliberately contrives in order to win Cordelia for himself, it is her refusal to acquiesce that strikes him with "amazement" and drives him to "frenzy."[26] In Boose's reading, however, Lear's psychology is more complex. Since his business, conscious or not, is to subvert the ritual passage of his daughter to a husband, there is a sense in which her failure to pass the love test gratifies him. Even in his repudiation of Cordelia, his retentive motives are expressed: "by disinheriting Cordelia, Lear casts her away not to let her go but to prevent her from going."[27] This circumstance shifts emphasis and interest to the second love test. The truly wrenching turn of events for Lear would come when France, recognizing that Cordelia is herself a dowry, takes her for his wife, without her father's grace or benison. Where Lear meant to frustrate the intentions of Burgundy and France, France instead frustrates Lear's intention to keep his daughter at home.

Had Shakespeare not made the king reveal that he hoped to set his rest on Cordelia's kind nursery—and had Bradley not concluded that this meant he intended to live with Cordelia—then there might be less cause to probe Lear's motives in this fashion. However, familiar readings of the play, while admitting, with Bradley, that the particulars of the division are already in place and that Lear's plan was to end his days with his youngest daughter, do nothing to reconcile the "kind nursery" line with Cordelia's marriage to a foreign prince. Instead, critics from Samuel Johnson to Germaine Greer stipulate the "obscurity and inaccuracy in this prefatory scene": "It is hieratic, unmotivated, preposterous."[28] Surely, as Granville-Barker observes, "A dramatist may postulate any situation he has the means to interpret, if he will abide by the logic of it after."[29] But Granville-Barker, as a man of the theater, would concede that performers and other readers are also under the necessity of interpreting the situation postulated. While it may be that Shakespeare presents Lear's "darker purpose" as a given, refusing the circumstantial explanation that would inform a comparable situation in a history play, Boose's essay, Dove and Gamble's essay, and differences and similarities between the source material and King Lear make it difficult not to conclude that Lear's division of the kingdom and the selection of a husband for Cordelia are more than coincidentally part of the same occasion.

The first scene of King Lear, then, is a paradigm of an enigmatic text, where accommodating a line that is usually ignored requires an elaborate and perhaps indulgent working out of the permutations of the scene, only to discover possibilities that invite us to rethink more than the opening moments of the play. Textually, there is no way to clarify the omissions or to resolve the inconsistencies of scene 1. But in deciding how to play the enigma, directors and actors are bound to sort through the available signals and to develop subtexts that will give the text sufficient clarity and cogency in production. The several approaches we have been considering, at the very least, bring certain issues into focus and encourage the attempt to see in scene 1 what G. B. Shand calls Lear's "full agenda."[30]

That agenda is expressed visually by the two properties that are explicitly demanded by the script—the map that Lear employs in the division of the kingdom and the coronet that he gives to Albany and Cornwall to "part" between them.[31] The common presence of these properties and the relationship of each to the love test affirm that Cordelia's betrothal is at least as central to the scene as the division of the kingdom.

The map figures importantly in the scene. Lear calls for it immediately on announcing his "darker purpose." Spread on table or floor, hung on the wall, or held in the king's or another's hand, the map is Lear's visual aid in the division of the kingdom, the documentation to which he refers after Goneril's and Regan's professions of love. But it is not merely the property that assists Lear in publishing his "daughters' several dowers." Prominently displayed, the map becomes, through its management, a means of exposition and a richly evocative visual diagram of the several but connected actions in the scene.

How is the map introduced? Wilfred Perrett suggests, "This map may be supposed to be in the hands of Kent or Gloucester when they enter discussing the division; and Lear's command 'Give me the map there' to be addressed to Kent."[32] If this is the case, then it may also be supposed that Kent and Gloucester speak knowledgeably about the division, despite their failure to mention Cordelia's "more opulent" third, and that they are privy to Lear's intention, perhaps even that, as trusted counselors, they concurred in it. This interpretation in production would be consistent with Gloucester's being absent when the king explains his "darker purpose" to the rest of the court and with Kent's protesting only when Lear rashly alters his original plan. But the map may just as plausibly be introduced, like the coronet, with the entrance of the royal procession, and Lear's command may be directed to an attendant. In that case, certain knowledge is centered in the king, and the information shared by the earls is more ambiguous. The impression created for the audience in the opening conversation would be closer to John Russell Brown's scenario:

> Two politicians talk about new, inside information. Gloucester is careful not to appear sure of what is to happen. Kent abruptly changes the subject. Their brief exchange can give a sense of foreboding, or resignation, or simply of awaiting future clarification.[33]

The instrument of clarification is the map.

Lear might, of course, have divided his kingdom without the map, conferring his daughters' dowers through verbal rather than visual lines. There is a special sense, however, in which the public display of the map complements the public declaration he calls for in the love test. Lear asks for expressions of love "That we our largest bounty may extend / Where nature doth with merit challenge." The ritual contest is also designed to affirm Lear's affection for his daughters and his recognition of their virtues. It is, therefore, appropriate that he, in demanding oral proof of their love, give visual proof of his own.

The lines designating the daughters' separate shares of the kingdom may be a significant feature of Lear's map. In production, these boundaries are often imaginary, to be traced on the moment by Lear with his scepter or staff, but, because the division is already settled, it is possible that the lines have been inscribed. In the only comparable scene in Shakespeare, the rebel nobles' division of the realm in 3.1 of 1 *Henry IV*, the map clearly has been so marked:

> *Glendower.* Come, here is the map. Shall we divide our right
>   According to our threefold order ta'en?
> *Mortimer.* The Archdeacon hath divided it
>   Into three limits very equally.
>
>   (67–70)

Mortimer goes on to describe the "three limits," admittedly with more geographical precision than Lear shows in his awards, and Hotspur is soon complaining that his "moi'ty, north from the Burton here, / In quantity equals not one of yours" (93–94). According to Kent and Gloucester in their opening conversation, the sort of "curiosity" (or close scrutiny) that Hotspur engages in can discover no such discrepancy to make either Albany or Cornwall envious of the other's "moi'ty." If the earls are, in fact, relying on personal knowledge, not just hearsay, their commentary again implies that the boundaries of the threefold division are inscribed on Lear's map. Lear himself speaks as though they may be seen easily: "Of all these bounds, even from this line to this. . . ." In the ceremony over which the king with this document presides, if the lines are conspicuously displayed, they become especially effective in suggesting the paradox of boundless love earning a bounded reward.

"The map," Marshall McLuhan remarks about the scene, "was also a novelty in the sixteenth century, age of Mercator's projection, and was key to the new vision of peripheries of power and wealth."[34] The love test couples the pragmatism of this "new vision" with the ritualism of an older vision. And if Terence Hawkes is right about the play on the antithetical meanings of "love"—to feel affection for and to estimate the price or value of—the pun exemplifies the ambivalence of Lear's exchanges with his elder daughters.[35] To express her boundless love, Goneril professes she loves her father "Beyond what can be valued, rich or rare." In response, Lear grants her the land within "bounds" he has prescribed, "With shadowy forests and with champaigns rich'd, / With plenteous rivers and wide-skirted meads." Asking to be "prize[d]" at Goneril's "worth" but claim-

ing to surpass her sister in love for Lear, Regan declares herself
"an enemy to all other joys / Which the most precious square
of sense possesses." Her father responds by granting her a share
"No less in space, validity, and pleasure / Than that conferr'd
on Goneril." Ironically, the very lines that Lear inscribes on
his map to define his loving fatherhood both affirm his pleasure
at his elder daughters' extravagant professions and place symbolic boundaries on the love that claims to know no bounds.
Were he himself to read the lines of his map, he would know
more of boundaries than Goneril and Regan's "large speeches"
would have him know.

Cordelia, by contrast, shows respect for bounds, not as the
"peripheries of power and wealth" but as the condition of
human bonds. Reacting to the love test, she asserts, "I love
your Majesty / According to my bond, no more nor less." She
cannot love her father all, for marriage will represent another
bond, claiming her love, care, and duty. In declaring both the
bounty and the limits of her love, Cordelia rejects the excesses
of her sisters and, more important, prescribes the boundaries
of love that Lear has reserved the right himself to prescribe.
In return for her modest profession, Cordelia receives not a
share of her father's love and bounty but nothing—which, paradoxically, knows no bounds. With her failure to please Lear,
the map intended both to offer and to reward love becomes
an ominous image of the incomplete ritual. For Cordelia's dower,
in all its opulence, stands unclaimed.

Once Cordelia disappoints Lear, the king may or may not
refer to the map again. In his disinheritance speech, he disclaims
his relationship to his youngest daughter: "And as a stranger
to my heart and me / Hold thee, from this, for ever." If the
"this" of his declaration refers to Cordelia's intended share of
the kingdom, then Lear's pointing to that designated cartographi-
cal space would complement and subvert the sequence of invitation, response, and reward that has characterized the love test.
The same gesture that showed his approval of Goneril's speech
and Regan's now confirms his disapproval of Cordelia's words.
If Lear's "this" is not read as the unclaimed land, then, after
Cordelia's disobedience, Lear does not refer to the map again.
In the absence of any direction for its removal, however, we
may assume that the map remains in place for Kent's defense
of Cordelia, for Lear's investment of power in Albany and Cornwall, and, most tellingly, for the restructured betrothal ceremony
with Burgundy and France.

If Lear had intended to give Cordelia in marriage to one of the two suitors at court, he now intends to publish his displeasure and her shame. Calling for France and Burgundy, he settles the redivision of the kingdom, then banishes Kent for pleading that he revoke his gift, before the two suitors appear. Once Gloucester escorts France and Burgundy into the room, Lear moves directly to the business at hand, which is not to give Cordelia's heart to a husband but to "give / Her father's heart from her." He bargains first with Burgundy over the price of his daughter, declaring her worthless and making clear that he offers nothing. When Burgundy refuses to "take" the woman, preferring to "leave" her, Lear offers her—or does not offer her—to France, making a point of her wretchedness and shame. But France, perceiving Cordelia's worth, challenges Burgundy's love—and Lear's: "Love's not love / When it is mingled with regards that stands / Aloof from th' entire point."

We never know what role Cordelia would have played in the selection of a husband had all gone well. Since France and Burgundy have wooed her for some time at court, she probably has a preference by now. But whether Lear would have let her choose or would himself have chosen her husband, we do not know. We do know that, even in this altered circumstance, Cordelia plays an active role. Witness to both suitors' reactions to her condition, she comes to her own defense when France wonders that she has so quickly fallen out of her father's favor. When Burgundy, offered her hand a second time, still refuses, she breaks her silence again. Her judgment, the same that she might have passed on her sisters, is sharp: "Since that respect and fortunes are his love, / I shall not be his wife." France, having heard Cordelia's defense of her honesty, has now only to hear Cordelia's farewell to Burgundy to know that Cordelia is "most rich being poor, / Most choice forsaken, and most lov'd despis'd!" If Cordelia's sacrificed share of the kingdom, still outlined on the map, is prominently in view, it becomes a potent sign that Cordelia's bounded love has nothing to do with the "peripheries of power and wealth" that Burgundy and her sisters value with the blind endorsement of Lear.

Throughout the opening scene, then—in the division of the kingdom, the love test, and Cordelia's betrothal—the map articulates visually the action of the scene. Particularly if its lines are deeply inscribed across its surface, it remains a reminder of Lear's intention to give most richly what he most suddenly and foolishly denied; of Cordelia's willingness to abjure so much for the integrity of her love; of France's readiness to relinquish as much for Cordelia; and of the divided kingdom that will occasion the appalling events of the play.

The second property present throughout the proceedings in act 1, scene 1 is the coronet. Of no less interest than the map, the coronet in the Quarto heads the royal procession announced by Gloucester's "The King is coming":

> Sound a Sennet, Enter on bearing a Coronet, then Lear, then the Dukes of Albany, and Cornwell, next Gonorill, Regan, Cordelia, with followers.

Where the coronet rests until Lear presents it to his sons-in-law at line 138 or how it gets on stage in the Folio version only production can determine. But its prominent, even primary, position in the Quarto and its dramatic use by the outraged Lear point to its significance in the scene.

In a paper presented at the 1986 International Shakespeare Congress in Berlin, published in *Shakespeare Quarterly*, Shand closely scrutinizes the coronet. Though in production the property is often represented as the royal crown, worn by the king and ceremoniously passed from him to the new rulers, Shand reminds us that, according to the *Oxford English Dictionary,* a coronet denoted a "dignity inferior to that of the sovereign."[36] One need only recall Casca's report of Marc Antony's offer of a crown to Caesar—"yet 'twas not a crown neither, 'twas one of these coronets" (*Julius Caesar*, 1.2.237–38)—to be assured that the two are different.[37] The coronation processional in 4.1 of *Henry VIII*, with its explicit stage directions regarding coronets and crowns, is especially revealing: the Garter King-at-Arms, "a gilt copper crown"; the Marquess Dorset, "a demi-coronal of gold"; the Earl of Surrey, "an earl's coronet"; the Dukes of Suffolk and of Norfolk, "coronet[s]"; the Queen, "in her hair, richly adorned with pearl, crowned"; the old Duchess of Norfolk, "a coronal of gold, wrought with flowers"; and certain Ladies or Countesses, "plain circlets of gold without flowers." Clearly, there was a hierarchy in Renaissance headgear, as G. K. Hunter, Frances Teague, and others have remarked,[38] a hierarchy that distinguished not only hats and caps and helmets but ceremonial head rings as well. Had Lear removed the golden ring from his own head as a signal of his divestiture, he would not have referred to it as a coronet. Shand introduces the possibility that Lear is speaking derisively of his crown, which, after Cordelia's betrayal, is but a trifle to him. But he dismisses the possibility as quickly as he raises it, finding it "difficult to justify" and noting the stage direction in the Quarto that objectifies Lear's reference to "This coronet."[39]

The argument for the coronet's not being the king's crown strikes us as irrefutable, despite the stubbornness of production in representing it as such. As with so many other aspects of this occasion, which repeatedly reflects the disparity between what Lear expected and what Lear got—what Marvin Rosenberg calls the "if-but-yet disequilibrium that energizes the play"[40]— the question of intention remains. Was the coronet intended for its recipients, Albany and Cornwall? Was it intended for Cordelia? Or was it intended for Burgundy or France? Once again, we are placed in the position of attempting to understand what would have happened had Cordelia professed she loved her father all.

By his own account, Lear had intended to divide the kingdom in three and to set his rest on Cordelia's kind nursery. Instead, he divides the kingdom in two and arranges to live by months with his elder daughters. The presentation of the coronet to his "Beloved sons" comes as a climactic gesture in Lear's furious revision of his plan. Still reacting to Cordelia's untenderness and to the attempted intrusion of Kent, Lear orders that France and Burgundy be brought before him, then turns to Albany and Cornwall, directing them to "digest" Cordelia's share of the kingdom with his "two daughters' dowers." In vesting them with "power, / Preeminence, and all the large effects / That troop with majesty," he confirms their joint rule with the line "This coronet part between you." There is no stage direction suggesting the manner of presentation or the manner of receipt; nor is there any clue as to whether Lear intends a literal parting of the coronet (accomplished in some productions with a swing of the sword). However, the singularity of the property and the context of the presentation indicate that it is only as a consequence of Cordelia's failure to please her father that her sisters' husbands gain possession.

Albany and Cornwall, though present throughout most of the scene, are essentially silent. In the Quarto, they say nothing; in the Folio, they have a three-word line, "Dear sir, forbear," directed at Lear when he threatens Kent (perhaps by drawing his sword). There is not even a stage direction specifying their exit. We are left to guess at their reaction to the confirming coronet. Yet its presentation forms the concluding frame for the division of the kingdom sequence. Where Kent and Gloucester have spoken in the play's opening lines only of Albany and Cornwall's shares of the kingdom, now, after considerable drama concerning the threefold division, Lear declares the kingdom divided in two, with Albany and Cornwall possessing equal shares and equal rule.

If the coronet was not originally intended for Albany and Cornwall, as Lear's timing in its presentation suggests, then it must have been intended either for Cordelia (as Dove and Gamble argue) or (as Shand argues) for Burgundy or France. In Dove and Gamble's reading, the coronet represents dominion over the most opulent share of the kingdom; it would have been presented to Cordelia after she earned that share. Noting that a coronet was a symbol of "ducal, a crown of regal authority," Dove and Gamble argue that it could not have been for Goneril and Regan, "who have been made duchesses by their husbands"; for France, who wears a king's crown; or for Burgundy, who wears "his own ducal coronet." As symbol of "some British territorial rule," the coronet would have gone to the unmarried Cordelia. Albany and Cornwall, after all, divide it as confirmation that they now possess Cordelia's third.[41] What Dove and Gamble fail to notice is that prior possession of a crown or a coronet does not eliminate the possessor as a possible recipient of another.

Shand, by contrast, sees the coronet as belonging not to the division of the kingdom but to Cordelia's betrothal. Claiming that there is no "darker purpose," Shand suggests that Lear, having selected a husband for Cordelia, would have presented the coronet to the betrothed suitor, who, at the moment of his acceptance of Cordelia, would become ruler of the kingdom's most opulent share. Shand's note that Lear ultimately presents the coronet not to Goneril and Regan but to their husbands lends force to his contention that Burgundy or France is the intended recipient.

Shand's reading is arresting because it acknowledges the richness of the coronet as a symbolic property. It is originally intended to represent Cordelia's betrothal and the share of sovereignty that is her dower. Lear's angry conveyance of the coronet to Albany and Cornwall divests the property of its original meaning, leaving it representative only of territorial rule. The point has often been made that the division of the kingdom would have been distressing, whatever the circumstances, to a Jacobean audience. That audience had been nurtured on the biblical maxim, "Every kingdom divided against itself is brought to desolation" (Matt. 12:25), as elaborated and applied to its own history in pulpit oratory, printed literature, and dramatic representations. It is no doubt true that this aspect of the opening scene had a force for Shakespeare's contemporaries that it does not have for us. But even a modern audience is likely to react with some uneasiness to Lear's flourishes with the map, his treatment of the realm as if it were so much real estate. Now, through the use of another property—"This coronet part between you"—the feeling of unease is intensified. We can only imagine the response of the Jacobean audience, sensitized as it was to the perils of divided rule, and, of course, we can only imagine the appropriate stage business. Shand neatly summarizes some possibilities:

> One perfect round, loaded with implications of broken arcs. The circlet form of the coronet carries with it all the necessary statements of the impossibility of division, even though it is not the regal crown. Perhaps Cornwall goes on to tip his violent hand, dividing the coronet himself. Perhaps he and Albany twist it out of shape. Perhaps they stand a moment, frozen by impossibility, before handing the coronet over to an attendant. . . .[42]

But even while the associations with a unified and a divided kingdom are present in the round when Albany and Cornwall receive it, so too is the association with marital love, traditionally symbolized by the wedding ring and memorably expressed in John Donne's "A Valediction: Forbidding Mourning" ("Thy firmness makes my circle just. . . ."). When Lear transfers the coronet to the dukes to part between them, the gesture is also in this sense symbolic, exemplifying the subversion of his daughter's passage in marriage.

Significantly, the coronet is not present in any of Shakespeare's sources, where the circumstances are altered in two respects: (1) the occasion of the division of the kingdom is also the occasion for the selection of husbands for all three daughters, and (2) none of the prospective husbands is on the scene. Had a coronet or some comparable trapping been intended for the bride, then the sources presumably would have contained three of them, one for each of the soon-to-be-wed daughters. Had it been intended for the groom, then the sources presumably would have contained none, for none of the prospective husbands is at court. In The True Chronicle Historie of King Leir, when the counterparts of Albany and Cornwall do arrive at court to receive their shares, three scenes after that of the love test, Leir has them draw lots, an action Perrett equates with the handing over of the coronet.[43] Shakespeare's revision of the source material, which makes Cordelia the only unmarried daughter and brings both of her wooers to court for the scene of the love test, may well imply that the one coronet in 1.1 is, as Shand suggests, meant for Burgundy or France.

Earlier, in discussing the map, we noticed one of Lear's lines in the speech that precedes his presentation of the coronet to Albany and Cornwall. In disclaiming paternal care of Cordelia, the king charges her, "And as a stranger from my heart and me / Hold thee, from this, for ever." We first suggested that Lear might indicate Cordelia's share of the kingdom by pointing to or touching the map. The "this," however, could just as readily refer to the coronet, prominently placed in anticipation of the betrothal. If the coronet was to confer Lear's blessing on his youngest daughter's marriage and the generous dowry that would accompany the match, then it is perfectly appropriate for Lear in his rage to deny Cordelia access not only to her inheritance and to his heart but to the symbolic coronet as well. In production, the line is perhaps most often played to mean Lear's breast, indicated by his placing his hand upon it. Of course, it may be taken as referring neither to a property nor to the speaker but to time, "from this time forth," a reading Bevington seems to favor by inserting commas around the phrase (there are none in the Quarto or Folio). As with other such ambiguous and apparently "gestic terms" in Shakespeare, a decision must be made in production.[44] Certainly, both the map and the coronet offer appropriate antecedents of "this," each reminding the audience of the presence of a stage image that collects several strands of action in the scene into a unified whole.

As much as the map, then, the coronet provides a visual articulation of Lear's full agenda. Carried at the head of the royal procession, the coronet acquires visual and symbolic primacy. Within view of the onstage and offstage audiences, it reminds all that Lear yet intends to confer it, along with his grace, his love, his benison. Passed to Albany and Cornwall in confirmation of their joint rule, it remains visibly indivisible, to be shared by two who will reign over a divided kingdom. Denied Cordelia or her husband, it becomes, as Boose suggests, "a parody of the ring rite," in which "Lear takes the golden round uniting king and country and parts it, an act that both dramatizes the consequences of dividing his realm and demonstrates the anguish he feels at losing his daughter to a husband."[45]

The opening scene prepares us for the enigmatic actions that characterize the play. In effect, the first scene of *King Lear* is like the play-within-the-play in *Hamlet*: the offstage audience is as interested in the reactions of the onstage audience as it is in the inner play. With Lear staging the division of the kingdom, the love test, and the proffering of his daughter's hand, the most telling signals will come from how others respond. If, for example, the court did not expect a threefold division, there might be murmurings or other expressions of surprise at Lear's declaration. If Goneril and Regan thought the kingdom was to be shared between them and then discovered that Cordelia was in on the competition as well, how might they appear just prior to their professions of love? When each receives Lear's prescribed share, is she self-satisfied, angry, disappointed, pleased? How do Goneril and Regan each react to the other's profession of love? And how is Cordelia positioned in relation to Goneril and Regan? The Quarto—and less clearly the Folio—directs that Cordelia enter with her sisters, the three together following Albany and Cornwall. Does she remain with her sisters, presumably close to the throne, perhaps closest to Lear, so that father and daughter form a couple along with the other royal couples? Or does she stand apart, outside the frame of the ritual, speaking her asides to herself or to the audience? If a space divides father from daughter, does Lear come to her or invite her to come to him on "Now, our joy . . ."? And what of the silent Albany and Cornwall? Are they delighted at their wives' excessive protestations? Who of the two—or both—receives the coronet? If the two remain on stage for the betrothal ceremony, do they stand, coronet in hand, for France and Burgundy to see? Indeed, where are the coronet and the map during the second love test, and how do these properties affect the suitors or shape the stage image the audience receives? How, in production, is what Bevington calls "The Language of Costume and Hand Properties," "The Language of Gesture and Expression," "The Language of Theatrical Space"[46] articulated in act 1, scene 1? How is Cordelia's plight staged?

In approaching these questions through the BBC and the Granada productions of *King Lear*, we will look at the two love tests chiefly through the productions' treatments of the map and the coronet.

Productions

The decor Miller and his designers adopted for the BBC production is "late-Renaissance," "about ten years past Shakespeare's death"; at the same time they sought "ultimate simplicity" of setting balanced by an "understated elegance" of costume.[47] Accordingly, the panoply of kingship is not much in evidence during the first scene before or after the entrance of Lear and the royal procession. The opening shot of the throne chamber, with the camera almost at ground level, shows an expanse of board flooring with a long table as a barrier midway and an unadorned throne at the upper end. A bench lines each side wall, and the walls all around consist of simple cloth drapes. Everything is monochrome, gray or black, and the chamber is relatively dark, as though lit from windows above. The costuming also, while expressing appropriate period elegance, is in shades of black or gray, with white or silver accents. The only bit of color in the first scene is the orange feather or coxcomb in the floppy hat of the Fool, who in this production is a silent witness to his master's folly. No sennet, only the sound of approaching footsteps on the boards, heralds the coming of the king and the royal family; nor do flourishes accompany the entrance of France and Burgundy or the exit of the king and the duke. When Lear enters, no coronet is borne before him, and he is himself bareheaded. The effect of the *mise-en-scène* is to preserve but minimize the atmosphere of a royal court and to assert the ambience of an aristocratic household. The emphasis shifts subtly from Lear's kingship to his fatherhood.

At the opening, Kent and Gloucester enter upstage and cross to a downstage position to speak confidentially of the division of the kingdom as some other members of the court mingle behind them. In this staging, Kent carries a rolled-up document, which he glances at significantly after delivering his first line. It is the map that Lear will call for to make public display of the division, and apparently Kent and Gloucester have scrutinized it. The question of whether the earls know of the threefold division seems settled. Since they share not only possession of the map but familiarity with the details of its intended use, they must know that Cordelia will receive a portion of the kingdom. Their discussion of Albany and Cornwall's moieties may

Cordelia's Plight. BBC Production. Frank Middlemass as the Fool, Brenda Blethyn as Cordelia. Courtesy of the British Broadcasting Corporation. Copyright © BBC.

be prompted by their speculation having proved false, or perhaps they have already discussed the most opulent share. The subsequent action, however, generates a residual ambiguity. Once the map is unrolled on the table, it is evident that no lines have been specially inscribed upon it. In apportioning the kingdom, Lear must create spatial boundaries with his hands. The map, then, offers no precise confirmation of the earls' knowledge that the kingdom will be divided in three, although this is strongly implied. Meantime, there are other signals to attend to.

While Gloucester softly expatiates on the division, Kent twice looks over his shoulder at Edmund, who stands at a respectful distance, looking away but probably listening. Once recognized by Kent, he joins the earls for the conversation about his bastardy, at which he smiles good-naturedly. This is broken off by Gloucester's quiet warning that the king is coming, and the three move stage left to make way for the royal procession.

Lear enters from the downstage left margin of the frame, his back to the camera, distinguished only by his height and a black robe with a fur collar. He is followed briskly by the royal family—Regan and Goneril, Cornwall and Albany, the Fool and Cordelia, with others—who assemble upstage as Kent deposits the map on the table at center stage, the position reserved for the throne in most productions. Notably also, when the family tableau forms by the upstage throne, Cordelia is not in it. Flanked by his elder daughters and their husbands, the still standing Lear, having dispatched Gloucester on his errand, announces his "darker purpose" and demands the map, adding "there" as an afterthought and pointing toward it. This is Kent's cue to unroll and spread the map, about three feet by two feet, on the table. A bit of business delays Lear's announcement of the threefold division. He walks to the table, examines the document, and points to its lower edge, then looks up as though satisfied and nods to Kent before returning upstage. Kent responds to the nod by himself glancing at the map. When the king declares his purpose, the face of Kent, who stands downstage left, his back to the camera, is not visible. Similarly, the deep focus shot allows only a distant view of the faces around Lear. The blocking teases. But no change of countenance is discernible in the group when Lear makes his declaration, and all remain erect and unmoving as he continues his speech. There is likewise no audible reaction, no expression of surprise, at his "darker purpose." On the line "Unburden'd crawl toward death," the old monarch sinks into his throne with a quaver in his voice, and the camera cuts to a closeup showing his face set and determined. Turning to Cornwall and then Albany, he is emphatic in his justification "that future strife / May be prevented now."

As Lear takes up the subject of the betrothal, the camera zooms out to catch the head and shoulders of Cordelia in the foreground, facing the family tableau but outside of it. Costumed in black like her sisters, she is distinguished from them by her nun-like bonnet and collar in white. When Lear speaks of "our youngest daughter's love," everyone looks toward her, including the Fool, whom we now recognize on the stage right margin of the frame. The frame remains fixed, with these two creating an inner frame for the beginning of the love test. Lear's challenge focuses attention on the elder sisters, whose reactions are suggestively different. Goneril, on Lear's left, seems frozen, her face masklike. Regan, on the right, seems energized by the proposed competition. Eager to speak first, she makes a movement toward her father, raising her hand, only to be stopped by Lear's command "Goneril, / Our eldest-born, speak first." Whatever their subtexts, whatever the components of surprise, resentment, or anticipation that inform their responses, it is clear that both sisters take the love test seriously, not as a mere formality. If the division of the kingdom is a *fait accompli*, they do not seem to know that it is.

In a medium shot, Goneril stands in place near her father as she begins her profession. Although she delivers the speech carefully, smoothly, and sincerely, she shows signs of distress, nervously clasping and unclasping her hands at her waist and never looking directly at the watching Lear. At "A love that makes breath poor, and speech unable," she places her right hand beneath her breast in visual support of her words. As she concludes, Lear nods complacently and rises; brushing a finger across the bottom of his nose, he expels a labored breath and walks forward to the table. There, cupping both hands over the map to form the boundaries of Goneril's share, he confers a third of the kingdom on his eldest daughter. Her face registering a quick smile of pleasure, she raises her hand and returns Albany's approving glance.

The two daughters and their husbands have assembled on either side of Lear at the table, and now he turns to Regan. In contrast to Goneril, Lear's middle daughter is unhesitating and even calculating in manner: she obviously means to outdo her sister. Looking right into her father's eyes, she speaks her words crisply, with appropriate touches of honey. When deprecating her sister's profession of love, "Only she comes too short," she leans and glares triumphantly at Goneril, prompting Lear to turn his head as well. The camera shows a Goneril incredulous at her sister's gall and a dismayed Albany. It then returns to the other half of the tableau for the skillfully articulated modesty of Regan's conclusion, at which an abrupt cut profiles the Fool and Cordelia in the foreground for the youngest daughter's aside.

In this production, neither of Cordelia's asides is, strictly speaking, an aside. Ignoring the lack of any indication in the text that the Fool should be a presence in the first scene, Miller makes him one, an old man in coxcomb and white face, the mute ally of Cordelia as she observes and reacts to the ritualized competition of her sisters. It is to him that she addresses her fretful lines. At her second comment, the Fool rests a comforting hand on her shoulder. As he offers Cordelia this solace, the camera returns to Lear and Regan, with the inquisitive Cornwall leaning forward between them, for the second award. The king makes it, using the same gesture he used to designate Goneril's share, though this time the map is below the margin of the frame. Regan seems momentarily doubtful, then smiles at her prize, gazing up at her husband. The camera again cuts to a deep focus shot, foregrounding Cordelia.

Having dispatched his business with the elder daughters, Lear turns with mellow voice to his youngest, addressing her first from a distance, then coming forward to confront her with the question "what can you say? . . ." Though Lear means to look into her eyes, Cordelia blinks and looks past him, turning her head briefly on "your sisters" to glance at them, who now stand together holding hands. Aware of the ocular attention of everyone at court, this is a Cordelia who is acutely uncomfortable and at the same time indignant that she should be made so. Lear towers over her, his command to speak full of expectancy: hers is the reply that he is really interested in. When it comes, it is curt, cryptic. Baffled, the king gives his head a little shake and smiles reflexively. During the taut exchange, Cordelia becomes bolder, returning her father's gaze. There are stirrings in the background as others react anxiously to her displeasing words. Kent steps forward to stand framed by the faces of Lear and Cordelia. His own face registers concern, Lear's disappointment and disbelief, Cordelia's an indignation that her modesty seeks to conceal. But she remains very sure of herself. Though she had resolved to be silent, she tries to explain to her father as she might to a child the nature and extent of her love. When she refers to marriage, Lear again shakes his head, and his lips move inaudibly as she concludes.

Lear's incredulity at Cordelia's "untender" truthfulness builds to rage at what he deems her ingratitude and arrogance. In pronouncing his oath of repudiation, he punctuates it on the lines "And as a stranger from my heart and me / Hold thee, from this, for ever" by moving upstage of Cordelia, but he does not gesture toward the map, which is screened by Kent. In this blocking, "from this" can only mean "from this time." He then turns back to Cordelia, still in profile, to shout his equation of the "barbarous Scythian" and his "sometime daughter." She endures her rejection tight-lipped and blinking, shutting her eyes on this last invective. Meanwhile, the camera cuts briefly to Regan and Goneril, huddled together, their eyes meeting in astonishment.

The camera returns to a two-shot of Lear and Kent, with the king silencing his counselor and showing his hurt as he admits he loved Cordelia most. Pacing left, he gives "her father's heart from her," and it is here that he gestures toward the map now visible on the table, near which Cordelia reenters the frame to form an upstage triad with Kent and the Fool. Isolated, Lear stops and calls loudly for France and Burgundy, then for Cornwall and Albany, who come forward to stand on either side of the king for the divestiture. On "digest this third," Lear again motions toward the map and rapidly states his conditions. But Lear presents the dukes with no coronet. This property the production simply omits. Incongruously, though Lear speaks the line and reinforces it with a staccato gesture, neither has a visual antecedent.

If Cornwall and Albany become less prominent through the omission of the coronet they are to share, so also do they lose their one opportunity to speak. When Lear threatens the protesting Kent by brandishing a dagger, it is his rejected daughter who pleads "Dear sir, forbear."[48] The change has the effect of bringing Cordelia, who rushes from the stage right margin of the frame, back into the action. She stands upstage, the Fool with his hands on her shoulders, as Lear forces Kent to kneel for the sentence of banishment. By the end of the sentence, Lear has himself stalked all the way up to the throne, and Kent moves to Cordelia for his farewell. The map is visible on the table behind them as he assures the aggrieved young woman that she has "most rightly said!"

On his exit from the state chamber, the spurned counselor nearly collides with the returning Gloucester, who leads France and Burgundy on stage for the betrothal sequence. Cordelia's expectant suitors appear from the same downstage entrance that served Lear and his procession earlier, their backs on the camera as well. Like those in the procession, they take stations on either side of Lear, who is center stage to greet them, the presiding figure over the two love tests. As the camera singles out Burgundy and Lear, Cordelia and the Fool are visible between them. Hearing his intended bride condemned and her dowry refused, the duke turns briskly into the camera and walks out of the frame. As Lear had earlier challenged Goneril on his left and Regan on his right, he now moves from Burgundy on his right to address France on his left. When France expresses bewilderment over Lear's displeasure, Cordelia advances to beseech, indeed, demand that her father exonerate her of any vicious blot. The king, in the foreground, will not deign to wish her unborn to her face. France beholds her, however, studying in turn daughter and father. As the impatient Lear walks upstage to a position behind Cordelia, the blocking readjusts: now Burgundy and France are downstage right and left, Cordelia a few paces upstage between them, and Lear in the background. When at the prompting of France Burgundy renews his request for the dower, Cordelia turns upstage to face her father. This time, after a pause, he requites her boldness. Approaching his daughter, he pushes his face up to hers to reply: an irrevocable "Nothing."

Even as Lear turns away from her and Burgundy disavows his suit, France claims Cordelia for himself. With the couple foregrounded, Lear upstage looks toward them but remains fixed. The camera also provides a shot of Regan and Goneril, still holding hands and now gazing directly at each other. When France concludes, aiming the word "unkind" at Lear, the king, who has stood in profile with his mouth working, comes forward to give his dowerless daughter officially to the foreigner. During the brief separation ritual, Lear keeps his eyes on France, acknowledging Cordelia's presence only by denial: "we / Have no such daughter." In spite of his rigidity, there is a tremor in his voice, and the camera records his anguished expression. Unwilling to yield, like Cordelia, he is already suffering the emotional cost. The passage complete, even in its incompletion ("without our grace, our love, our benison"), Lear exits the same way he came in, his entourage following.

Throughout the betrothal sequence, the map has remained spread across the table, visible occasionally in the background. But if France and Burgundy notice the map, they never register their awareness. The most interesting staging in this version comes not in its modest use of one property, which will be put to special use in scene 2, or in its neglect of the second but in the reaction shots, which record silences and gestures that speak with the dialogue to the feelings of the characters.

The collective reaction to Lear's announcement of his "darker purpose," the threefold division, and Cordelia's betrothal betrays no sign of surprise or disturbance among those assembled. The audience must presume that this much is understood by the participants in the occasion. If Lear's intention to marry Cordelia to a foreign prince conflicts with his intention to give her a third of the kingdom or to repose on her "kind nursery," then Miller allows the inconsistency to stand. Similarly, Lear gives no indication, in his references to France and Burgundy or otherwise,[49] that he means to sabotage Cordelia's marriage, nor do the responses of others support that interpretation. It is the love test that causes a sensation, especially among the daughters. It takes them by surprise, puts them on their mettle, and provokes them to make significantly different responses. Neither of the elder sisters is certain of the material outcome, and each in her own way enters the competition. For Cordelia, already outside the family group, the love test is a crisis of affection and conscience, and it is her interaction with Lear that shapes the rest of the scene. Finally, however, Lear is the one who is tested. And his reactions to both love tests suggest the incestuous proprietorship that Boose adumbrates. The Fool silently and Kent vocally supply appropriate commentary. In contrast to Regan and Goneril, whose responses the camera consistently records and who begin as adversaries and end as allies, their husbands are background figures, present only to help dramatize certain moments, their roles further diminished by the preempting of their one line and by the absence of the coronet.

While in scene 1 the map is used to good effect as a stage image primarily in the division of the kingdom and not in the betrothal, the transition to scene 2 in this production restores and extends its symbolic primacy. Just as at the outset Kent and Gloucester spoke confidentially, with Edmund framed between them, so at the end of the scene Regan and Goneril are engaged in confidential conversation, when Edmund appears in the distance between them. Unobserved, he stands in silence watching the sisters "hit together." Ending the conversation, Goneril notices the young man, and both sisters look at him and exchange smiles with each other before exiting. The camera then moves in on Edmund, who stands behind the table looking at the map, his left hand resting on it. Though he may not know all that has happened in the previous scene, having apparently followed his father to fetch Burgundy and France (as some modern editors propose), he now delivers his self-defining soliloquy with the map as a prop.

Where the map has in scene 1 been a visual reminder of a daughter's deprivation, now Edmund complains of his own as a son, the consequence for him not of integrity but of bastardy. At his resolve to remedy the situation by securing his brother's inheritance, he again looks down at the map and reflects on the stratagem that will lead him to counterpoint Cordelia's "Nothing" to her father by making the same disclaimer to Gloucester moments later. With the map and the single figure composing the stage image, the association of the map with the "new vision of the peripheries of power and wealth" is reasserted to initiate the underplot in the BBC production.

GRANADA

The Granada-TV *King Lear* represents a different tradition in the staging of the play. Elliott chose to evoke not Shakespeare's era but ancient days, pre-Christian and druidical, mysterious and mythic. The opening shot shows the rising sun framed by the monoliths of a temple like Stonehenge. An elevated camera then drops and pans beneath a sheltering barrier for the antescene involving Kent, Gloucester, and Edmund. Around them, the dawning light filters through towering posts and lintels. Two sennets, joined by rising background music, herald the coming of the king, and, as the camera follows the earls into the central open space, waiting courtiers disperse to reveal a large wooden throne, studded and gilded, resting on animal skins in the midst. With the camera moving to the right of the throne, the figures who make up the royal procession enter singly and in pairs from behind an upstage monolith, silhouetted in their progress against the backdrop of the sun. Unlike the brisk entrance of the royal family in the BBC produc-

Cordelia's Plight. Granada Production. Anna Calder-Marshall as Cordelia.
Courtesy of Granada Television. Copyright © Granada T.V.

tion, this one is slow and ceremonial, with Lear and his youngest daughter entering last, preceded by a sword-bearer. On reaching the throne, a white-haired Lear releases Cordelia from his embracing arm and stands in place, garbed in a fur-collared robe and adorned by a magnificent golden crown and a massive pendant of state. An overhead shot shows the solitary figure encircled by the monoliths and the members of his court, who now prostrate themselves at his feet. If this Lear is every inch a father, he is also a king and a priest.

While evoking a world that is remote and even primitive by comparison with the BBC's Renaissance *mise-en-scène*, the Granada version presents a society that is highly structured and self-consciously ritualistic in its behavior. These qualities are also reflected in its dress, which is suggestive, anachronistically but effectively, of Anglo-Saxon and Norman styles. In the opening sequence, the three bearded men wear heavy earth-colored tunics, cloaks draped about their shoulders, and ornamental headbands. Kent is distinguished from his fellow earl, however, by a chain of office, a blue cloak, and a gold headband. The primary sign of Gloucester's rank, apart from his easy familiarity with Kent, is a headband in silver. Edmund's headgear is mere leather. The costuming of the young bastard is, in fact, of particular interest. Although the BBC Edmund is elegantly appareled from the start, the Granada Edmund is not: the altering and enriching of his accoutrements become the visible index of his rising fortunes. There is a corresponding divestiture of Kent, Edgar, Gloucester, and Lear. In this respect as in others—circles and wheels, for instance—the production reflects a special effort to embody linguistic motifs in stage images. At the beginning of the play, the procession into the temple gains in ceremonial splendor because of the richly colored fabrics and ornaments that bedeck the members of the royal family. Yet there are interesting differences to notice. The subdued Goneril, in purple, is dressed more severely than the bold and radiant Regan, in blue; Cordelia alone wears white, a simple smock, with an embroidered yoke and light blue cape framing her long blond hair. Clearly, costume is meant to be expressive of personality as well as rank or office.

In this staging, neither Kent nor Gloucester carries a map at their entrance, and they at once sound a note of uncertainty concerning the division of the kingdom. Kent's opening line is somewhat accusatory, and Gloucester's reply seems apologetic, as though it was he who led Kent to suppose the king's preference for Albany, contrary to the apparent outcome. The sense of their uncertainty is strengthened through the cutting of Gloucester's commentary on the equality of the dukes' moieties. Kent's acknowledgment of Edmund, who only now appears on camera, changes the subject. It is a hearty, obtuse, and rather vulgar Gloucester who confesses his fathering of the unsmiling Edmund to the embarrassed Kent. When offstage horns sound the sennet, the old earl abruptly breaks off, raising his hand to urge silence, and the three move into the circular throne chamber.

The Granada treatment of the processional calls for the separate entrance of each component of the royal family. Goneril and Albany are the first to come into view, both looking ill at ease as they position themselves stage right of the throne. Regan and Cornwall appear next, she confident and he scowling, to take their places on the left. Behind the shadow of the sword-bearer, Lear and Cordelia enter in a posture of affectionate intimacy, the old king with his right arm wrapped around his daughter's shoulder as they enjoy a private talk. When Lear releases Cordelia, who takes a position downstage of the throne, the camera moves to a lingering closeup of his aging, nearly beatific face. It is hard to say whether it is wisdom or complacency that the long years have etched in the handsome lines of that countenance. His eyes gaze around at the group before it becomes prostrate before him.

When Lear sits and speaks, it is with an old man's voice, in a nuanced high register. As he dispatches Gloucester, all rise to hear the mild announcement of his darker purpose. In response to "Give me the map there," an overhead shot shows two attendants carrying on the huge rolled map, for which the designer Roy Stonehouse had four cowhides stitched together,[50] and spreading it on the ground before the throne. Approximately eight feet by eight feet, a sea of blue with yellow land masses unmarked by boundaries, the document assumes a central position in the setting. With the camera again focused on Lear, he announces the division, emphasizing "three," but, since the camera stays on the king, it is impossible to gauge whether the emphasis surprises those present. When he finally names the dukes, the reaction shots are mixed, with Cornwall and Regan looking receptive and Albany and Goneril apprehensive. At the mention of France and Burgundy, the camera provides a deep focus shot with a partial view of Cordelia, blond tresses tumbling down her back, in the foreground and upstage the

enthroned Lear, one hand on each knee. It then records Cordelia's girlish face, eyes wide, lips pursed in a slight smile, her
head nodding at Lear's "And here are to be answer'd." She
alone, up to this point, registers definite signs of informed expectancy, perhaps the consequence of her private talk with her
father at their entrance. But, like the others, she is unprepared
for the sequel.

As though now done with the items on the official agenda,
Lear settles back in his throne and becomes expansive, allowing
a melodic tone to enter his voice as he proposes the love test.
He makes the challenge seem playful, teasing, but it is not so
taken by the earnest Albany and the uneasy Goneril. Stepping
forward in response to Lear's "Speak," with misgiving in her
face, the eldest daughter kneels and begins, "Sir," only to be
interrupted by her father's gesture of pointing to the map, whereupon she falls forward to kiss it and then resumes her kneeling
position to continue. In spite of her discomfiture, she manages
to generate a breathless enthusiasm and even a smile in delivering her speech, which culminates in a whispered "I love you"
so intense that it sounds like a lover's passion. During this
performance, for that is what it obviously is, the camera has
glimpsed Lear hanging on every word, and now, in another
aerial view, he demonstrates his pleasure. Rising to his feet
and taking the ceremonial sword from an attendant at his left,
he walks to the center of the map and traces out with the sword
point the kingdom's northern regions for Goneril and Albany.
The couple, standing on the stage right margin of the map,
are balanced by Regan and Cornwall, standing on the left. A
shot of the recipients registers their subdued relief, and a resounding cheer emanates from the assembly.

Still standing on the map, beaming his satisfaction, Lear turns
to challenge his "dearest Regan." Unlike her sister, Regan is
at once ready and resourceful, dropping to her knees with a
loving look at her father, kissing the map, then kissing his hand,
which causes him to chuckle and her to smile. With her hands
clasped before her breast, in an attitude of prayer, she professes
her love so sweetly and surely that she draws audible sighs
from Lear, and when she offers the reflection, pointed by a
glance in her sister's direction, that Goneril "comes too short,"
she commands a delighted chortle. At her triumphant conclusion, which she seals with a second kiss on her father's hand,
Lear happily repeats the pattern of the first award, granting
with his sword point the southern portion of the kingdom to

his second daughter and her husband. Regan smiles and Cornwall blinks in satisfaction, and another cheer rises from the court. It is a Lear who has enjoyed every minute of this charade who now nods his head at Cordelia.

Stationed downstage of the throne and the map, and out of sight during the ritual of challenge and reward, Cordelia has, of course, reacted to the professions of each of her sisters in turn. For her first aside, she is foregrounded, turning her face to the camera to whisper her dismay. Delivered as "What? Shall Cordelia speak?" rather than as "What shall Cordelia speak?" the aside signals her predicament, which is not *what* to say but *whether* to say. Though she decides to love and be silent, she will soon be compelled to use her voice. For her second aside, she speaks again from the foreground, looking over her right shoulder and confiding to the audience that her love is "more generous" than her tongue. Whereas the shot for the first aside had included Goneril and Lear in the background, the daughter kissing her father's hand, the shot for the second includes Regan offering the same token to a smiling Lear. Now, in the third deep focus shot, the camera shows Cordelia facing her nodding father and then switches to a closeup of her face, her eyes large and liquid, as she braces herself to reply. Clearly expecting a treasury of love from his "joy," Lear has returned to his throne to savor her words. Sitting comfortably, he is arch with her, wondering what *she* can say, and, on his command to speak, he lifts both hands to his mouth and opens them out to her, almost as though blowing a kiss.

Looking grave, Cordelia says "Nothing, my lord" rapidly, her voice tight. Alternating closeups of both speakers, the camera shows a puzzled, uncomprehending Lear, glancing away and then, with his eyes fixed on his daughter, cupping his hand over his ear, as though he has not heard well, and only partly articulating his "Nothing?" in response. When Cordelia repeats herself, averting her own eyes, Lear is seen with his right hand to his chin, his index finger across his white beard, still trying to assimilate the word. Shrugging, he smiles and coaxes her to "Speak again," giving her another chance. But Cordelia's denial of mere words coupled with the affirmation of her bond is strong, in spite of her distress, and this time it penetrates her father's defenses. Calling her name, with the same musical intonation of each syllable that he will use in 5.3 to urge his dead daughter to speak, he invites her to "Mend your speech a little" and then whispers his fatherly advice, "Lest [it] may mar your fortunes." Cordelia's firm reply, her longest speech so far, is punctuated by a stern glance at her sisters, when she asks why they have husbands, and by a voice raised in anger, when she concludes with the assertion that she will never marry "To love my father all." By comparison with her BBC counterpart, this younger Cordelia declares herself with less composure and more emotional force.

Cordelia's display of emotion is mild, however, when matched with the shocked and shocking reaction of Lear, which ranges from whimpering incredulity to raging invective. When Cordelia replies to his halting questions with an emphatic "So young, my lord, *and true*," the old king sits back, head raised and eyes narrowed, to decree her truth her dower. Disclaiming "all my paternal care," he gestures grandly and grotesquely, touching his breast, extending his arms outward, then repeating the movement as he identifies his heart as the subject of his "Hold thee, from this, for ever." At the intervention of Kent, who puts his arm around Cordelia, just as her father had done earlier, Lear responds furiously and next sentimentally, nearly weeping at his admission that "I lov'd her most. . . ." Shouting "Hence, and avoid my sight!" he shuts his eyes to shut his daughter out and again waves his right arm in a gesture of repudiation. The camera shows Cordelia staggering back under his fury, obviously appalled at this reaction to her "truth," and standing with Kent as Lear gives "Her father's heart from her."

As Lear calls for France and Burgundy, then Albany and Cornwall, the camera again provides an aerial view, exposing the map to which Lear points when he instructs Albany and Cornwall to digest Cordelia's third. That map, spread before him, defined the physical divide between father and his best-loved daughter, the space over which this collision of wills is enacted. Now it forms a visual square, with Lear at its head, Goneril and Albany at one side, Regan and Cornwall the other, and Cordelia barely visible on the remaining edge.

The camera moves in on Lear's face for his divestiture speech, shifting briefly to Goneril and Albany, who look astonished, to Regan and Cornwall, who look grim, and to the shaken Cordelia and Kent, holding hands. In this production, the map and the coronet become companions when, at "This coronet part between you," Lear wrenches the crown from his head and, in an overhead shot, sends it tumbling onto the surface of the map. Visually, the two properties acquire immense power in their union, yet the reading of the coronet as the royal crown both fights Lear's intention to retain the name and all the addition to a king and denies the property any connection with the betrothal.

Neither Albany nor Cornwall bends to pick up the crown, but both stand by as Kent kneels to plead with and rises to provoke his master. At first quietly threatening, "Kent, on thy life, no more," the bareheaded Lear furiously sputters his next line, "Out of my sight," again shutting his eyes, and then loses all control. Rising in his wrath, he wrests the huge ceremonial sword from his attendant and brandishes it over Kent's head, only to be restrained when his sons-in-law seize his arms. Thwarted in this act of physical violence, he stands leaning forward on the sword, its point embedded in the map, his arms still held by Albany and Cornwall, as he imposes on the kneeling Kent the violence of banishment.

While Kent exits downstage, Cordelia looking after him, the voice of Gloucester behind the throne announces the entrance of France and Burgundy. A sustained flourish of horns recreates an ambience of decorum, and an overhead camera records the appearance of order restored. The two suitors position themselves on either side of the king, who has lowered himself onto the throne and now stands partially to bow to France on his right. The foregrounded Cordelia advances a few steps to become part of the tableau. The map and discarded crown remain in the midst. (The crown, though off the eastern shores of Britain at its fall and lying on its edge, now rests, upside down, more centrally on the map.) Burgundy, it should be noted, wears a broad blue and gold headband, apparently a ducal coronet, and France a gold crown, lighter and far less elaborate than Lear's. If either notices the map or the crown that lies unclaimed, he gives no sign.

The camera now alternates between closeups of the speakers and wide shots of the group, with Cordelia in the downstage right margin of the frame. Lear's disingenuous offer of his dowerless daughter to Burgundy, accompanied by a gesture and a sneer, seems designed to humiliate her; though his manner with France is more deferential, it reflects the same vindictive spirit toward Cordelia. In response to France's dismay, she can no longer contain herself: she falls on her knees to protest, accusatory in tone despite the subservience of her posture. Lear shows her only bitterness, "Better thou hadst / Not been born . . . ," reiterates "Nothing" emphatically, then offers the quiet assurances "I have sworn" to Burgundy, "I am firm" to France. A wide shot highlights France's climactic action. With Lear's eyes riveted on him, the foreign king strides downstage across the map of Britain, seizes Cordelia's hands, and lifts her from her knees, consummating the implied stage direction in "I take up what's cast away." Ironically, in this last glimpse of the map, it has become the locus not of Lear's triumphant self-enhancement, as he expected it to be, but of his frustration and defeat. France now stands with his arm encircling Cordelia, in place of her father, and declares her his queen. From the throne, Lear makes the pronouncement that he has "no such daughter," resolutely attenuating the line, but, as he shakily rises, his voice is shaking, "nor shall ever see / That face of hers again," and tremulous as he turns his back on her, denying his blessing by word and by a limp wave of the arm. As the old king exits upstage supported by Burgundy, to a final cheerless flourish of horns, downstage Cordelia, in tears, turns away and into the arms of France. Behind the couple, Goneril and Regan join to bid their sister farewell, amazed by their father's infirmity and determined not to fall prey to it.

The Granada version of the play stages the opening scene with a ritualistic formalism that is progressively subverted by the monarch whose office commands and whose person should validate it. The temple setting, the large-scale symbolic properties, the expressive costuming, the ceremonial business and blocking all serve to create a world of sacramental imperatives, of which the royal procession is an exquisite announcement. The atmosphere thus generated is enriched by the action of the camera, as when an aerial shot shows the imposing figure of Lear with the entire court prostrate around him. Yet it soon becomes apparent that the ritual homage accorded this king, priest, and father is being put under a strain and that the source of the tension is Lear himself. Though it is in the nature of ceremony to be uniform and predictable, the master of ceremonies is in this case capricious and unpredictable. The note of uncertainty concerning his actions is sounded in the opening exchange between the earls on the division of the kingdom, and it is sustained even during the opening processional as the several components of the royal family register their different reactions to the occasion. Cordelia alone, who enters in private conversation with her father, exhibits assurance; however, she is immediately unsettled by the announcement of the love test. No one seems to be sure of what is happening. Still, again except for Cordelia and later Kent, all seem ready to comply with whatever demand Lear may make, to abide by the ritualized form of obedience to a monarch with a whim of iron.

This Lear is distinguished initially by his great power and his handsome presence—"Yet looks he like a king." The early closeups readily suggest a Lear as seasoned and sage in affairs of family and state as the Lear that Jaffa postulates.[51] But this impression is steadily eroded. Lear's treatment of the official agenda is mild, matter-of-fact, perfunctory; Olivier seems to be playing against the charged language of the lines. Is the slight emphasis on "three" significant? How is the threefold division intended to prevent "future strife"? By what means will France and Burgundy "be answer'd"? Such questions are not answered, because this Lear is not very interested in them. The love test is the thing, and there is a marked change in his manner as he proceeds to it. Though playful and pleasant in proposing the ritual, he is strictly attentive to every detail of its execution and increasingly flamboyant in his responses to each stage of its progress. Cordelia's rebuff, once he absorbs it, provokes him to childish excesses of emotion and Kent's protest to the extravagance of physical violence. Lear puts an intolerable strain on the loyalty of those who truly love him, and it is, of course, paradoxical that the only way Cordelia and Kent can show him love and loyalty is by rejecting his demands for a showing. The consequence is the disintegration of the rituals associated with these values, a process epitomized when Lear wrenches the royal crown from his head and propels it across the map of Britain. The pattern is repeated in the betrothal sequence. There is an apparent restoration of ceremonial order with the entrance of France and Burgundy, but Lear's bitterly teasing offer of his daughter's hand is a perversion of the betrothal ritual, just as Boose says it is. The dismayed suitors know not what to think. While Burgundy proves cooperative, France does not. It remains for the French king to rebuff Lear and to reassert the value that has somehow become "mingled with regards that stands / Aloof from th' entire point" (though the line is cut, its meaning is not). He takes up Cordelia on the map that now represents her father's repudiation of her. The physical infirmity that Lear shows at his exit is the fitting correlative of his debilitation during the scene as king, priest, and father.

The BBC and Granada productions exemplify two different approaches to the enigmatic text. The BBC version minimizes Lear's kingship and stresses the disruptive effects of his incestuous preoccupation with his youngest daughter. The Granada version emphasizes Lear's kingship in order to stress his self-regarding neglect of the responsibilities of his position, including his fatherhood. Neither resolves the ambiguities of the text, but each offers a largely coherent attempt to accommodate them. In neither production is coherence complete. Both directors stumble over the coronet: Miller tries to finesse the property by omitting it; Elliott adopts the expedient of substituting the royal crown. Thus both versions of act 1, scene 1 remain partial responses to Shakespeare's "darker purpose."

2

The Wicked Sisters: 1.4 and 2.4

In *The Empty Space*, Peter Brook talks of his experience with a woman who had neither read nor seen *King Lear*. He asked that woman to read Goneril's speech in the opening scene, in which Lear's first-born daughter professes her love to her father. The woman read the lines simply, with "eloquence and charm." When Brook explained that Goneril was a wicked character and asked the woman to read the lines for hypocrisy, she had difficulty doing so, for the "simple music of the words" resists such a reading. Still, anyone who knows *King Lear* and who has witnessed Goneril's monstrous behavior later in the play would read into the unmeasured love expressed in these early lines the hypocrisy of a wicked daughter. Brook's point is that such preconceptions too often shape production, simplifying character relationships and producing what he calls "deadly theatre."[1]

The admonition is instructive, particularly for those who have been seduced by foreknowledge or theatrical convention into believing in the inevitable. There is, in fact, nothing in either Goneril's or Regan's professions of love to suggest that these two are the wicked stepsisters of the Cinderella fairytale or even the pettily malicious young women who appear in the second scene of *The True Chronicle Historie of King Leir*.[2] Clearly, the Goneril who plots against her husband (4.2) and who poisons her sister (5.3) is wicked, as is the Regan who tortures Gloucester and thrusts the blind man out of the gates, letting him "smell / His way to Dover" (3.7), and who competes with Goneril for Edmund's visits to the "forfended place" (5.1). But a production in which either or both of the sisters grow into evil is every bit as possible and as plausible as one in which the two are implacably wicked from the start. Indeed, given the complex network of relationships in *King Lear*, such a production is more likely to serve what Rosenberg calls the changing "dramatic equation" of the play.[3]

When a troupe of British actors, sponsored by the Alliance for Creative Theatre, Education, and Research (ACTER), was in residence at our campus in 1985, they premiered their five-actor, empty-space *King Lear*. In that production, Sheila Allen's Goneril and Pippa Guard's Regan offered their expressions of love in earnest: these were women who did indeed love their father. Their voices were those of complaisant daughters, willing to play their father's public game, to express, in the excess appropriate to the occasion, a love that is nonetheless sincere. Allen and Guard declined to present the two elder sisters as malignant from the outset. Instead, they took the risk of showing Goneril and Regan progressing from conventional daughterliness to vicious perversity.

Allen's Goneril was prompted by a rash father's stubborn insistence that she house his ill-mannered knights and by his overreaction to her resistance. When Lear pronounced his curse in scene 4 of act 1, praying for Goneril's sterility, the astonished daughter fell to her knees, then groveled on the ground, her mouth agape in horror. This was a woman who was herself sinned against and who reacted by sinning. In her vulnerability at the hands of an irrational father, she recalled Cordelia in scene 1, as well as Kent; unlike those two, she embraced self-serving hostility instead of responding to Lear's terrible rebuke with selfless decency and love.

Guard played Regan as an apparently sensible woman who is rather shocked by the behavior of her father. When she greeted him in 2.4, she was affectionate, becoming patronizing only in response to Lear's extravagance. With the arrival of Goneril, she showed confidence in her sister but tried to reason with her father, speaking many words while Goneril spoke few. Lear's raging was what hardened her against him. For Guard's Regan, the irreversible hardening in evil occurred in 3.7, with the blinding of Gloucester. Angry at the opening of the scene, she became increasingly excited, taking the initiative in plucking out the old man's eyes. Though at first horrified by the act, she was soon exhilarated by it, gloating over Gloucester's misplaced trust in his bastard son—almost as though she were gloating over her own betrayal of Lear.

Such an approach to Goneril and Regan in production, we think, extends the interpretive dialectic of the play in performance. By way of developing it, we shall concentrate on 1.4 and

2.4, since the proposition that the two characters are not implacably evil from the start makes these scenes particularly telling.
In them, each of the daughters interacts with Lear for the first
time after the division of the kingdom. The dynamics of that
interaction serve to recall the daughters' earlier professions of
love and to seal their subsequent cruelty. The audience's response to the Goneril of 1.4 and the Regan of 2.4 becomes
the measure by which it judges these "unnatural hags."

There may, of course, be a clue to the elder sisters' potential
for ingratitude as early as the opening scene, not in their public
professions of love but in Cordelia's private conversation with
the pair at the end of the scene. As the disinherited daughter
bids farewell to her sisters, in her first and only speeches to
them, she leaves them with less than salutary words. Acknowledging they are "the jewels of our father," she claims to know
more about them—"I know you what you are"; only her sibling
loyalty restrains her from speaking their faults. When Regan
retorts "Prescribe not us our duty" and Goneril points to Cordelia's own fault—"You have obedience scanted"[4]—Cordelia expresses her sense of a moral order that her own experience
has just suggested may not prevail: "Time shall unfold what
plighted cunning hides, / Who covers faults, at last shame them
derides" (1.1.282–83). Given the circumstance—and without entertaining preconceptions—how much trust can an audience
place in Cordelia's judgment? Clearly accustomed to her father's
favor, she has just witnessed her sisters' excessive but eloquent
protestations of love. Herself unable to heave her heart into
her mouth, might she envy the ease with which her sisters
respond to her father's demand? Cordelia knows her love for
her father is greater than her sisters', yet they have won the
prize. When she confronts them with their faults, she cannot
name them, even as she was unable to name her love for Lear.
In the context of Cordelia's special affection for her father, her
verbal reticence, and the rebuff she has just sustained, one could
hardly expect salutary words, even from the fair Cordelia. An
audience seeking to know Goneril and Regan better must await
the sequel.

Cordelia's farewell to her sisters is significant, then, not because it reveals something certain about their characters—it
rather reveals something uncertain about Cordelia's—but because it urges the pragmatic pair into fortifying themselves
against Lear. They know well that their father has always favored
Cordelia, yet in a gross display of "poor judgment" he has "cast

her off." The sisters conclude that they are up against an "unruly waywardness that infirm and choleric years bring with them." They must be ready to protect themselves from "Such unconstant starts."

The sisters' assessment of Lear is an accurate one, reflecting both Kent's judgment in scene 1 and our own. For defending Lear's best-loved daughter from Lear's proud and capricious ire, Lear's faithful follower earns banishment. Like Goneril and Regan, Kent sees Lear's repudiation of Cordelia as folly, a "hideous rashness," perpetrated by a "mad . . . old man."

That rashness appears to prevail as Lear begins his alternative residencies with his daughters. When next we see Lear's first-born, in scene 3, she is complaining to her servant Oswald of the behavior of Lear and his retinue. Oswald confirms that her father struck her gentleman "for chiding of his fool," apparently only one of a series of misdeeds:

> By day and night he wrongs me! Every hour
> He flashes into one gross crime or other,
> That sets us all at odds.
>
> (1.3.4–6)

Unwilling to tolerate such behavior in her home, Goneril instructs her servant and his fellows to "Put on what weary negligence you please" without regard for Lear's displeasure. She will feign illness, absenting herself while she writes to Regan, who, she knows, will support her.

At the very least, the Goneril who approaches Lear in 1.4 is out of patience. The price she has paid for her share of the kingdom is higher than she had expected: as she put it to Oswald, she must suffer an

> Idle old man,
> That still would manage those authorities
> That he hath given away! Now, by my life,
> Old fools are babes again, and must be us'd
> With checks as flatteries, when they are seen abus'd.[5]
>
> (1.3.17–21)

By her account, Lear "upbraids us / On every trifle," and his one hundred knights have disturbed her placid household. When she complains to Lear, she accuses his "insolent retinue" of carping and quarreling, "breaking forth / In rank and not-to-be endured riots," which Lear not only endures but endorses.

It is not easy to assess the relative truth or falsity of these charges. Lear's own wayward and preemptory disposition lends plausibility to the accusation that his followers have behaved badly. Yet, as Stephen Booth points out, the "one representative knight we meet," in 1.4.55–65, "is not only notably civil and decorous himself but particularly sensitive to incivility and indecorum in others."[6] In the action immediately following, however, the disguised Kent, newly accepted as "Caius" into Lear's service, treats Oswald with "just the kind of bluff, cheerful brutality that one would expect from the entourage Goneril describes."[7] Booth's point is that Shakespeare's treatment of the tension between Goneril and Lear is systematically ambiguous, evoking "contradictory responses"[8] in the audience.

Goneril's conversation with Lear is repeatedly punctuated by the Fool's commentary, in which he acridly suggests that her complaints pervert the natural order: daughter telling father what to do is akin to the young cuckoo biting off its surrogate mother's head or to the cart that draws the horse. Indeed, having observed that "Old fools are babes again," Goneril means to treat Lear like a child, resolved that his recent caprices have changed him "from what you rightly are." Lear too understands the impropriety of Goneril's counsel, coming as it does from a daughter who is being less than daughterly. "Are you our daughter!" he asks, then mockingly seeks to affirm that he is—or is not—Lear:

> Does any here know me? This is not Lear.
> Does Lear walk thus? Speak thus? Where are his eyes?
> Either his notion weakens, his discernings
> Are lethargied—Ha! Waking? 'Tis not so.
> Who is it that can tell me who I am?
>
> (1.4.222–26)

But Goneril's admonishing of Lear for his "pranks" does not go without sympathetic notice, for it is followed by a speech of consummate sobriety, Goneril's most reasoned plea to her father to restore the order of her home:

> I do beseech you
> To understand my purposes aright.
> As you are old and reverend, should be wise.
> Here do you keep a hundred knights and squires,
> Men so disorder'd, so debosh'd and bold,
> That this our court, infected with their manners,

Shows like a riotous inn. Epicurism and lust
Makes it more like a tavern or a brothel
Than a grac'd palace. The shame itself doth speak
For instant remedy.

(1.4.234–43)

The exchange delicately balances conflicting notions of propriety and order. Lear himself upset the natural and social order by relinquishing his kingdom prematurely, delivering his lands and his responsibility into the hands of his daughters while still maintaining the name of king. Though his eldest daughter was quick to obey in the opening scene, proffering her love as Lear commanded, now she claims dominion over her own household, her father included. As the uprooted subjects and servants of a king in title only, Lear's knights may well have become unruly, responding to the breach of social order that Lear imposed upon them. Lear's faithful supporter, the Fool, reproaches Goneril for her attempt to make Lear an "obedient father," yet he himself suffers from the effects of Lear's actions: since Cordelia went to France—since Lear divided his kingdom—he "hath much pin'd away." Lear reacts with astonishment and fury to Oswald's arrogance and Goneril's accusation: "You strike my people, and your disorder'd rabble / Make servants of their betters." The only name he can give to this evocation of disorder is "Ingratitude." But an audience—and it was probably true of Shakespeare's audience as well as a contemporary one—cannot help measuring Goneril's violation of order in the context of Lear's. In this situation, what may be said to constitute propriety and order?

For Lear, there is no ambiguity and no mitigation of his eldest daughter's fault, which makes Cordelia's seem "small": Goneril's unnatural treatment of her father deserves punishment in kind. Now in the presence of Albany as well as his offending daughter, he pronounces a terrible but fitting malediction, that "nature" either curse her with sterility or inflict on her the disfiguring "torment" of a "thankless child":

Hear, Nature, hear; dear goddess, hear!
Suspend thy purpose, if thou didst intend
To make this creature fruitful!
Into her womb convey sterility;
Dry up in her the organs of increase,
And from her derogate body never spring

A babe to honor her! If she must teem,
Create her child of spleen, that it may live
And be a thwart disnatur'd torment to her!
Let it stamp wrinkles in her brow of youth,
With cadent tears fret channels in her cheeks,
Turn all her mother's pains and benefits
To laughter and contempt, that she may feel
How sharper than a serpent's tooth it is
To have a thankless child!

(1.4.272–86)

Lear also has a practical solution: he will turn to Regan, who, he is sure, will not only treat him as a daughter should but will, with her nails, flay the "wolvish visage" of her sister. He joins this imprecation, in his final words, with a threat to resume his cast-off power.

It is an alarmed but practical Goneril who responds. In the Quarto version of this scene's end, she is all business, brushing aside Albany's misgivings, dispatching the Fool, and issuing instructions to Oswald. The Folio text includes thirteen additional lines between the exit of the Fool and the entrance of Oswald (1.4.319–31), all but one spoken by Goneril. These show her, as Steven Urkowitz suggests, "thinking aloud during the intervals between her brusque comands."[9] There is no wisdom, she reflects ironically, in permitting Lear a hundred armed knights to "enguard his dotage with their pow'rs / And hold our lives in mercy." To Albany's objection that she may "fear too far," she replies, "Safer than trust too far." Knowing her father's "heart," she has written of her fear to Regan, apparently proposing the reduction of Lear's retinue—and thus preparing the audience for 2.4.[10] Finally, in both versions, Goneril gives Oswald license to embellish her message as needed and secures from Albany his uneasy acquiescence in her actions.

More important than her husband's assessment of Goneril's initiative is, of course, the audience's. How serious a threat to her household has Lear been? Might she have been more accommodating of a king who has so recently yielded his kingdom to her and who is, after all, her father? Is her violation of the bond of kinship a justifiable act of self-defense or a spiteful assertion of power? How is Goneril affected by Lear's response to her plea that he return to his rightful self? How is she affected by his curse? Given the last public encounter she had with her father, which won his approval, how does this public rejection affect her? Certainly the events in 1.4 are damaging: to

Lear, to Goneril and Lear, and to Goneril. But how an audience feels about Goneril as Lear and his attendants head off to Regan's depends on how a production shapes the progress of this father-daughter exchange.

Had Brook extended his argument against preconceiving the elder sisters, he would undoubtedly also have warned against monocular vision of them. Though in the opening scene Cordelia addresses Goneril and Regan as though they shared the same faults, and though Regan herself claims to be made of the "self mettle" as her sister, subsequent appearances of the middle daughter suggest that she and Goneril are not the interchangeable Dromios of *King Lear*. Brook could well argue that the Regan of scene 1 is not yet wicked, yet were he to ask the anonymous woman for a reading of Regan's love speech, that woman's "simple eloquence" might become more complex. For while Regan passes her test with aplomb, flattering her father with expressions of unmatched love, just as Goneril does, Regan also scores a well-placed point against her sister:

> I am made of that self mettle as my sister,
> And prize me at her worth. In my true heart
> I find she names my very deed of love;
> Only she comes too short. . . .

> (1.1.69–72)

The "Only she comes too short" may simply be a rhetorical strategy, Regan's way of valorizing her own utterance; it may signal a playful spirit; or it may reveal the malignity that Brook proposes may not be there.

Lear's love test has three parts, and because the third of these, involving Cordelia, is distinct from the first two, it is easy to see the elder sisters as made of the same mettle. But the Regan of scene 1 chooses not simply to offer evidence of love that will satisfy Lear; she chooses as well to claim superiority over her sister. In the BBC production, Regan even takes a step toward her father when he asks, "Which of you shall we say doth love us most?", making his "Goneril, / Our eldest-born, speak first" Lear's concession to propriety. While Goneril is halting in speech until she is sure of her course, Regan responds with confidence to the competition and shows pleasure when Albany's and Goneril's faces register shock at her having put her sister down. In the Granada production, Lear gestures to Goneril to kiss the map on the ground before professing her love; when

Regan's turn comes, she falls to the ground and kisses the map without instruction, then kisses Lear's hand and smilingly delivers her lines. This is a Regan who knows how to please her father and proceeds to do so. At "Only she comes too short," the old man raises his eyebrows in sport, complementing the gesture with a hearty "Oh ho." Regan's performance in the love test earns her more than "this ample third of our fair kingdom"; it earns her a closer look as "one o' the pairings."

Each of the elder daughters figures prominently in certain scenes following act 1, scene 1 and prior to act four. In 1.3, 1.4, and 2.4, Goneril is preoccupied with her father, and most of the time she is in his presence. As a consequence, an audience has no measure of her behavior apart from the context of the intolerable domestic crisis her father has caused. In Regan's case, however, the audience has the advantage of seeing her in action on various occasions both before and after 2.4 and at a time when Lear has not yet dwelled in or disrupted her home. When she arrives with her husband at Gloucester's residence in 2.1, to be sure, she has been "well inform'd" by her sister and is seeking to avoid Lear and his "riotous knights"; but her attention is simultaneously engaged by the wounded Edmund's show of filial loyalty, which prompts Cornwall to take the handsome bastard into his service. This scene serves to situate Regan with respect to both the Lear plot and the Gloucester plot. The two occasions that frame her first meeting with Lear since the love test similarly encompass both plots—the stocking of Kent (2.2) and the blinding of Gloucester (3.7). These provide the specific context for Regan's treatment of her father in 2.4. Together, the three scenes may well track a progression in evil, the realization of the potential for malignity at least suggested by Regan's reproach of Goneril's too moderate profession of love.

If 2.1 finds Regan in flight from her father rather than at home preparing to receive him and his knights, 2.2 finally shows her shaming him in the person of his servant. This episode is complicated, however, by the extravagant belligerence of the disguised Kent in his outrage at the presence of Oswald. Once the one-sided fight between the rival messengers is broken up, Kent greets Regan and Cornwall with a display of insolence and insult that provoke them into stocking him. Though he means to serve Lear, his behavior proves, as Rosenberg observes, a "special kind of disserving service to Lear."[11] Kent loses whatever opportunity he might have had to be Lear's spokesman.

His "saucy roughness" is received not as evidence of righteous indignation but as proof of Goneril's report: "This is a fellow of the self-same color / Our sister speaks of. Come, bring away the stocks!" Still, the balance in the scene shifts when Cornwall orders the stocking of the king's surrogate. Moreover, Regan compounds the insult to her father. Unable to resist topping Cornwall (as is her wont), she extends his sentence on Kent— "Till noon? Till night, my lord; and all night too!"—then responds to Kent's "Why, madam, if I were your father's dog, / You should not use me so" with the final word to the astonished messenger: "Sir, being his knave, I will." Though she preferred to "further think of it" when Goneril proposed they "hit together" in the first scene, now Regan clearly has taken sides. In spite of Gloucester's pleadings on behalf of her father, she expresses concern only for the sensibilities of her sister:

> My sister may receive it much more worse
> To have her gentleman abus'd, assaulted,
> For following her affairs. Put in his legs.
>
> (1.2.151–53)

For Lear, the humiliation he endured at the hands of Goneril is replayed and intensified in 2.4. Earlier, he had been able to redress the chiding of his Fool by striking Goneril's gentleman; now, facing the stocked Kent, he can do nothing but register suffocating disbelief and shock. In act 1, scene 4, Albany, at least, remained ignorant of how his wife had offended Lear; here Cornwall is accomplice to the deed. In 1.4, Goneril had feigned illness, unwilling to receive her father; now both Regan and Cornwall absent themselves from him, sending word that they are ill. In 1.4, Lear had to negotiate through Oswald, who treated him with disrespect, refusing even to respond to the king's query, then offending him further by calling him "My lady's father." That episode ended happily for Lear, however, who took pleasure in Kent's tripping of the "clotpoll." In 2.4, Lear must go off to fetch his daughter himself, but he returns with Gloucester instead. And Gloucester, though sympathetic, presumes to caution the king about "the fiery quality of the Duke, / How unremovable and fix'd he is / In his own course." At first appalled, Lear insists that Gloucester command them to come, then, struggling for patience, concedes that the Duke might be ill. Finally, noticing Kent, Lear decides that Cornwall and his daughter are in fact snubbing him. If, like Edgar, Lear had thought in 1.4 that "I am at the worst," he must surely realize now that "I am worse than e'er I was."

Still, when Regan finally appears, it is not with Goneril's frontlet but with a warm and reverent welcome: "I am glad to see your Highness." Lear responds to her welcome with reassurances, then tells her of her sister's "Sharp-tooth'd unkindness." As incredulous now recalling Goneril's depravity (he can "scarce speak") as he was listening to Kent (now released) accuse Regan and Cornwall of putting him in the stocks, Lear looks to his second daughter for affection and comfort. But her response throws him off balance: if Goneril complained, Regan is certain her sister had cause. Within moments of their reunion, Lear finds himself in mock performance, responding to Regan as he had to Goneril in 1.4. At Goneril's suggestion that he was not what he should be, he had turned to his men, pretending not to know himself, pleading for someone to tell him who he is. Now, at Regan's suggestion that he ask Goneril's forgiveness, he falls to his knees, begging his absent daughter to provide him with "raiment, bed, and food." Regan's response, "Good sir, no more! These are unsightly tricks," strikingly recalls Goneril's "This admiration, sir, is much o' th' savor / Of other your new pranks."

This repetition of events gives an audience good cause to regard the sisters as the interchangeable characters of an Ionesco play, and Jan Kott might argue that such a reading helps elucidate the absurdist vision of Lear. Indeed, a discussion of the progress of Lear from unseeing arrogance to insightful madness could profit from a communal catalog of the daughters' "unsightly tricks." But a discussion of the "wicked sisters" is necessarily more discriminating, and an audience responding to the similarities in Lear's encounters with Goneril in 1.4 and with Regan in 2.4 should notice, as it did in the opening scene, the variation as well. The fact is that, both in her profession of daughterly love and in her manner of receiving their father, Regan does her sister one better. And in the unnatural bonding that brings 2.4 to its climax, she takes the lead in action and utterance.

Up to the point of Goneril's entrance, Regan manifests a regard for her father and a confidence in her sister that is sweetly reasonable. Her firm insistence on Lear's age and its attendant infirmities is punctuated by expressions of respect ("O, sir," "Good sir," "I pray you") and even piety: "O the blest gods! So will you wish on me, / When the rash mood is on." Though she sounds a note of vexation in this last speech, she does not couple it, as Goneril did, with an ultimatum. It is only when Lear describes her "tender-hefted nature" by cataloging her obligations to him that she brings him up sharply, "Good sir, to th' purpose," and provokes the furious question he has avoided: "Who put my man i' th' stocks?" The blast of Goneril's trumpet and the appearance of Oswald interrupt the exchange. Stung by the sight of the steward, Lear repeats his question, now making explicit the test it implies: "Who stock'd my servant? Regan, I have good hope / Thou didst not know on 't." In the Folio version, he addresses this to Regan after the entrance of Goneril at line 186: in his preoccupation with his middle daughter, either he does not see the eldest or he does not at once acknowledge her.[12] However, he is soon twisted into recognition first of her offending presence and then of the sisters' common cause: "O Regan, will you take her by the hand?" When the agonized king vents his fury and disappointment by asking a third time, "How came my man i' th' stocks?" and gets an answer from Cornwall, even he knows the question is futile.

The entrance of Goneril is obviously a turning point in Lear's interaction with Regan, and yet the pattern of variation between the sisters continues. While Goneril bluntly dismisses Lear's protest as "dotage" and remains crisply ruthless throughout the rest of the scene, Regan, by comparison, is expansive, explanatory, diplomatic. Goneril is already hardened against her father, but Regan is still in the process of revealing and possibly discovering her own nature. Though insisting on his age and weakness, she continues her exchange with Lear in the same accents as before, explaining that she is not yet prepared to receive him in her home, defending her sister's judgment, and pointing out the difficulties and dangers of accommodating Lear's many followers—"'Tis hard, almost impossible." Even at this point, line 242, Rosenberg notes, "Regan still does not absolutely reject Lear."[13] But the informing dynamic of Regan's personality has already taken over. In a parodic inversion of the love test, she enters into a competition with her sister to deprive Lear of the prerogatives due him as king and father. The fifty knights that Goneril will allow in Lear's retinue Regan reduces to twenty-five. Lear's response repeats his foolishness in measuring love and compounds his humiliation: just as he had bargained with his daughters in the first scene, now he equates numbers with love, telling the Goneril he has condemned that he will go with her: "Thy fifty yet doth double five-and-twenty, / And thou art twice her love." Following her sister's lead, Goneril reduces the retinue to ten, then five, leaving Regan, again, the final word: "What need one?" The moralizing Regan ends the scene by counseling Gloucester to shut up his doors on Lear. When Goneril rebuffed him, Lear sought refuge with her sister; when Regan rejects him, there is no refuge but the heath.

Clearly Regan has treated her bemused father cruelly. Both daughters will look like the "unnatural hags" Lear calls them when, in his reunion with Cordelia, the old man laments,

> I know you do not love me; for your sisters
> Have, as I do remember, done me wrong.
> You have some cause, they have not.
>
> (4.7.75–77)

Cordelia replies, "No cause, no cause." Unlike her sisters, Cordelia has known from the start the meaning of a father/daughter bond, within which none of the elder sisters' unkind behavior could claim cause. But in responding to the elder sisters, an audience also recognizes its bond, which is to consider not only principle but motivation as well. The question in judging Regan is not simply whether she was justified in violating her bond with Lear—there she could claim no cause—but whether Shakespeare gave her the motivation to do so, as he did Goneril.

The elder daughters have proven themselves pragmatists, both in the love test and in their confidential conversation at the end of the first scene of act 1. It is in part pragmatism that prompts Goneril to speak with her father about his riotous knights and to write to her sister for support. It is pragmatism that urges Regan to begin her interview in 2.4 sweetly; until she has the strategic advantage, she will proceed with care. But cutting Lear's retinue to twenty-five and, eventually, to none when Goneril has already reduced it to fifty carries pragmatism to excess. The need, indeed, cannot be reasoned, nor need it be. Yet Regan, showing no sign of the abundant love she professed in act 1, scene 1, has made reason supreme, the kind of reason she appeals to when she admonishes her father, "For those that mingle reason with your passion / Must be content to think that you are old . . ." (2.4.234–35). Were it not that Shakespeare provides suggestions that such rationality is consistent with wanton cruelty, all that Regan does in this sequence of scenes might be explained as prompted by "common sense."

The most persistent of these suggestions resides in the pattern of Regan's need to outdo the doings of others. But structurally there are suggestions as well. Shakespeare places Regan's cruelly pragmatic approach to her father after the shameless stocking of Kent. And, more importantly, he provides a corollary of her treatment of Lear in Regan's next appearance: the blinding of Gloucester in 3.7. There, in an act that recalls her baiting of Kent, she ignobly plucks at Gloucester's beard. Then, as Cornwall sets his foot on Gloucester's eye, she urges "One side will mock another; th' other too!"—just as she had added to her father's torment by further reducing his train. Finally, it is she who moralizes Edmund's treachery and orders Gloucester be "thrust . . . out at gates," recalling her similar treatment of Lear. The blinding of Gloucester becomes a physical correlative of the torture she inflicted on her father, which, seen now in this context, is irredeemably severe. Gloucester's assessment of Regan for her cruelty to Lear seals the connection: he sent Lear to Dover "Because I would not see thy cruel nails / Pluck out his poor old eyes."

By now, of course, an audience has witnessed the consequences of Regan's rejection of her father, having followed the mad king on the heath. The scene of Gloucester's blinding, the consequence of his own son's betrayal, confirms the growing feeling that Regan's reactions are grotesque: it is not Gloucester and Lear who are treacherous; the traitors are their "bastard" children, whether bastard by birth (Edmund) or by paternal proclamation (in 1.4, Lear calls Goneril "Degenerate bastard"; in 2.4, he greets Regan by saying were she not glad to see him—she soon proves she is not—"I would divorce me from my mother's tomb, / Sepulchring an adultress"). All three have been unnaturally vicious. But Regan, without the prompting of riotous knights or the deprivations of illegitimacy, seems once again to have topped the others. In this world of broken allegiances and brutal action, it is a fitting touch that the judgment of Regan's wickedness is finally secured not by the complaints of Lear or the condemnations of Gloucester, nor by the sympathy generated by their unhappy lots, but by the rebuke of her husband's servant. Though this anonymous servant has been faithful to Cornwall all his life, when the Duke gouges out Gloucester's eye, he draws his sword to stop and then mortally wound his master. During the confrontation, he puts it to Regan, "If you did wear a beard upon your chin, / I'd shake it on this quarrel!" Astonished at the servant's breach of propriety ("A peasant stand up thus?"), though she has done the same with lesser cause, she seizes a sword and kills him.

Regan's offenses are rank, and by 3.7 her wickedness smells to heaven. And though less prominent in these middle scenes, Goneril is her ally in abomination: if Regan participates in the blinding of Gloucester, it is Goneril who exhorts "Pluck out his eyes." Yet the progress of each to this point has been discrete. Goneril began hers by responding to a provoking event, an upheaval in her home. But Regan, like Edmund, seems driven by an insistent psychological need. She is, finally, the richer character in her malignity, though probably the more difficult sister to play. For with Regan, the progress of evil—from the opening scene through the first scenes of act 2 to 2.4 and 3.7—is marked not so much by the dramatic action as by the emphases an actress brings to the role.

Productions

BBC

The Goneril of both the Quarto and the Folio is a woman who does not suffer fools gladly. Taunted by Lear's Fool in 1.4, she reacts with a contemptuous sneer for the fooling servant and a patronizing rebuke for his foolish master. This is the woman who, in 1.3, expressing chagrin at the behavior of Lear and his followers, announced (in the Quarto) that "Old fools are babes again." The Goneril of the BBC production makes much of these textual signals. In 1.4, she initially shows her father unrelieved condescension, reasoning with him indeed as one would with a child. While the Fool hovers near her shoulder and Kent as Caius remains at her back, in a chamber filled with the king's retainers, she stands in the foreground face to face with Lear, eyes focused on his, waving and clenching one hand as she admonishes him. In the accents of parental authority, she proffers first her complaint—his "insolent retinue" hourly carps and quarrels—and then her disappointment:

> I had thought, by making this well known unto you,
> To have found a safe redress, but now grow fearful,
> By what yourself too late have spoke and done,
> That you protect this course. . . .
>
> (1.4.202–5)

The Wicked Sisters. BBC Production. Penelope Wilton as Regan, Gillian Barge as Goneril, Michael Hordern as King Lear. Courtesy of the British Broadcasting Corporation. Copyright © BBC.

Lear has not only failed to keep his followers in line; he himself seems to have encouraged their "riots." If he has, she warns shaking her head, it is such a "fault" as "Would not scape censure."

Perhaps it is unlikely that Goneril's parental manner might ever have prevailed with Lear. But the tactic is bound to fail in the present circumstances. The old man has just sustained the impudence of Oswald, who identified the king as "My lady's father," and the taunting of a particularly truculent and merciless Fool, who reproached the king for having made "thy daughters thy mothers." Rather than endure further humiliation, Lear insists on asserting his own parental identity and authority. Turning from Goneril, he moves upstage through the corridor formed by his company of men, histrionically asking, with a false chuckle, "Does any here know me?" In the foreground, Goneril assumes the expression and posture of the long-suffering, exasperated mother, now with both hands on hips, now with one hand fingering her collar, as she waits for her father's charade to end. On Lear's return, when he touches her arm with his riding crop, she bats it away and then stiffly meets his mockery with a scolding for his "new pranks," again the accusing mother to the misbehaving child. Whereupon she suddenly abandons the pose.

A closeup camera, fixed on Goneril's face over Lear's back, marks her shift into a mode of earnest entreaty: "I do beseech you," and she pauses, "To understand my purposes aright." Lear quickly catches the change in tone. As the camera returns to a two-shot for Goneril's sober, almost whispered catalog of his knights' misdeeds, he raises his hand and shushes her lest she offend them. This abrupt concern for decorum is ironic but fitting. It is Goneril and Lear, along with the Fool, who have engaged in indecorous displays; the behavior of Lear's knights has been singularly mild and inoffensive throughout the scene. The silent testimony of the knights forms a commentary on the principals, calling in question both Goneril's charges and Lear's extravagant reaction. In the context of this discussion, though, Goneril's altering style is what invites special scrutiny.

It appears that Lear's eldest daughter is not the self-assured woman that her confident and patronizing demeanor, here and in 1.3, may have suggested. Though she seeks to control occasions, she cannot control her reactions to them. Certainly, she proves to be not a strategist but a tactician in her dealings with her father. At the end of act 1, scene 1, worrying that Lear's poor judgment would touch her, she had warned her sister "We must do something, and i' the heat," but she apparently remained uncertain as to what this quick action should be. Days or weeks later, in her own home, she complains to Oswald of her father's wronging her, resolving "I will not speak with him. Say I am sick." But the moment the horns sound Lear's arrival, she decides not simply to insult her father by not receiving him but to confront him with her gripe. Directing Oswald to slight the king and neglect his knights, she proposes to "breed from hence occasions." Having created such an occasion through her servant's effrontery, she follows her plan, treating Lear like the child she observed he was. When that tactic fails, she shifts to an earnest plea that her father understand her purposes and agree "A little to disquantity your train." When Lear responds with outrage, however, styling her a "Degenerate bastard" and calling for his horses, she too relinquishes her composure. As he storms to the upper end of the room, she shouts loudly and angrily after him: "You strike my people, and your disorder'd rabble / Make servants of their betters."

Goneril has exhausted her tactical repertory and lost control. When Lear strides back downstage a moment later, dragging Albany by the arm, she stands in helpless silence, clasping her hands in front of her, pinned by her father's glare. Though she manages a tight smile at Lear's praise for his men and an irritable grimace for Albany, she quails under her father's curse of "sterility." On the word, her firm lips part, her face turns toward the camera, and her hands hold her midsection; as Lear denies her a "babe to honor her," she shuts her eyes and then opens them to face him aghast, spreading her right hand over her breast and her left over her stomach. "Never afflict yourself," she says to the bewildered Albany, on the mass departure upstage of the king and his men, but her voice rises and breaks at the end of the speech, betraying her own affliction. When the shouting Lear returns, now with only Kent and the Fool in his train, Goneril raises her hand to cover her mouth and her distress at the prospect of another encounter.

Like Cordelia, whose name Lear invokes just before pronouncing his malediction, Goneril has endured the ultimate expression of her father's wrath. As the younger daughter had stood silent and shocked at Lear's disavowal of paternal care, so Goneril stands silent and shocked at Lear's curse. The filming of the two scenes in counterpoint, with the frame accommodating Lear and his daughter, Kent or Albany in the background between them, with others watching, endows the moment with an ironic resonance and elicits a residual sympathy for Goneril: as she feared it might, the "poor judgment" that Lear showed in casting off Cordelia has at length touched her.

But Goneril does not respond with a chastened assertion of her love: she is not in a forgiving mood. Bracing herself, she turns with her hands again on her hips, her head and frame thrown back, a picture of haughty composure, to confront her father. Though Lear rages at the order she has issued to dismiss fifty of his knights, in the now almost empty room, she is unmoved by his anger or by his shame at being so shaken. Only when Lear threatens her "wolfish visage" with Regan's nails does she raise a protective hand to her cheek. On his parting threat, to resume the shape of the authority he shed in his folly, Goneril tosses her head and sighs self-righteously, overacting her exasperation with an emphatically drawn out "Do you mark that."

Clearly, in spite of her waxen countenance, Goneril is unsettled by her father's rage. Fidgeting with her left hand, the other on her hip, she dismisses the Fool; then, in a high, strained voice, she explains to her husband that permitting Lear to keep so many knights is neither politic nor safe, punctuating her speech with a nervous laugh and pulling away from Albany with distaste when he reassures her that she may "fear too far." But just as clearly, Goneril is bent on action. "I know his heart," she says, facing the camera and making a fist. Confident in her instructions to Oswald, who will deliver her report to Regan, she firmly tells Albany she has no patience for his "milky gentleness and course."

In mounting the BBC production, Miller was apparently loath to yield to a preconception of Goneril. For Miller, scene 4 of act 1 is pivotal in Goneril's initiation into the evil that characterizes her later in the play. At first put-upon but superficially sure of herself, as the sequence progresses she is shaken in her judgment of herself and her father. By the scene's end, she is a woman prepared to pursue non-gentle means to protect her interests and to minimize the damage her formidable father has caused or may cause.

The BBC Regan, like her sister, is an elegant lady, after the style of Jacobean aristocracy, in dress, in manner, in formality of utterance. But the pair are suggestively differentiated. Where Goneril is calculating but flappable, Regan is the more impulsive but determined of the sisters. Moreover, Regan can be charming.

In 2.1, when she and Cornwall make their surprise visit to Gloucester's estate, she offers an impressive display of sympathy for the offended father and indignation at the offending Edgar, evidently, on the reports of her sister and the plausible Edmund, a companion to her father's "riotous knights." At the close of the scene, she approaches Gloucester earnestly and affectionately, seeking advice and giving comfort, smiling and stroking the gray hair of "Our good old friend." This gesture, though cruelly ironic in the sequel, wins Gloucester's heart and may well warm that of the audience. In 2.2, with the stocking of Kent, Regan is less winning. In the background through most of the scene, subdued but alert, she is not only assertive but smug when she extends Kent's sentence and sharply defends her sister's interests to the protesting Gloucester. Because she has proved, unlike Goneril, capable of showing warmth as well as asperity, we are the more curious about her confrontation with Lear.

Cornwall and Regan enter in 2.4 to receive Lear decorously, he with a bow and she with a curtsy. The formality of this acknowledgment signals the spirit in which Regan means to conduct the interview. Her greeting, "I am glad to see your Highness," is notably cool, as is the careful folding of her hands before her. Lear himself has been guarded in his greeting, and now, standing at full height, he pauses before responding. When it comes, however, the response is ingratiating, a plea for sympathy and affection: ducking and nodding his head, he crosses to Regan, clasping first one hand and then both over hers as he makes his appeal, "Regan, I think you are . . . Beloved Regan, / Thy sister's naught." In his absorption, he scarcely notices the release of Kent. Repeating her name a third and a fourth time, "O Regan," he gives her hands a loving shake and gazes into her eyes. Though Regan in return counsels patience quietly, almost reassuringly, the contrast in manner between father and daughter becomes increasingly pointed. Having indicated her bias earlier, she again defends her sister's action and deprecates Lear's reaction, prompting him to expel a breath and pull away his hands from hers, which, it is now clear, did not return his clasp. Sweetly rational, and smiling at her own suggestion, she urges her father to return to the "wrong'd" Goneril. As Lear falls to his knees, facing the camera, in mock supplication to his eldest daughter, the others on the scene gather behind Cornwall to watch. Lear's mocking tone changes to anger on the last line, to be met with an impatient "Good sir, no more" and a curt demand that he return to Goneril. But it is only when Lear rises to renew his curses on Goneril that he excites emotion in Regan. Shouting furiously "So will you wish on me," she turns her face away from him, lips trembling and eyes blinking. The closeup camera tracks the embracing Lear's reassurances and Regan's sulky return to calm, containing them both in the frame until she once more turns her face to him.

Regan's resistance to the burdens of filial affection recalls Lear from his wishful fantasizing to the reality of present affronts, the stocking of his servant and the entrance of Goneril's servant Oswald to herald the arrival of the mistress. When Goneril does arrive, far upstage, Lear turns away to invoke the heavens, then turns back to behold, along with the camera, Regan and Goneril together making a stately progress towards him, arm in arm and soon hand in hand. Though he protests, this time Goneril is ready for his rebukes, dismissing them with a supercilious air. Meanwhile, Regan gravely urges the old man to return to his eldest daughter.

With Regan taking the lead, both sisters are insistently reasonable in mercilessly proposing cuts in Lear's retinue until it is reduced to none. For most of the negotiation, the camera frames them in a medium shot, Regan on the right, and Lear downstage facing them. The sisters play off one another especially well in this production, suggesting not only a cooperative spirit but a competitive one as well. Neither wants to accommodate Lear and his knights in her home. Goneril smiles when she thinks Lear will go with Regan, and Regan looks anxious. When Goneril suggests that their own household servants attend Lear, Regan, struck by the reasonableness of the idea, emits an approving "Mmmmm." When Lear chooses Goneril because she is "twice her love," Goneril frowns, and when Regan delivers the crucial line, divesting Lear of all his men, she pokes her head forward toward him, stressing each word, then returns it to place, well satisfied.

Now, with the company forming a circle around him, Regan and Goneril still holding hands on the right, Lear meditates on reason and need, cries for patience, and promises unspeakable revenges on these "unnatural hags." Amused at the threats, Goneril tilts her head and smiles at her sister, but Regan remains tight-lipped, taking them in. In the aftermath of Lear's upstage exit, which the sisters observe from the center foreground, they continue to play off one another. While Goneril puts a gloved hand to her chin, Regan raises her eyes and blows a noiseless sigh. As thunder rumbles in the background, Regan is shrilly self-justifying, "This house is little," alternately folding and spreading her hands, the latter to assure both sister and husband, almost musically, that she would "gla-adly" receive Lear alone. Goneril is more subdued, touching her sister's hand, but quietly implacable. The signal that Regan may be the mistress of more than casual cruelty is her strident declaration over the protests of Gloucester that Lear has procured his own injuries. "Shut up your doors," she commands, adding that it is in the interest of public safety. This is the mixture of malice and moralizing that will take a more terrible shape in 3.7.

We can only guess at what transpires in Regan's life between 2.4 and 3.7, while her father is on the heath, but when we see her in the blinding scene, there is little doubt that Lear's judgment of her in 2.4 holds: she is indeed an "unnatural hag." The advance in malignity is abruptly indicated. Opening with a two-shot, the camera shows Cornwall soberly advising with Goneril and handing her a letter; when he calls for the "traitor Gloucester," Regan suddenly enters the frame close behind her sister, on the right, placing her hand on Goneril's shoulder to suggest, "Hang him instantly." Goneril looks back at the smiling Regan with her own proposal, "Pluck out his eyes," and both sisters laugh. At Cornwall's deadly serious "Leave him to my displeasure," Regan herself becomes sober, raising her hand to cover her mouth, perhaps intimidated by Cornwall, perhaps apprehensive about what is in fact to come. About this, when they are alone, Cornwall counsels her; as the couple walk toward a tracking camera, he assures her that it will be a "court'sy to our wrath."

Regan proves to be an aggressive pupil. When Gloucester is dragged in upstage by two servants and on Cornwall's order bound to a chair in the center of the chamber, Regan with an imprecation circles up and faces her host and prisoner, instructing the servants to bind him "Hard, hard." The blocking is such that we cannot see Gloucester's face, only the back of the heavy chair, with Regan upstage fronting it and the sinister Cornwall in the foregound still facing the camera. We watch the woman who once stroked her old friend's head pluck his beard and hold her trophy to the light, "So white, and such a traitor?" She is learning the pleasures of bitter mockery as well as of ruthless interrogation—"Wherefore to Dover?" she insists, apparently digging her nails into Gloucester's unseen face. By now she has been joined by Cornwall, and when he proceeds to pluck out Gloucester's eye, Regan again brings her hand to mouth, watching fixedly as the old man screams. The gesture registers fascination, not disgust, at the spectacle and culminates in a smile. Her next move may astonish even her husband. Smiling, she pushes against him and kisses him, then, hanging on his shoulder, stares at Gloucester's mangled face and recommends that the other eye be gouged out as well.

At this point, both servants intervene, one restraining Cornwall and the other Regan. In the scuffling around the chair, Cornwall sustains his mortal hurt from the sword of the first, and Regan, energized by violence, kills the first servant with the sword of the second. Once Cornwall has taken Gloucester's other eye, Regan returns to front her old friend for the last time. The blocking is an ironic variant of the earlier arrangement, with Cornwall again in the foreground, this time on the right and gasping for his life, and his wife upstage absorbed in torturing Gloucester with the disclosure of Edmund's perfidy. She punctuates her gloating revelation with an elaborate curtsy when remarking that Edmund is "too good to pity thee," and, on the reflection that the blind man "can smell / His way to Dover," she snickers and rejoins Cornwall. But her buoyant smile vanishes at the sight of her husband. She seems puzzled at the recoiling of violence on its perpetrators. The partners exit together, the husband draped on the wife, to Cornwall's offstage death.

In presenting the spectacle of the blinding, this production does not feature onscreen bloodletting. However, it suggestively underscores the horror of the episode by playing off the actions of the principals against the reactions of minor figures. Though the servants' concluding dialogue from the Quarto is cut, as in so many productions, the director compensates by having both of the servants who are assisting Cornwall intervene and by introducing a third servant who is only a presence but a compelling one. The third servant is a very old man, with snow-white hair and beard, matching his stiff collar. He remains far upstage throughout the blinding sequence, but he reacts to each phase of it. When Gloucester's first eye is taken, we see him beating his head helplessly. When the other is gouged out, we see him holding the second servant in his arms. As the scene ends, the final shot is of the old man approaching Gloucester's chair. He will, of course, appear in the next scene, 4.1, leading the blind man. In the blinding scene, he is the mute measure of Cornwall and Regan's monstrosity.

For that is what Regan achieves in this scene. She has found a new tone, one that marks not only the ease but the delight, even the passion, with which she does injury to others. Though the BBC production does not definitively dramatize the point at which Regan chooses to make evil her good, the production does trace her evolution through that point. The stages of Regan's villainy, if not its specific progression, are clear.

GRANADA

The Goneril of the Granada production is of a decidedly different stripe from her counterpart in the BBC. She shows herself, by contrast, both capable of and probably intent on evil almost from the start. In 1.3, questioning Oswald, whom she holds roughly to her, she is angry, not amazed, by her father's striking of her man. Her outrage modulates to a series of grim orders and rasping invectives. Omitting the reference to old fools and babes, she vehemently reflects on the "Idle old man" who still presumes to manage forfeited "authorities," an appropriate emphasis for this Goneril.

Sinister music accompanies her sudden appearance before Lear in 1.4, music that is pierced by the sharpness of her tongue. Older than the BBC Goneril, shorter, and buxom in a purple V-neck gown, she abjures any archness of manner. Seeking neither to school nor to persuade her father, she expresses her anger to the king and his assembled retinue in full-voiced complaints. In response, Lear too is angry. Enthroned at table as she faces him, he rises to meet the attack with bitter questions, looking about to read "Who is it that can tell me who I am?" not as mock inquiry but as an expression of withering contempt.

Goneril is unimpressed. She relentlessly pursues her bill of complaints, laughing briefly on the observation that Lear "should be wise" and raising her voice to denounce his followers, which draws from the assembly a roar of disapproval. Ordering his people from the chamber, Lear barely acknowledges Albany and then pauses to look upward and pronounce his curse. For this, the closeup camera focuses on the old man. Goneril is at some distance on his right, and only twice, as he looks or gestures in her direction, does the camera cut to her stony face. On the second cut, a jutting lower lip and a slight enlargement of the eyes are the only signs of a reaction to the terrible words. In fact, she is moved merely to a venomous commentary on Lear's "dotage." Having undertaken to overbear

The Wicked Sisters. Granada Production. Dorothy Tutin as Goneril, Diana Rigg as Regan. Courtesy of Granada Television. Copyright © Granada T.V.

her father, she has matched force with force and proved the stronger. Now obviously vulnerable, the frail king storms helplessly at the loss of his knights, pushes his fists into his eyes, and departs with a threat and a burst of confidence that seems unconvincing even to himself. This Goneril's "Do you mark that" is quietly understated but scornful, the expression of a woman intent on winning any confrontation that may ensue. Her voice and anger rise again when she dismisses the Fool and when, pacing furiously, she numbers her fears and prospects. Now, however, there is not only intense anger but hatred in her voice and manner, a hatred she moderates only slightly in response to her ineffectual husband's placating words. The sequence ends with a closeup of Goneril in profile, setting her jaw.

The Granada Goneril is hardly an appealing character, but she is a consistent one. Already vicious at the beginning of 1.4, she vents her wrath without care for kinship or kingship, wielding her power with certainty of success. Unlike her counterpart in the BBC production, this Goneril appears determined from the start to divest her father of any remnant of power. And she wins no sympathy for her method of doing so. Moreover, the closeup camera work on Lear during his curse discourages any association of Lear's rejection of Goneril with his rejection of Cordelia in act 1, scene 1, staged in a different mode. An audience can only feel that this splenetic Goneril has earned her father's curse.

Still, in the Granada production, Goneril's cause for complaint is manifest. Lear enters her home noisily, riding his horse into the chamber and calling loudly for dinner, joking and laughing boisterously with his one hundred knights. The trumpet sounds frequently, dogs bark, and the knights drink, arm wrestle, and generally make their presence known. If the presence of the carousing retinue supports Goneril's claim, though, it also supports Lear's cause, becoming a leering, cheering, complaining chorus as Goneril catalogs their faults and abuses their king. In the end, the absence of the knights is as significant as their presence. Once the knights and, finally, Lear and the Fool have departed, the room becomes cavernous in its silence, as the lamps and braziers flicker light on the empty tables, benches, and throne chair, leaving Goneril the presiding mistress of nothing.

The Granada Regan creates an impression strikingly different from that left by her sister. In the BBC production, while the two sisters are carefully distinguished, they still have much in common. Their Granada counterparts share very little, with respect to looks, manner, or personality. Goneril bears the stigma of being the homely sibling. Though erect in carriage and impeccably groomed, she still evokes dowdy middle age. In her first appearance (1.1), she looks ill at ease, apprehensive, and though she manages to offer a convincing performance for Lear in the love test, her relief when it is over is evident. In fact, she disdains subtlety of manner, as her confrontation with Lear in 1.4 makes abundantly evident. By this time, her self-serving resentment and anger have surfaced, to modulate only in intensity as the play progresses. By contrast, the tall and shapely Regan is not only beautiful in appearance, with her cameo complexion and luxuriant hair braided over her ears, but confident and winning in her ways. She smiles her way through the love test, easily topping her sister, while charming Lear into effusive murmurings of pleasure. As a character, this Regan is a consummate performer. Her manner, of course, masks motives every bit as self-serving as Goneril's, and in the end she will prove even more diabolically malignant. But she exhibits far greater range and variety in revealing her true nature.

Interestingly, the hints of this appear earlier and more strongly than they do in the BBC production. Since Goneril takes the urgent initiative in the private conversation between the sisters at the end of the opening scene, we learn there only that they share the same concerns; though there is a slight twist to her mouth as she delivers it, Regan's final line is quietly pensive, "We shall further think of it." When she appears with Cornwall at Gloucester's estate in 2.1, she shows the requisite indignation at Edgar and sympathy for Gloucester, but she offers no special gesture of endearment to her "old friend." Instead, this production creates a suggestive interaction between Regan and Edmund. Three times during the scene, the two exchange pointed glances, with the closeup camera recording each: when Edmund confirms that Edgar was of her father's "consort"; when he promises to serve Cornwall and Regan "Truly, however else"; and when Regan gratuitously turns away from Gloucester in speaking of "businesses, / Which craves the instant use." Perhaps unsurprisingly for this Regan, a sexual motive is already operative. At the stocking of Kent, in 2.2, there is a hint of something more vicious. Though standing by cool and imperious for most of Cornwall's interview with Kent, she not only steps forward to extend the sentence but, over Gloucester's protest, walks all the way downstage herself to slam the stocks shut on Kent's legs, smiling as she draws a cry of pain. The various signals Regan has given in her early scenes begin to cohere in 2.4 and culminate in 3.7.

The Granada Regan of 2.4 greets her frail and failing father with a radiant smile. As the gasping Lear half listens to the Fool's story of "kindness," the camera reveals that Regan and Cornwall have entered upstage behind him. Lear turns tentatively, to see Regan approach him with her greeting and her smile. The old king is pitiful as he tells of Goneril's behavior, ending his first speech by putting his hands up to his face to cry. Regan offers comfort, "I pray you, sir, take patience," pressing close to him and speaking with soft but certain reason in defense of her sister. But there is condescension in her gentle daughterliness, which even Lear seems to detect when, in response to "My curses on her," Regan touches his chin to stay him and informs him of his age. Because Lear's mock supplication is cut in this production, she has no occasion to speak of "unsightly tricks." She remains smoothly, even brightly, persuasive. When Lear turns to the camera to renew his angry curses on Goneril, however, Regan reacts with studied indignation, tinged with apparent fear: "So you will wish on me." After listening impassively to Lear's reassurances, which end in a whining reminder of her debt to him, she drops the mask, with a dismissive "Sir, to th' purpose."

Trumpets, but no Oswald, announce the arrival of Goneril. Her entrance is highlighted. As Lear is in the midst of his grim question about Kent, a bustle in the chamber turns him around, and, with a surge of ominous music, the camera zooms on the eldest sister glaring into it and tossing the train of her cloak over her arm. In effect, she is already present, though the audience hasn't yet seen her, when Lear says "Who comes here?" and registers his shock. When the camera cuts from Lear's reaction back to Goneril, Regan is with her taking her hand; at Lear's query, the defiant Goneril punctuates her answer by kissing her sister on the cheek. The two women stand in unruffled solidarity.

Lear's bitter exchange with Cornwall brings Regan back to him with the patient admonition, "I pray you, father, being weak, seem so," though she gives a sharp edge to the "weak." As the blocking develops, the sisters are at a distance with Lear between them, moving from Regan to Goneril and then back to Regan. Regan continues to maintain her tone of patient understanding as she speaks her damaging words, but the edges get progressively sharper. At "Not altogether so," she overarticulates, breaking her saccharin smile. As the sisters close in to orchestrate their assault, they turn Lear's head into a spinning tennis ball as he listens to each in turn. Regan's smug "And in good time" no longer conceals the dagger in her smile. The sisters stand side by side when Lear finally screams, "O, reason not the need!" A brief cut shows an unsmiling Regan almost interrupting this speech, but the tormented Lear's vaunting and futile threats stop her. At the end, he breaks down, weeping and howling, to go off in the arms of the Fool.

While thunder breaks and the wind whistles, the sisters stand, still side by side, now with Cornwall behind them, staring after Lear. For the moment, the three are matched in mood. Regan is visibly angry and decidedly in control. She briefly resumes her suasive manner, affecting a last smile, to admonish Gloucester about "willful men," then drops it and sharply orders the stunned retainer to shut up his gates. In a final long shot, with lightning flashing and rain falling, the gates are shut on the camera.

Though we are better prepared for the Regan we see in 3.7 of the Granada production than we are for her counterpart at the same point in the BBC, she still shocks us, as does the entire scene. No doubt this is true of any performance of *King Lear*; it is part of the design of the play. Strictly speaking, there can be no preparation for the atrocity of 3.7 any more than there can be for the catastrophe of 5.3. What is especially shocking about the Granada Regan, perhaps, is her exquisite embodiment of the Shakespearean motif of fair-seeming evil. The blinding scene provides the bold and beautiful Regan with the occasion to reveal that she possesses the appetites and capacities of a fiend.

While the scowling Cornwall presides at a table over the early business of the scene, he does not control it for long. The focus shifts to the sitting sisters for their sinister pronouncements on Gloucester, about which there is nothing girlish. When Goneril rises to depart with Edmund, she stands behind the handsome bastard smiling, but then Regan surprises everyone by offering Edmund a loving farewell kiss. As Goneril bristles and Cornwall's scowl deepens, Regan turns to her husband with a look of brazen placidity. The mood is the uglier when the hapless Gloucester is brought before the menacing couple.

Regan at once advances on the "filthy traitor" and spits in his face. As soon as the old man is bound in the chair, where he remains for the most part visible in this production, she strokes his cheek, then plucks some of his beard, caressing the white fuzz for a moment before letting it float to the floor. Meanwhile, Cornwall rolls up his sleeve. The two engage in staccato cross-questioning of Gloucester until Regan sinks her nails in his cheek and he roars out his cry for vengeance. At this, Cornwall topples the chair backward to take the first eye. While Cornwall flinches at his own act, the camera in closeup showing the bloody socket, Regan laughs with excitement and, seizing the head with both hands, calls for the other eye. Only one servant intervenes here, and Regan ends the sword-play by stabbing him, with her own dagger, in the back. By this time—and it is an appalling touch—she seems bored with the proceeding. She observes the second blinding from a distance, while the audience again sees the mutilated face in closeup, and then, with casual disgust, tells the weeping Gloucester it was Edmund who betrayed him. Ordering the blind man thrust out, she holds up her bloody hand, not wanting to soil her purple gown, and nonchalantly wipes it clean with a towel.

In the foreground, Cornwall hangs over the now empty chair beginning to feel the death throes. Looking up to Regan, he faintly tells her of his hurt, screams his outrage against the dead servant, and, now pleadingly, asks Regan to give him her arm. The camera captures her stony face, as she stands motionless, refusing to budge. Returning to Cornwall, it tracks his collapse in death, but it comes to rest, finally, on Regan's expressionless face.

Unlike the Cornwall and Regan of the BBC production, this couple are partners only in violence, not in love. While both Regans are exhilarated by cruelty, finding erotic excitement in inflicting pain, the Granada Regan tires of it, not in revulsion but in boredom. It is the difference between the neophyte in evil and the jaded veteran. The opportune death of Cornwall suits not only the Granada Regan's convenience but her disposition. Her mind is already elsewhere, contemplating other things.

Both the BBC and the Granada versions of Lear's elder daughters lend credibility to Brook's direction of Goneril's love speech in the first scene. In different ways, both productions seek to eschew facile preconceptions about Goneril and Regan, the presumption "that somewhere, someone has found out and defined how the play should be done."[14] In each case, the wickedness of the "wicked sisters" is not simply announced but permitted to emerge.

3

The Mock Trial: 3.6

For the tragic protagonist and for the audience alike, 3.6 of *King Lear* promises a moment of respite. After the ordeal of the storm-swept heath, the maddened Lear and his little band of shocked and shaken allies are provided by Gloucester with shelter "where both food and fire is ready":

> Here is better than the open air; take it thankfully. I will piece out the comfort with what addition I can. I will not be long from you. (3.6.1–3)

Such comfort, however, gives Lear no relief from the "tempest in my mind," and the developing scene projects the audience into the realm of the phantasmagoric. Apparently seizing on the ordinary furnishings of the place, the suffering king's hallucinating imagination transforms it into a court of law for the purpose of arraigning and judging those "she-foxes," his daughters Goneril and Regan. The scene becomes a grotesque expression of Lear's new concern with justice as he appoints his fellow sufferers as judges, the "naked wretch" Poor Tom, the frantic Fool, and the agonized Kent.

Harley Granville-Barker thought the episode "admirable on the stage," and others have echoed his verdict.[1] Yet surely the scene poses a complex challenge to anyone interested in performance. Precisely because it is "technically 'daring,'" it puts special demands on director and actors and presents a series of puzzles to students of stage images. Indeed, the omission of the mock trial itself (17–55) from the Folio may indicate that the heart of the scene was not always performed by Shakespeare's own company. Modern productions, however, rarely omit this highly theatrical sequence.[2]

The mock trial sequence embodies at least three theatrical components that prove to be powerfully suggestive elsewhere in the play: the ritual, the trial, and the use of dramatic artifice.

Rituals, those ceremonial occasions, usually reflecting arche-typal models, by which society seeks to order itself, are exem-plified in the play by the formal love test in scene 1, the reconciliation of Lear and Cordelia in 4.7, and the chivalric trial by combat in 5.3. Even when the performance of the rituals is ill-advised or flawed, as in the case of the love test that Lear couples with the division of the kingdom, these occasions still exhibit the characteristics of being "public," "deliberate," and "predictable, in outline if not in detail."[3] Though indubita-bly an attempt to invoke a time-honored social ritual, Lear's mock trial shares none of these qualities. It is carried out not in any public arena, whether castle or camp, but in a place of concealment, a farmhouse or outbuilding on Gloucester's es-tate, among a group of outcasts. It is not deliberate but unpre-meditated, the sudden production of crazed inspiration on Lear's part. And it is completely unpredictable, in both outline and detail, with respect to its course and outcome. There is, in fact, no outcome, since the trial is abruptly broken off with the imag-ined escape of the imagined defendants. In short, the invoked ritual has been converted to parody.

A *trial* is, of course, a certain kind of ritual, involving more or less formal arraignments, judgments, and sentences of alleged offenders against the values and hence the well-being of the community. The play offers plenty of instances: Lear's disinheri-tance of Cordelia and banishment of Kent in 1.1; Gloucester's rush to a verdict on Edgar in 1.2 and 2.1; Cornwall's stocking of Kent in 2.2; Goneril and Regan's judgment on Lear in 2.4. All these occur prior to Lear's mock trial. It is immediately followed by the scene in which the "form of justice" is the blinding of Gloucester at the hands of Cornwall and Regan. Ironically, Lear's court is made up of those on whom judgment and punishment have been visited by the powerful, of those now at the farthest remove from authority. The only other char-acter in the scene is Gloucester; not actually present for the trial, he exercises the authority he retains on borrowed time, as 3.5 has made clear, and he will suffer terrible punishment for the good offices he performs for Lear and his fellows. But the supremely ironic presence is Lear himself, now the victim of his own original failure as a dispenser of justice; he presides at a trial where he is also a plaintiff and really a defendant. Formally, this trial is again a travesty of legal procedure. How-ever, as Granville-Barker remarks of the stage picture conjured up, "Was better justice done, the picture ironically asks, when

[Lear] presided in majesty and sanity and power?"[4] Curiously, Lear's mock trial is the only one among the many that achieves anything like a just condemnation of the truly guilty. As there is wisdom in folly and reason in madness, so there is justice in legal anarchy.

If rituals and legal proceedings are analogous to theater, the third component of the scene—*dramatic artifice*—partakes more directly of the thing itself. No doubt Edmund is the most consciously skillful actor and improviser of such fictions that we encounter, beginning with the elaborate deceptions he perpetrates on both father and brother in scene 2 of act 1. While Edmund chooses to practice the theatrical art as a means of securing status and power, others have it thrust upon them and pursue it more tentatively. Kent becomes Caius in 1.4 because it is the only way he can continue to serve Lear. Edgar becomes Poor Tom in 2.3 out of fear, desperation, and the aching sense that "Edgar I nothing am." Circumstance forces him to sustain and elaborate his role-playing in ways he cannot anticipate, and, at length, as he grows more accustomed to performance and more convinced of its transforming effects on himself and others, he invents well-meaning fictions, such as the solemn charade with Gloucester on Dover Cliff in 4.6. As the theatrical art is associated with Edgar's existential progress through the play, so it is with Lear's. But with Lear, the practice is less conscious and more willful. In effect, as king, as father, and as mere man, he repeatedly stages scenes in which he casts himself in the dominant role as either the primary agent of justice or the primary victim of injustice. Yet, as Robert Egan observes, Lear's expanding vision of experience discredits his various attempts at dramatic artifice.[5] By the time he reaches the farmhouse in 3.6, he has been thoroughly unhinged by his ordeal, and in this setting he mounts what is ostensibly the most artificial of his dramatic fictions.

With the words "It shall be done; I will arraign them straight," Lear seeks to transform the rude shelter into a courtroom. Immediately, he begins to assign roles and block his characters. The gibbering Tom o' Bedlam is directed to take his seat as a "most learned justice" or, as he is later styled in acknowledgment of his blanket-wrapped loins, "Thou robed man of justice." The hysterical Fool, a "sapient sir," benches by his side, "his yoke-fellow of equity." Even the long-suffering Kent, in sorrowing sanity, must take his part: "You are o' th' commission, / Sit you too." To be sure, a trial requires defendants to answer charges as well as evidence to incriminate them, and Lear calls for both: "Bring in their evidence"; "Arraign her first; 'tis Goneril . . ." Here an ultimate tax is put on the theatrical imagination, that of performers and audience, since both evidence and defendants are improvised. Though Lear's own madness is the most cogent evidence of the injury done him, he is hardly in a position to offer it as such. Instead, he claims that Goneril "kicked the poor King her father," a demonstrable abuse, and, in doing so, he may well point to physical "bruises," correlatives of the internal hurt he has endured. The Fool, if not Lear himself, invents the correlative for the defendants:

> Fool. Come hither, mistress. Is your name Goneril?
> Lear. She cannot deny it.
> Fool. Cry you mercy, I took you for a joint-stool.
>
> (49–51)

Seizing on the device, Lear now indicts Regan, "another, whose warp'd looks proclaim / What store her heart is made on." Then, with the strain on illusion at its greatest, Lear suddenly announces the disappearance of one, and thus both, of the defendants: "Stop her there! . . . False justicer, why hast thou let her scape?" At this point, the trial collapses, Poor Tom muttering to the perplexed old man, "Bless thy five wits," an allusion to the deranged mental powers that generated the illusory spectacle.

At once solemn and absurd, Lear's mock trial remains the truest dramatic fiction he has created. It is Egan who notes that the involvement of others, the community of participants, gives it special force:

> For the fiction . . . is not, like his previous visions, a private attempt to wield his experience into an orderly aesthetic pattern; it depends for its fulfillment not merely on Lear's own imagination and utterance but on those of a gathered, ritually participating community as well. . . . For a moment, a true moral need is thus expressed and fulfilled through dramatic artifice.[6]

The nature of this "moral need" is clarified in Victor Turner's *From Ritual to Theatre*. An anthropologist who employs the suggestive analogues provided by drama in analyzing social conflict, he offers a summary formulation of the way groups react in a state of crisis:

As the conflict swells to crisis and the excited fluidity of heightened emotion, where people feel at once more enclosed in a common mood and loosened from their social moorings, ritualized forms of authority—litigation, feud, sacrifice, prayer—are invoked to contain it and render it orderly.[7]

Lear and his fellows, in this bizarre episode, are making such a response to their own crisis. But the small, disenfranchised, and alienated community that participates in the mock trial cannot possibly "contain" the chaos in the larger world of the play; it is rather a "ritual of affliction" that they perform. Still, it is the means by which they give sacramental expression to human values betrayed or abrogated in that larger world; as David Bevington puts it, "Ceremony is all the more precious because it is so terribly perverted to unjust ends, and conversely the picture in Shakespeare of disrupted ceremony gains significance because of the ideal of ordered behavior that it implies."[8] Here the whole process entails a curious inversion. The interruption of a ritual act or its conversion into parody ordinarily robs it of its sacramentality.[9] But in the "liminal" state through which Lear and his fellows are progressing, the ordinary sanctions are suspended. In this transitional phase of the rites of passage, images of disorder may become images of order. The same is true of the mock trial viewed as a dramatic artifice. The trial collapses when the defendants escape, but, as Egan points out, the trial as play includes within its fictional frame the disruption that ends it:

> Much of the efficacy of the play-trial and the stability of the image of moral order it sets forth derives from its participants' awareness that they are enacting not a real trial but a ritual imitation of a trial, and from the artwork's formal recognition of the chaotic realities over which it has no material power.[10]

While it is arguable that Lear, at any rate, can distinguish the imitation from the thing imitated, the fact remains that he dramatizes and thus encompasses formally the "corruption" he can neither deny nor evade.

The language of the scene, like the stage imagery, is rich in complex associations. Virtually all of the leading motifs in the play are represented. There are references to gods and demons, sanity and madness, majesty and misery, parents and children, human beings and animals as well as to sight, sex, sleep, clothes, food, fire, and "nature." Especially persistent and powerful in the scene are Edgar's evocations of the fiends that haunt and torment Poor Tom:

Frateretto calls me, and tells me Nero is an angler in the lake of darkness. Pray, innocent, and beware the foul fiend. (6–8)

At the outset, he conjures up a picture of hell and its punishments, where Nero, as the type of the tyrant, fishes, perhaps for his lost soul. Lear, an "innocent" and yet "A king, a king!", seems to respond by extending the imagery of hell: "to have a thousand with red burning spits / Come hizzing in upon 'em—." Such associations help to establish the nightmarish quality of the scene and provoke in Lear the vision of judgment of which his trial is the corollary. Fraught as it is with apocalyptic imagery—"Arms, arms, sword, fire! Corruption in the place!"—the scene anticipates Lear's expanded vision of "this great stage of fools," with its extremities of suffering and injustice, in 4.6. Similarly, shortly before he surrenders to exhaustion, Lear will put one of the insistent questions of the play: "Is there any cause in nature that make these hard hearts?" The scene is thus proleptic also of the catastrophe, the "promised end" or "image of that horror."

In mounting the scene, director and designer must sort out the verbal images and decide which among them are merely imagined or hallucinated and which might have some relation to actual stage images. In a realistic or highly representational staging, for example, there might actually be a fire in a fireplace over which meat is broiled on spits—Gloucester promised "food and fire"—all of which Lear converts to the iconography of hell. More stylized renderings would depend less on properties and more on the actors and the language, perhaps even eliminating properties altogether. In such renderings, ambiguities would abound, as they were probably meant to. The only physical properties that Shakespeare's script, and thus Shakespeare's staging, seems to call for are cushions, one or two joint-stools, and maybe a bench. Even if all properties were eliminated, there would still be plenty of interpretive choices to be made. For example, when Lear declares the court in session and turns to the "she-foxes," Edgar exclaims, "Look, where he stands and glares. Want'st thou eyes at trial, madame?" Is the "he" who stands and glares the judge who faces the accused? Is this in the nature of a stage direction for the actor playing Lear? Or

is the bedeviled Poor Tom, whose last and next speeches fix
on the "foul fiend," conjuring up an infernal spirit? That is,
should Poor Tom be played as fully entering into Lear's make-
believe trial or as merely pursuing "his own train of delirious
or fantastick thought," as Samuel Johnson supposed?[11] What
is the meaning of his question about Goneril or Bessy or whatever "madame" wanting "eyes" at the trial? Eyes of spectators
to look at her? Eyes like those of Lear or the fiend that glare
at her? Or eyes of her own to see with? According to the way
Edgar, by gesture or delivery, nuances the line, he may project
for the audience a woman who is primping or one who is fright-
ened or one who is blind and struggling to see. One might,
as those who mount a play must, go through the sequence line
by line putting such questions to the script. In fact, the choices
to be made, like Poor Tom's devils, are legion. And we have
said nothing about costuming and decor, blocking and movement, lighting and sound, all of which involve critical decisions
about stage images. The best way of suggesting some of the
theatrical possibilities of this visionary sequence is to examine
the treatments of it in the BBC and the Granada productions.

Productions

BBC

As the scene opens in the BBC version, Gloucester and Kent
speak downstage in near darkness, the flame of an open lamp
flickering between them. It is hard to tell much about the setting
at first because of the prevailing darkness, and the details continue to be obscure throughout the scene because the guttering
lamp remains the only effective source of light. The shelter
is, in any case, a rude one, with a large opening upstage left,
through which now and again lightning flashes in the distance
as thunder rumbles. The reminder of the storm and the chiaro-
scuro technique employed in lighting the scene create an appro-
priately eerie effect.

We gradually make out the other characters, with an important
exception. Behind Gloucester and Kent, the aged Fool sits at
a wooden table where the lamp rests, and the nearly naked
Edgar stands in the background by the entrance. But Lear is
not in evidence. Not until Gloucester and Kent fade upstage

The Mock Trial. BBC Production. Anton Lesser as Edgar, Michael Hordern as King Lear, John Shrapnel as Kent, Frank Middlemass as the Fool. Courtesy of the British Broadcasting Corporation. Copyright © BBC.

and Edgar comes down to the table do we detect his presence. When the Fool begins his question, "Prithee, nuncle," a bundle to his right moves and makes a sound, and suddenly Lear raises a shrouding blanket from his head to answer, "A king, a king!" For this "discovery," the camera guides our attention to Lear's wild and wrinkled face, and then it moves back to fix the frame in a medium shot of the table and its occupants illuminated by the lamp. Turned toward the Fool, Lear seems to take his inspiration for the trial from his companion's self-consciously sage advice about misplaced trust. Announcing the trial, he calls on Edgar, who stands behind, to sit at the table on his right hand. Kent remains standing just upstage of Lear and the Fool. This is the basic blocking for the trial sequence.

On "Now, you she-foxes," Lear himself rises and bends forward over the table gazing downstage left. Looking up, Edgar sees Lear "stand and glare" and then turns his eyes in the same direction; his gibe at "madame" draws an approving laugh from Lear. Lear's eyes remain on "Her," his mouth moving slightly, as the Fool intones his lines about Bessy and as Edgar rubs his belly and rebuffs the "black angel." His engagement with the visionary woman is so intense that he virtually ignores Kent's appeal that he rest. Kent, in turn, ignores Lear's attempt to seat him with the others, turning away briefly and then looking back sadly. "Let us deal justly," says Edgar, suddenly dignified. Arraigning Goneril, Lear raises his hand to recite his oath and make his charge. Though the line is a mere formula as Hordern delivers it, its very inconsequence sorts ironically with his earlier oaths and maledictions. When the Fool addresses the accused by name, Lear speaks to him confidentially, and when the Fool equates her with a "joint-stool," Lear laughs.

In a stage production, a director would have to make certain decisions about the joint-stool. Is there really to be one (or two)? Does Lear point it out? Or does the Fool first make the equation? But since this is television, the camera determines what the audience sees or doesn't see, expanding or confining the space within the frame. Here the frame stays fixed on the group around the table, with the attention of all directed beyond the frame. It is up to us, responding to the mix of signals given, to imagine what may or may not be there. The effect is uncanny. By refusing to illustrate the text, the director forces the audience to do so, letting us create our own surreal combinations of fact and fantasy, our own stage images.

Lear's demented playfulness abruptly dissipates. Even as he

gestures toward "another" with "warp'd looks," he cries out, "Stop her there!" In his anxiety and frustration at the escape, he turns to Kent and the Fool, reproaching the Fool, and then stands helpless, yelping in his distress. This marks a new phase in the sequence, characterized by a gathering together of the others in their care and concern for Lear. The Fool, now silent, reaches out to touch and stroke Lear's arm. Kent combines "pity" with an anguished rebuke for Lear's failure to retain "patience." And Edgar, who in this production is not only bare and begrimed but crowned with thorns, momentarily drops the mask of Poor Tom: "My tears begin to take his part so much," he says, with eyes shut and hands folded, "They mar my counterfeiting." As Poor Tom again, he chases the dogs that bark at Lear—"Tray, Blanch, and Sweet-heart." A tide of pathos threatens to engulf the scene, when Lear sinks to his seat again. But Lear's next action counteracts it. From a dish, he picks up a mangled meat-bone and probes it: "Then let them anatomize Regan." He pulls off a strip of flesh and eats: "see what breeds about her heart." He flourishes a morsel: "Is there any cause in nature that make these hard hearts?" He puts the question offhandedly, chewing. This blend of the pathetic and the grotesque is more compelling than either would be alone, and it expresses the spirit of the whole sequence.

Having asked an ultimate question, Lear is ready to accept the ministrations of Kent, who comes to the table and leads him upstage to his long-delayed rest. As the old king settles on the cushions, he pulls imaginary curtains around him and collapses under his blanket in exhaustion. The faces of first Edgar and then the Fool in the foreground also reflect pain and weariness. The Fool, with almost all of his clownlike makeup wiped away, pronounces his final line like an epitaph and then literally puts down his head and sleeps at the table. But there is to be no rest. The remainder of the scene is given over to Gloucester's urgent warnings and the rapid decamping of the others with the comatose Lear. Only Edgar remains at the table in the flickering lamplight, taking what comfort he can from the "fellowship" of suffering.

When all is said, the BBC treatment of the scene is rather conservative. It is spare, though effective, in its use of stage images and close to the received text. By comparison, the Granada version is baroque in its imagery and prolific in its cuts. The pattern of difference seems clear. While Miller in the BBC version exploits the medium of television, he still treats *King*

Lear as a play. Elliott, in the Granada version, means to turn the play into a film.

GRANADA

The Granada version reduces the scene by one half, omitting about sixty lines. Some of the same lines were also cut in the BBC production, such as Edgar's pastoral effusion (41–45) and his exorcism of the dogs (65–74), probably at no great loss. The largest single piece of text omitted is Edgar's soliloquy at the end of the scene (102–15). This is also missing from the Folio, but it is not a matter of Elliott's following the Folio rather than the Quarto text, since he also includes lines from the Quarto and omits others from the Folio. Some of the cuts are surprising, such as Lear's initial naming of the judges (21–22), his outcry against "Corruption in the place" (54), Edgar's aside on his tears (59–60), and, most of all, Lear's anatomizing of Regan and his question about "hard hearts" (75–77). There are also some changes in the readings of lines, of which more will be said later. The point is that these modifications involve a remaking of the scene.

What is lost in language and the meanings it may convey Elliott seeks to supply in cinematic images. As the scene begins, with a rush of background music, the camera is zooming through a driving rain over a thatched rooftop. It zeros in on a hole in the roof to offer an aerial view of the white-haired Lear sitting on a bale of hay, the Fool also sitting and clinging to his right arm, and the convulsive Edgar thrashing at his feet. This tableau is presented four times from various angles. Now inside the barnlike structure, the camera at ground-level offers a rear view that includes in the background Kent standing and Gloucester planting a torch in an upright. Other torches are already in place, and the scene is brightly lit throughout. The camera cuts to a closeup of Kent and Gloucester for their brief exchange and, with Gloucester's exit, back to the rear view of the Lear group with Kent approaching it. As the angle is reversed, we see Lear, still in his kingly robes, staring down at the gravelly voiced Edgar muttering his hellish imprecations and then turning to the Fool, young but wan, to answer "A king, a king!" The next ten lines are collapsed into three, all Lear's: the excited "To have a thousand with red burning spits / Come hizzing in upon 'em" inspires "It shall be done; I will arraign them straight." The gesturing king attempts to rise on the last line

The Mock Trial. Granada Production. Laurence Olivier as King Lear, David Threlfall as Edgar, John Hurt as the Fool, Colin Blakely as Kent. Courtesy of Granada Television. Copyright © Granada T.V.

but, weak as he is, can do so only with the help of the Fool and Kent. Once on his feet, he turns on his next line, "Now, you she-foxes!", and the camera shifts away to show Lear and the others in the background and a single joint-stool looming large in the foreground. Now standing on Lear's right, Edgar points downstage with the line, "Look, where she stands and glares." The ambiguities in the text are eliminated by changing the gender of the pronoun and by eliminating the second half of the line. One may say that the camera angle does make the joint-stool seem formidable.

Swelling music signals a change in mood as the trial begins. Gone is the lassitude Lear showed in the early tableaux. The ritual invigorates him. Busily, he arranges Edgar, the Fool, and Kent to his left, who stand rather than "bench," the camera following him closely and then returning downstage to frame the joint-stool. As Edgar rasps out his call for justice, Lear points at "Goneril," cranes his neck toward the "honorable assembly," and waves his arms for the charge. Also gesturing, the Fool takes a step downstage to address the defendant, his high-pitched voice counterpointing Lear's sonorous assurance. Unable to contain himself, Lear bustles downstage on the line "Here's another" and scrambles to the right of the joint-stool after a cackling hen, which he seizes in triumph. "Ha," he cries, holding it up, "'tis Regan!" This reading replaces "Stop her there!" The director thus eliminates another ambiguity and introduces an action and an image. We are shown Lear's chortling triumph and then, as the hen flutters from his grasp, his whimpering defeat. Moreover, as played here, it is a defeat at his own hands. Turning to pursue the escaping bird, he reproaches not one of the others but himself as the "False justicer."

The collapse of the trial leads directly to the collapse of Lear. While Kent and Edgar rush to his side, Lear weeps openly and sinks onto the bale of hay. His disappointment is inconsolable. He also shows self-pity. Hallucinating the "little dogs," he lovingly remembers "Sweet-heart" and makes kissing sounds, only to whine in protest that "they bark at me." As he lies back to rest, he gasps out his last lines faintly. Here pathos is the dominant note. The cutting of lines 64–80 excludes any qualifying dissonance. And the handling of the rest of the scene reinforces the pathos. Lear's "We'll go to supper i' th' morning" is immediately followed by a closeup of the stricken Fool for his "And I'll go to bed at noon." The bustle of Gloucester's urgent return still permits the camera to linger over the sleeping

Lear and his tender removal by Kent and Edgar to the litter. There is also a closeup of the departing and despairing Edgar. But the end of the scene is given to the Fool, in a style that recalls its beginning. We first see him from the rear sitting alone on the bale of hay as the others leave. After the cut to Edgar, the angle is reversed for the camera's zooming return to the abandoned and shivering figure. That last shot is of the Fool's face, mouth twitching and eyes shut against the pain of approaching death.

That Lear's mock trial should fare so well in such different productions takes us back to the power of the sequence as a theatrical event. While the text may be variously realized in performance, since production remains interpretation, Shakespeare has provided the distinctive components on which to raise a structure of compelling stage images.

4

Dover Cliff: 4.6

Act four of *King Lear* opens with Edgar ruminating on his beg-
garly condition. As Poor Tom, the "lowest and most dejected"
of men, he is consoled by the knowledge that he cannot get
worse. But when the blinded Gloucester enters, led by an
Old Man, Edgar's presumption about the extremity of his own
wretchedness shatters. Seeing his father's misery, the young man
cries:

> O gods! Who is 't can say "I am at the worst"?
> I am worse than e'er I was. . . .
> And worse I may be yet. The worst is not
> So long as we can say "This is the worst."
>
> (4.1.25–28)

Edgar reproaches himself for playing the "fool to sorrow,"
for deceiving his pitiful father, who believes he is a Bedlam
beggar; but he retains the disguise, winning the blind man's
sympathy and trust. Gloucester sends the Old Man off to fetch
raiment for the "naked fellow," then asks Poor Tom to guide
him to Dover, giving him his purse and promising him more
if he will take him to a particular place:

> There is a cliff, whose high and bending head
> Looks fearfully in the confined deep.
> Bring me but to the very brim of it,
> And I'll repair the misery thou dost bear
> With something rich about me. From that place
> I shall no leading need.
>
> (4.1.73–78)

The scene ends with the madman offering the blind man his
arm: "Poor Tom shall lead thee."

Four scenes intervene before we see Edgar and Gloucester

105

again, presumably close to the top of Dover Cliff. While the pair are making their way toward Dover, Albany presents himself a changed man, repudiating Edmund's treachery, reviling his wife as a fiend, and defending the wronged Lear. Goneril and Regan seal their rivalry—and their doom—by making separate overtures to Edmund. Cordelia returns to reclaim her father and to fight for his right. And, apparently, a mile or two along the way, the Old Man brings decent clothing for Poor Tom. The first sequence of the Dover Cliff scene, 4.6, begins with the entrance of Gloucester and Edgar—"When shall I come to th' top of that same hill?"—and ends at the entrance of the mad Lear (4.6.1–80).

Like so much of Shakespeare's dialogue, the exchange is rich in implied stage direction, in what John Barton likes to call "hints to the actors"[1]—and to the director—as to how the moment should be staged. But this sequence of 4.6 is also rich in deception: Edgar, disguised as Poor Tom, leads his suicidal father to the precipice of a cliff, which is not a precipice at all. As Gloucester readies himself for the fall, Edgar explains in an aside, "Why I do trifle thus with his despair / Is done to cure it." If it has not already been clear to an audience, it is clear now that Edgar's deception involves more than his disguise. For the actors and the director, however, a provocative and practical theatrical problem presents itself throughout the sequence, for, in the context of Edgar's fiction, Shakespeare's implied directions frustrate rather than guide.

The initial exchange between father and son signals the problem. When Gloucester asks when they will come to the top of Dover hill, Edgar responds, "You do climb up it now," offering their labor in proof. When Gloucester expresses doubt— "Methinks the ground is even"—Edgar immediately contradicts him with "Horrible steep." Then, building his case, he asks whether Gloucester hears the sea, which Gloucester does not. To account for the disparity between what he claims they are experiencing and what Gloucester perceives, Edgar dismisses his father's other senses as "imperfect," made so by his "eyes' anguish."

Whether this initial exchange is part of Edgar's deception or not may easily be shown in production. If a director stages the sequence on an incline, then, apparently, father and son have arrived at Dover Cliff and are indeed laboring to climb it. Gloucester's sense of the climb is distorted by his loss of vision and, as Edgar suggests, by the flawed sensations that accompany the loss. Clearly, Edgar does not place Gloucester at the edge of the precipice, but, until the moment of clarification, the two may well be approaching it. If, on the other hand, a director stages the sequence on an even plane, then, apparently, father and son have not arrived at Dover Cliff; the hill is part of Edgar's deception. The staging, then, would remove the ambiguity of place, offering an audience visual confirmation of whether or not the pair are at Dover Cliff.

But in both cases, we have used the word *apparently* to remark on place, for the formulation is simple, the location *apparent*, only if one assumes realism. In a production that is not dependent upon the realistic mode, the physical properties of the space would not be the measure of Dover Cliff; rather, dialogue and action would be. How, then, would an audience assess Edgar's claim that the climb is steep? Is this a direction from Shakespeare to the audience identifying place? Or is it Edgar's misdirection to Gloucester, a lie designed to convince the blind man that they are where they are not? When realism is not the prevailing mode, the audience, like Gloucester, has no ocular proof.

Nor is aural confirmation available to either. Gloucester has no eyes and has not yet developed sufficient confidence in his other senses to trust them above Edgar's report. But his ears encourage suspicion. While he does not hear the sea, he does hear a change in the beggar's voice, noticing the shift signaled by the prose of 4.1 and the blank verse of 4.6. Edgar is quick to deny that he is now "better spoken" and to return the conversation to the visual, where his authority is not open to challenge. The audience, of course, knows of Edgar's disguise, but, unless sea sounds are piped into the theater, it has not heard the ocean either and has no surer sense of where Edgar and Gloucester are than Gloucester does.

With the blind man, it must heed Edgar's assurances and warnings, which echo Gloucester's earlier account of the cliff: "Come on, sir, here's the place. Stand still. How fearful / And dizzy 'tis, to cast one's eyes so low!" Edgar confirms Gloucester's prior knowledge of the place and plays upon the expectations of the audience by offering in dizzying perspective a view of the scene below: of soaring crows and choughs that appear as small as beetles, an herb-gatherer hanging on the cliff, mice-sized fishermen on the beach, and a tall ship reduced to its cock-boat. Again, with Gloucester, the audience must listen to Edgar retract his intimation of sea sounds and confirm their absence: "The murmuring surge, / That on th' unnumb'red idle pebbles chafes, / Cannot be heard so high."

When David Rintoul and John Burgess, in residence with ACTER, experimented with this sequence in our Shakespeare in Performance class, they asked students to close their eyes through the first run-through, putting them, like Gloucester, in the position of seeing the world through Edgar. The exercise proved instructive, precisely because it was, finally, gratuitous. Our students understood that, unless the Dover Cliff sequence is staged realistically, an audience, even with its multiple eyes open, cannot read what is before it. Until Edgar's aside, its advantage over Gloucester consists solely in its knowledge that the Bedlam beggar is no beggar at all but Gloucester's son. The madman's words are leading the blind.

Moreover, Edgar's guidance and misdirection extend beyond the physical: Shakespeare's use of theatrical artifice also informs the spiritual lesson that Edgar offers his disillusioned father. When Edgar first encounters the blinded Gloucester in 4.1, he decides immediately to remain Poor Tom, in spite of the alteration in circumstance and in his father's attitude toward him. He has heard Gloucester's bitter self-reproach—"I have no way, and therefore want no eyes; / I stumbled when I saw"—his longing to be reunited with his abused son—"Might I but live to see thee in my touch, / I'd say I had eyes again!"—and, most telling, his judgment on the cruelty of the gods—"As flies to wanton boys are we to th' gods, / They kill us for their sport." Actuated by the desire to restore his father's faith in the beneficence and the justice of the gods, Edgar takes on the role of physical and spiritual guide. Ironically, though his evangelism succeeds, the "miracle" that is Edgar's proof-text is itself an illusion, one not shared with Gloucester by the audience.

Edgar is intent on rescuing his father from despair, by whatever means he can contrive. Having positioned Gloucester on the imaginary precipice, he listens as the blind man utters a kneeling farewell to life, a prayer that expresses alienation from the world and the "mighty gods" and ends with a blessing on Edgar. Moments after Gloucester falls forward and, presumably, faints, Edgar adopts yet another verbal disguise, pretending to be someone at the seaside. In speeches that counterpoint in visual detail his account of the view from above, Edgar offers his reviving father a view from below, of a perpendicular cliff stretching higher than ten ship-masts set end to end. From the beach, "the shrill-gorg'd lark so far / Cannot be seen or heard."

Feigning astonishment at Gloucester's survival of a fall from such a height, the spiritual instructor presents a judgment: "Thy life's a miracle." When the wretched man does not immediately accept the judgment, complaining rather that his failure to die makes him worse than he was before, Edgar moves surely into the second part of his moral play: seen from below, the "thing" that parted from Gloucester was not "A poor unfortunate beggar" but a creature with moons for eyes, a thousand noses, and horns—in short, "some fiend." Invoking the same superstition that inspired Horatio's fears for Hamlet in the presence of the Ghost—"What if it tempt you . . . / . . . to the dreadful summit of the cliff / That beetles o'er his base into the sea, / And there assume some other horrible form" (1.4.69–72)—Edgar convinces Gloucester that his attempt at suicide was the work of the devil, neutralized by the gods. Taking heart, Gloucester promises to bear affliction and to endure.

Though prompted to acknowledge the justice of the gods, Gloucester experiences not a miracle but a hoax, perpetrated by one who, though he himself believes, can bear no effective witness to his belief. Unable to rely on the gods to preserve his father, Edgar creates an artificial example of their justice, then provides the moral:

> Therefore, thou happy father,
> Think that the clearest gods, who make them honors
> Of men's impossibilities, have preserved thee.
>
> (4.6.72–74)

As Alan C. Dessen remarks in *Elizabethan Drama and the Viewer's Eye*,

> given a simple, nonrepresentational staging, the audience (unlike Gloucester) could not possibly accept Edgar's explanation of the miracle. Edgar (and Shakespeare) have placed the audience in a curious position. In questioning (or rejecting) the "miracle" and the moralization, the viewer is simultaneously questioning (or rejecting) . . . the accompanying assumptions about heavenly intervention in man's affairs. The obvious fiction created by Edgar and accepted by Gloucester *prevents* the audience from sharing that comforting illusion.[2]

By the time Edgar points his moral, the audience is certain of his act of deception. Though the opening moments of the sequence may have been fraught with ambiguities, Edgar's aside signals that he is trifling with Gloucester's despair in order to cure it.

When presenting the sequence in the classroom, in a neutral space just as their stage would be for the full performance of the play later that week, Rintoul and Burgess tried out two stagings. In the first, Rintoul as Edgar supported the illusion of the cliff by labored movement as he led Burgess to the precipice. Describing the scene below, he knelt by Gloucester's side, gesturing and gazing into the distance, standing again and looking away on "I'll look no more." With Gloucester poised on the verge, he moved upstage, as though departing, to a position where he turned and spoke his aside directly to the students. In the second staging, Rintoul's Edgar trusted language to create the illusion of the cliff for Gloucester but made no effort to preserve it for the audience. He pulled the blind man indiscriminately around the stage, not respecting the point that became the imagined verge. On reaching that point, he described the scene while looking up with eyes closed. When departing, he walked downstage of the kneeling figure, into the space that would have sent Gloucester tumbling to his death had the precipice been there, to tell the audience near at hand that he was deceiving his father. In the full performance, which happened to be the premiere of this production, the actors combined the strategies of both stagings. In the early part of the sequence, Edgar engaged in labored movement and respected the imaginary verge, sustaining the illusion for Gloucester and the audience alike. But when describing the view from the cliff, Edgar shut his eyes, as though conjuring the spectacle, and when he said his farewell to the poised Gloucester, he came downstage to address his aside to the audience. Given any of these approaches, the audience knows that, when Gloucester falls, he is not in danger and that, when Edgar continues the charade with his reviving father, the "dread summit of this chalky bourn" is a verbal creation. It is possible, of course, to conceive of other stagings, including some that, by their treatment of Edgar's aside and Gloucester's "fall," might sustain the ambiguity of the situation a little longer—but certainly no longer than Edgar's next aside, which immediately follows the "fall": "Had he been where he thought, / By this, had thought been past." Though variously uncertain at first, the audience finally knows that it is witnessing a hoax—and looks with skepticism on the moral thus enforced.

In the storm of 3.4, the audience has heard Lear pray not

to the gods but to "Poor naked wretches," the unaccommodated man for whom Poor Tom is emblem, and to those who represent "pomp," especially himself. It is human agency, according to Lear, that must "show the heavens more just." Now the audience sees Edgar, not the gods, create a "miracle" to preserve Gloucester's life and to restore his faith. For the audience, the discrepancy between illusion and reality articulates in its grimmest voice the frustration that denies the justice of the gods and in its most optimistic voice the frail hope that humanity may affirm itself. In staging a "miracle," Edgar has comforted his father and discomfited us. As Robert Egan puts it, Edgar has provided Gloucester

> by illusion with a grounds of belief, a moral and metaphysical means of structuring his experience, which reality has not afforded him. This is, of course, the same end toward which our own theatrical expectations instinctively lean; we would like to come away from our experience of *King Lear* just as Gloucester has come away from the dramatic image Edgar has created for him, with confidence that all experience, suffering included, is contained within a greater plan of cosmic order.[3]

But, Egan continues, *King Lear* not only fails to satisfy such expectations; it specifically frustrates them.

If Edgar's miracle leaves Gloucester with a truth and the audience with an illusion, what effect does Edgar's own drama have on himself? It is evident that Edgar's art and Shakespeare's are at odds: the play-within-the-play that Edgar contrives for Gloucester is designed to affirm the very premise that Shakespeare's play questions. As Edgar constructs, Shakespeare deconstructs. Edgar, like any good dramatist, seems to believe in the art he practices. Even as he acts as agent of a justice the gods have refused, he endorses his fiction by counseling Gloucester to "Bear free and patient thoughts," as though the gods' vindication were earned. But Edgar is not permitted to rest in his consoling vision. The sequel provides this manipulator of truth with experiences that his conception of order cannot accommodate. Within moments of Gloucester's conversion, Edgar is face-to-face with the mad Lear, a "side-piercing sight." And, shortly after, he not only witnesses but, ironically, causes his father's death.

Just before Edgar is to engage in single combat with his brother, Edmund, he reveals himself to Gloucester. He does so to ask blessing from his father, who had asked blessing for him at

Dover. There, Edgar saved his father from death, but now his suit for blessing precipitates Gloucester's end. By Edgar's account in 5.3, Gloucester's "flaw'd heart" "'Twixt two extremes of passion, joy and grief, / Burst smilingly." If there is justice in this perverse twist of events, it rests in the promise of the dying Edmund's response: "This speech of yours hath mov'd me, / And shall perchance do good." Once again, however, promise is frustrated: Edmund's gesture at saving the lives of Cordelia and Lear comes too late; the earlier writ of death prevails.

Experience will finally prevail upon Edgar to modify his confident view of the gods' concern for humankind, even as it had earlier urged him to modify his contention that "I am at the worst." If indeed the final four lines of the play are Edgar's (as in the Folio), then, at play's end, he is no longer willing to say "what we ought to say." But at Dover Cliff, Edgar has not yet understood the significance of his own moral play.

The Dover Cliff sequence offers, then, through the interplay of Edgar's art with Shakespeare's, not only an ingenious bit of metatheater but a revisionist's vision of the world. Textually, the interplay between fiction and fiction is everywhere apparent. The challenge in production is to preserve enough of this interplay to tease an audience into questioning the lesson that Edgar's drama provides. We turn now to the BBC and the Granada productions of *King Lear* to see how the Dover Cliff sequence is realized.

Productions

BBC

In Miller's BBC mounting, the opening moments of the sequence are staged in a setting that simulates a neutral space. When Edgar and Gloucester appear, they are at the far end of a relatively flat expanse, moving stage left toward a downstage camera. The BBC production has already accustomed its audience to the realistic mode, and hence the topography of the setting must be recognizably natural. Since the effect of the realistic mode, as we remarked earlier, is to remove the teasing ambiguity that Shakespeare has built into the scene, Miller's compensating strategy is all the more interesting. His method throughout the Dover Cliff sequence is to provide the audience

Dover Cliff. BBC Production. Anton Lesser as Edgar, Norman Rodway as Gloucester. Courtesy of the British Broadcasting Corporation. Copyright © BBC.

not with visual evidence that either supports or exposes Edgar's deception but with signals that do both.

We initially see the two figures, Edgar like Aeneas carrying his father on his back, against the horizon, the land rising slightly behind them, perhaps to Edgar's thighs. There is nothing higher than they. The terrain is rocky and barren, such as might typify a high place. Yet the ground that Edgar traverses is essentially "even," not "Horrible steep." He is not climbing, though he says he is, and he is not laboring, even under the burden of Gloucester's weight. What is the audience to make of what it sees and hears? Miller's technique is daring, since he might have dispensed with this sustained long shot, keeping the camera tight on the figures, as he does for the moments on the verge. But, instead of preserving ambiguity the easy way, he does so by showing at once the plausibility and the implausibility of the charade.

Deprived of both sight and the sensation of walking, Gloucester is almost completely dependent on Edgar for his sense of the situation. And Edgar, moving slowly downstage through the opening exchange, at first contradicts his father's impressions and finally puts off the remarks on his altered idiom by announcing, "Here's the place," and setting the old man down. Meantime, the camera has been closing the distance so that the place where they stand is not visible when Gloucester alights. The camera continues to move in as Edgar orders his father to "Stand still," and, by the time he crosses behind to remain close on Gloucester's right, it is fixed on their heads and shoulders.

The ensuing description of what lies below is not the report of one surveying the scene. Edgar casts a perfunctory glance downward; then, shutting his eyes through a long pause as though to raise the vision, he whispers it almost directly into Gloucester's ear. He makes no gesture in the direction of the cliff, no effort to lean forward to see the herb-gatherer or the ship riding at anchor. Listening intently, the blind man nods and, as Edgar continues, smiles in recognition. It is a poignant moment between son and father, the one now soberly attired in a friarlike habit and the other in bloody bandage and shirt-sleeves, the ruff at his neck standing out wildly, the one painfully creating the picture that the other accepts with a despairing joy. Nevertheless, at this point, the moment seems to involve an obvious deception.

When Gloucester asks to be set where Edgar stands—an unlikely request since his son stands close, clasping his shoulder—

Edgar makes little concession to plausibility. Taking the blind man's hand, he guides him forward a step or two and warns, "You are now within a foot / Of th' extreme verge." As Gloucester prepares for death, Edgar steps back slightly, looking off to the right and projecting a loud farewell into the distance; in the same position and posture, he quietly mutters his aside. Then he returns his gaze to his father for the prayer and the leap.

If the ambiguity seems effectively dissipated by now, Miller unexpectedly reclaims it in staging the fall. With the camera in closeup, the audience is still ignorant of the space the two men confront. Moreover, Gloucester does not kneel but remains standing for his prayer of renunciation. When he concludes with his blessing for Edgar, the blind man stretches out his hands, pauses with open mouth, then with a cry throws himself forward—out of the frame. The camera stays focused on the space where Gloucester had stood, lowering slightly and tilting as the horrified Edgar looms in the frame and looks down to marvel at his father's determination to "rob / The treasury of life." For that brief moment, we do not know how far Gloucester fell.

Even Edgar's reassuring "Had he been where he thought . . ." leaves us in some doubt whether Gloucester is "Alive or dead?" Only with these words do Edgar and the camera drop to the prone figure. Now speaking in a different voice and accent, Edgar half lies on his motionless father, bending over the old man's head and embracing his back. Face down, the exhausted Gloucester breathes painfully while Edgar as disinterested by-stander celebrates the life-preserving "miracle." Gloucester is, of course, incredulous and anguished at his fortune and must at length be hauled to his feet by Edgar. It is not until the "stranger" describes the monstrous "thing" on the cliff that he engages Gloucester's full attention. For this, the closeup camera shows the profile of the blind man in the foreground and the full face of Edgar behind watching narrowly his reaction to the account of the "fiend" and the moral it enforces. Edgar's face softens in pity and relief when Gloucester nods in remembrance and, vowing to bear affliction, earnestly endorses the vision of good and evil that Edgar has offered him.

In staging this sequence, Miller means to manipulate his audience. He wants the episode of Gloucester's false death to seem both plausible and implausible, and he manages to achieve the effect first by neutralizing the medium's imperative of realism and then by using the opportunities it affords him for selective focus. The long opening shot establishes the ambiguity he proceeds to exploit through direction of the actors and closeup camera work. Edgar's manner finally discourages the audience's belief in his charade. In the staging of Gloucester's leap, however, Miller creates uncertainty at precisely the moment when there should be no doubt: Edgar's purpose is to cure his father's despair, not to seal it by permitting his suicide; surely he would not allow the old man to "Topple down head-long." What is especially engaging about Miller's handling of the moment is that it generates concern for Gloucester's life even in veteran Shakespeareans as they react to the contrary signals. The old man's scream, which fades as he falls out of the frame, prompts the thought that the "cure" may be the release of death. While this is not what Edgar has in mind, the sequel to the leap compels the audience to react to his real purpose. The reaction involves mixed feelings of relief at seeing Gloucester safe and resentment at having been tricked along with him. If the audience is likely to concede Edgar's good intentions, it is less likely to put much faith in his pious affirmations.

GRANADA

Elliott's Granada version, which must also present the sequence in the context of an otherwise realistic production, continues the cinematic mode that has characterized it throughout. To swelling music, the opening shot pans on Edgar and Gloucester moving left behind a border of high, wind-swept grass that conceals all but their shoulders and heads. Edgar leads the way, leaning forward and supporting his progress with a staff; the blindfolded Gloucester follows, head tilted upwards, his outstretched hand holding on to Edgar's shoulder. The pair remain in this posture for a few moments until they come into fuller view. As Edgar grasps his staff with both hands to pull himself along, Gloucester overtakes him and walks at his left, impatient that they have not yet arrived at the "top of that same hill."

The camera now accommodates nearly their full body lengths, highlighting the disparity in manner and movement between the two. Grunting and breathless, Edgar hunches over his staff and labors heavily, providing histrionic evidence for his claim that the ground is "Horrible steep." Gloucester, though he has no eyes, proceeds with relative ease, carrying a walking stick lightly in his left hand. The nature of the terrain is itself uncertain: though the land seems to fall away behind them, the back-

Dover Cliff. Granada Production. David Threlfall as Edgar, Leo McKern as Gloucester. Courtesy of Granada Television. Copyright © Granada T.V.

ground is obscured by mist. It is the discrepancy in the behavior of the two that suggests that all is not as it seems.

For Gloucester, the journey across what he thinks is flat land is a frustration. The old man's voice is querulous as he articulates his doubt. Unable to confirm that the beggar has carried out his employment, he tests the ground with his walking stick. Sensing his father's distress, Edgar quickly extends his arm to stop Gloucester and asks whether he hears the sea. When Gloucester replies with a furious "No, truly," thrashing the air with his stick, Edgar's specious comment on the blind man's imperfect senses serves to calm him to a resigned "So may it be, indeed." Putting his arm around Gloucester's back with a hearty "Come on, sir," Edgar guides him downstage five steps and chortles, "here's the place."

Everything that Edgar says is in the character and voice of Poor Tom, his somewhat altered idiom notwithstanding. Indeed, it is notable that, in cutting the sequence (some thirty out of eighty lines), Elliott omits the exchange in which Gloucester insists that his guide is "better spoken." This Edgar is determined to play out his adopted role on the "cliff" site. Though his nakedness is now covered, his dress and demeanor are ragged and wild, unlike those of his BBC counterpart. The viewers know, of course, that Edgar's role as Poor Tom is a guise. What they do not know for sure is the extent of his role-playing on the verge. Does it encompass his account of the place or not? In putting on an act for his father, he is also putting one on for the audience.

As in the BBC production, the viewers here remain ignorant of the space the pair confront. This Edgar, however, gives them every reason to suppose it is a sheer drop. As though at a height, he shambles ahead and looks down, then stops the following Gloucester with a sudden raising of his arm and an urgent "Stand still." In closeup, he himself stands behind the blind man's right shoulder to describe, his voice colored by awe, what he sees from his dizzying vantage. Throughout, he complements his words with gestures, moving his hands, pointing with his fingers, and changing his facial expression. When he speaks of the herb-gatherer, he cups his hand over his mouth as though shouting to the laborer, "dreadful trade!" As he nears the end of his report, he comes forward a few steps, kneels, and looks toward Gloucester, crying "I'll look no more, / Lest my brain turn" and pointing to his head. During Edgar's account, Gloucester has stood motionless, helpless, two red blotches on the ban-

danna where his eyes should be, taking it all in; now he tells
Edgar, "Set me where you stand," which is in this staging a
plausible request. When Edgar guides him to the "extreme
verge," the camera offers first a closeup of Edgar's face, over
Gloucester's bloody sleeve, as he earnestly warns the old man
of the danger, and next one of Gloucester's face, as he orders
Poor Tom to let go his hand and leave him.

At this point, the ironies accumulate and intensify. Edgar
stands to utter a jovial "Now fare ye well, good sir," touching
his father's shoulder, and takes several paces upstage to lean
on his staff; as he moves off, Gloucester completes the line,
with a joyful shake of the head: "With all my heart." Fraught
with emotion, this conventional tag becomes a particularly
poignant expression of the old man's determination to fare well
in his impending journey to death. It is immediately capped,
however, by a closeup on Edgar for his revealing aside. Facing
the camera but not looking into it, Edgar speaks in his own
voice for the first time in the scene, addressing himself. As
he muses on trifling with despair, he shifts and blinks his eyes
and rolls his tongue over his lips. The delivery of the aside
is not simply meditative but apprehensive and anxious: it
sounds self-justifying, and, of course, it is. The camera shifts
to the figure of Gloucester as he drops to his knees, fixes on
his face for the prayer, then moves back to include both figures
again. As the old man half-sobs his blessing for his son and
then shouts his farewell to the "fellow," Edgar turns upstage
in an obvious gesture of pretense to project into the distance
his "Gone, sir. Farewell—." The situation is now much the same
as it was in the BBC production. But the outcome and its effect
are quite different. With Edgar looking on, Gloucester lifts his
arms through a long pause, emits a sustained moan, and falls
forward. Even as he falls, the melodramatic music that has
served as background suddenly ceases, yielding to the ordinary
wind, and just as suddenly the camera cuts to an overhead
shot of Gloucester lying flat on his face in a patch of sand,
with Edgar standing on the grassy margin. It is a stunning anticli-
max.

The deception is on the instant patent to the audience, and,
in the altered atmosphere of the moment, no longer charged
with swelling music and histrionic gestures, the charade seems
grotesque. Elliott does not, however, conclude the sequence
flatly. He so directs it as to recharge the occasion with emotion,
modulating to a new emphasis and making Gloucester's recon-

ciliation to life tantamount to a reunion between father and son.

With the camera still overhead, Edgar remains motionless, studying the gracelessly prostrate figure in the sand pit, and then he moves quickly to Gloucester's side, with the camera returning to ground level for a reaction shot. Wondering "Alive or dead?" in his natural voice, he falls to his knees and presses his chest to query in a deeper voice, "Ho, you sir! Friend! Hear you, sir! Speak!—" Still looking for signs of life, he touches the fainting Gloucester's back, then pulls his hand back to his own heart, reassured that the old man "revives." At "What are you, sir?" Gloucester rolls over on his back, asking to die. When Edgar as stranger animatedly describes the precipitate fall, stressing the "miracle," the camera focuses on Gloucester's hand as it gradually opens and then pans along his arm to his bloody chest and face. When the old man expresses doubt, pain, and, finally, fury that he still lives, Edgar seizes the same hand and arm and pulls him to his feet. With the camera on both, Edgar, who had previously denied Gloucester's sensations, now joyfully confirms them: "Up—so. How is 't? Feel you your legs? You stand."

The reclaiming of Gloucester is managed through a series of closeups. With the blind man's face profiled and the young man on his left gazing at him, Edgar describes the "fiend" that Gloucester thought a "beggar." The camera is tight on the old man as he wonderingly accepts the revelation and then on Edgar who, with wet eyes, slowly, emphatically, and tenderly pronounces the moral, "There—fore, thou happy father," his face almost touching Gloucester's on "preserved thee." The pattern is repeated for the reaction of the father, who nods and looks toward heaven, and for that of Edgar, who, again with wet eyes, smiles gratefully and punches his concluding line: "Bear free and patient thoughts."

In this version of the Dover Cliff episode, Edgar's specious moral seems less important than the good will and sympathetic affection he finally shows his father by means of his deception. In order to reinforce this impression, Elliott makes certain adjustments in the text. He reshapes the concluding dialogue so that Edgar's identification of the "fiend" is immediately followed by Gloucester's reflection on his duping by the "thing" that "led me to that place." This reflection then prompts Edgar's moral on the old man's preservation by the gods, which in turn elicits Gloucester's expression of determination to endure

(75–77), now his final lines. To the same effect, Elliott treats the sequence as a scene, complete in itself. In Shakespeare's text, and in the BBC version, the exchange between father and son is interrupted by the sudden appearance of the maddened Lear, a "side-piercing sight" that makes Edgar's assurance ring all the more hollowly. (Though Lear does appear in the next scene of the Granada production, he is first shown serenely washing his garments in a stream.) Elliott, on the contrary, enforces closure with Edgar's "Bear free and patient thoughts." The camera offers a final overhead shot of Gloucester and Edgar standing together in the sand, the son holding the father's hands. Then Edgar puts his arm around Gloucester, and they begin to move downstage right, resuming their journey. This is the image on which the scene fades out—father and son, physically and spiritually joined in spite of the tragic misfortune that has overtaken them.

Both productions, then, though bound by realism, manage to transcend its limitations. Each generates ambiguity in its own way, teasing an apprehensive audience, and each does so to underscore Edgar's act of deception. Yet the effects of each version are, finally, quite different. The strategy of Miller's version, which closely follows Shakespeare's text and apparently Shakespeare's lead, qualifies sharply Edgar's moral vision while acknowledging his benevolent purpose. Elliott's strategy, while attentive to Edgar's devious means, serves to shift the emphasis to the son's salutary recovery of his father from despair and death and to the restoration of the bond between them.

Veteran RSC actor Patrick Stewart has occasionally spoken with groups of Shakespeareans, both professional and amateur, about the role of the anonymous Captain who utters two-and-one-half lines in 5.3 of *King Lear*. The Captain is on stage for an exchange with Edmund that immediately follows Lear and Cordelia's departure for prison and precedes the arrival with a flourish of Albany, Goneril, and Regan. Working inductively, Stewart likes to explore the production possibilities in this fourteen-line passage of dialogue, teasing them out for whatever time he has, which is never enough. The point is that the passage is so rich that it may provide a paradigm for performance-oriented inquiry. For this small patch of Shakespeare's text yields a harvest of interpretive choices for anyone, whether director or actor, teacher or student, who approaches it with performance in mind. We would like to consider some of those choices and then to show how the BBC and the Granada productions interpret the sequence. But first, since the passage is so brief, we will quote it, beginning with the end of the previous sequence. (Bevington's edition, like all modern editions, relies on the Quarto for the inclusion of the Captain's second speech [39–40].)

> *Edmund.*   Take them away.
> *Lear.* Upon such sacrifices, my Cordelia,
>   The gods themselves throw incense. Have I caught thee?
>   He that parts us shall bring a brand from heaven,
>   And fire us hence like foxes. Wipe thine eyes;
>   The good-years shall devour them, flesh and fell,
>   Ere they shall make us weep! We'll see 'em starv'd first.
>   Come.   *Exit [with Cordelia, guarded].*
> *Edmund.* Come hither, captain; hark.
>   Take thou this note; . . . go follow them to prison.
>   One step I have advanc'd thee; if thou dost
>   As this instructs thee, thou dost make thy way

To noble fortunes. Know thou this, that men
Are as the time is. To be tender-minded
Does not become a sword. Thy great employment
Will not bear question; either say thou 'lt do 't,
Or thrive by other means.
Captain.   I'll do 't, my lord.
Edmund. About it; and write happy when th' hast done.
   Mark, I say, instantly, and carry it so
   As I have set it down.
Captain. I cannot draw a cart, nor eat dried oats;
   If it be man's work, I'll do 't. *Exit Captain.*

                                        (19–40)

We have included Lear's parting lines to evoke the contrast
between the two moments, one the expression of loving self-
sacrifice, the other of ruthless self-interest. Even as Lear shows
that he is beyond caring about anything but his joining with
Cordelia, a union that is usually sealed by their physical contact, Edmund gives the Captain the death warrant that will sun-
der them. We also want to notice, however, that Lear's last line,
the monosyllabic "Come," is repeated and continued by Edmund, "Come hither, captain; hark," an irony that may be variously pointed in production. There is bound to be a difference
in the way each character utters the imperative: Lear is offering
comfort to his daughter; Edmund is issuing a command to a
subordinate. But Lear may also be directing his attention to
his guards or even to Edmund, who ordered that the pair be
taken away, in which case he might speak defiantly. As for
Edmund, whether he is matter-of-fact or urgent in his manner,
he is in any case imperious, addressing his subordinate by rank,
not name, and concluding the line with another command.

   The line thus shared by Lear and Edmund is, of course, a
line of verse, but it represents a departure from the norm, seven
syllables instead of ten. From the perspective of actors like Stewart and directors like John Barton, a short line is a signal from
the playwright. Barton comments on this in *Playing Shakespeare:*

> I believe Shakespeare is giving hidden stage-directions to the actor.
> When there is a short line, we can be pretty sure that he is indicating
> a pause of some sort. . . . Shakespeare's short lines can always tell
> us something, usually about the character's intentions.[1]

If the pause is to tell us something here, however, we must
decide where it occurs. A commonsense suggestion is that it

is meant to cover the exit of Lear and Cordelia, separating the first "Come" from the second and ensuring that Edmund's call to the Captain is unheard by the two. But most exits occur at the ends of lines, not in their midst. Suppose Edmund doesn't hesitate to speak and Lear and Cordelia overhear his abrupt and ominous imperative; it becomes an intrusion on their serenity, a tainting of their solemn joy. Certainly other spots in the line may accommodate a pause. Edmund's "hither" implies that the Captain must come up to him; a pause following "Come hither, captain" would permit him to do so. Or, if the Captain is already close by, the pause may follow "hark," generating anticipation on the part of the Captain as to what Edmund may want of him. Edmund might well pause after the "hark," since he means to impose on the Captain an extraordinary task, the killing of Britain's king and France's queen. If Edmund does not fully trust his subordinate or if he doubts that he will secure immediate assent, he might cautiously hold the moment to find both the words and the tone to convince the Captain to perform the deed. Even the villainous Edmund may require an emphatic silence to prepare for this seduction. It is, of course, possible to ignore these contingencies by ignoring the verse line, a practice familiar enough in many productions. However, if the verse line is to be taken seriously, as Barton insists, there is a constraint on the choices to be made.

Yet another tantalizing possibility suggests itself. There may be more to the seduction than the masterly rhetorical appeal that follows. Suppose that the pause does occur after "Come hither, captain." While it would be a practical means of allowing the officer traveling time, it could also signal a sudden rise in his fortunes: the man summoned by Edmund may not have been a "captain" until this instant. This may be a battlefield commission, granted by Edmund as an enticement to the soldier to do his bidding. Edmund himself lends plausibility to the idea when he observes, in line 29, "One step I have advanc'd thee." Though it may be that Edmund has previously advanced him and recalls the promotion as an earnest of the "noble fortunes" he now promises him, it may also be that Edmund is exhibiting his power and his bounty before our eyes. If this is so, then the astonished—and presumably pleased—"Captain" would surely hesitate before reacting, perhaps looking about to be sure Edmund was addressing him. The strategy would be typical of the unscrupulous Edmund, who, in being "as the time is," has consistently followed his own advice. The occasion calls for an agent bound to his service, and Edmund may well see the on-the-spot commission as the means of securing unquestioning obedience.

If so, Edmund couples the gesture with a neatly modulated appeal. His second line, like his first, consists of imperatives: "Take thou this note: go follow them to prison." But his manner quickly becomes persuasive and admonitory as he invites the Captain to consult his own interests and to serve the time without scruple, a doctrine that counterpoints ironically Lear's serene repudiation moments earlier of worldly ambition and the "ebb and flow" of political power. Though Edmund thinks he knows what "men / Are" in giving the Captain his "great employment," he concludes by offering a choice that is also a threat: "either say thou 'lt do 't, / Or thrive by other means."

Not surprisingly, the Captain's first words are "I'll do 't, my lord." The response not only echoes Edmund's phrasing, but it completes his last line. Again, Barton comments on Shakespeare's device of splitting the blank verse line between two speakers:

> He does it over and over, and almost always we'll find that it means one thing. The second speaker is meant to pick up the cue at once, as surely as if Shakespeare had written in the stage direction, "don't pause here."[2]

Admitting the Captain's prompt acquiescence, the actor playing the part still needs to decide at what point in Edmund's speech he knows that he will take on the task. If this is a battlefield commission, he may well be resolved the moment Edmund calls him "Captain." Or one of Edmund's several arguments may have prevailed with him, depending on the particular nature of his vulnerability. Is it the promise of "noble fortunes"? Is it the understanding, reinforced by his witnessing the battle's political outcome, that men must be "as the time is"? Is it Edmund's challenge to his soldiership, which should be as impervious to feeling as the weapon he bears? Is it Edmund's flat refusal to brook discussion of such "great employment?" Or is it the concluding ultimatum? If the Captain does not "do 't," he must "thrive by other means." Does this imply merely that he will have to seek "noble fortunes" in other ways, or does it mean that he will lose the position he now enjoys, that is, be stripped of his commission and dismissed from Edmund's service, if he refuses?

This last possibility becomes especially compelling as the

sequence continues. Edmund—perhaps relieved, or self-congrat-
ulatory, or simply eager to get on with it—repeats his promise
and orders the Captain to do the deed "instantly," cutting off
his charge with a short line: "As I have set it down." The reso-
nant line ends the deal, sealing Cordelia's and Lear's doom.
It may be that Shakespeare truncates the line in order to give
the audience a pause, one in which it assimilates the enormity
of Edmund's villainy and anticipates the appalling consequence
of his command. The audience should remember that not long
before, in his soliloquy at the end of 5.1, Edmund vowed that
Lear and Cordelia would never see Albany's pardon. Or the
audience may be meant to reflect on the moral deformity that
actuates these two opportunists and pervades their world. The
handling of the silence on stage is not likely to diminish its
uneasiness. It is for the Captain an opportunity to renege. He
does not depart immediately in the Quarto, despite Edmund's
insistence. Might he be having second thoughts? Might the Captain in this instant reclaim his humanity and decide to sacrifice
himself in the spirit of Lear's parting speech? Or might he need
the moment simply to review the practical situation? His response suggests that he has considered both options and yielded
to the occasion: "I cannot draw a cart, nor eat dried oats; /
If it be man's work, I'll do 't."

The anonymous Captain has made his choice, frustrating any
hope for a redemptive gesture that the audience might still have
entertained. He frames his response in pragmatic terms: he is
unable or unwilling to work and feed like a beast, which Edmund's displeasure would reduce him to; he will do "man's
work" instead. His final line is another short one. While the
pause will cover his exit, more probably the line is short to
permit its powerful irony to be absorbed. In denying his own
bestial nature and embracing "man's work"—his "great employment" being the murder of Cordelia and Lear—he has opted
for the enterprising bestiality that has threatened to redefine
humanity throughout the play. Man is not merely a "poor, bare,
forked animal" (3.4.106) in his vulnerability; he is actively bestial in his deeds. Though an incidental character, the anonymous
Captain in this chilling vignette prepares us for the shattering
frustration of the redemptive process when Lear next appears,
Cordelia dead in his arms.

There is another, more obvious decision about this sequence
that must be made in production, one that pointedly involves
stage business. When does Edmund give the "note" to the Cap-

tain? Bevington, like most modern editors, includes a stage direction (which we omitted) after Edmund's "Take thou this note," indicating that the transfer of the paper containing the commission should be made at this juncture. Here Bevington and others are relying on Malone, however, rather than on the texts of the Quarto or the Folio, where the action is unspecified. In fact, Edmund might hand the note to the Captain at any point during his two speeches or at the end of the second or even at the end of the sequence, during the emphatic pause. When he does so may be just a mechanical decision determined by convenience and comfort, but it may also be an interpretive choice. Edmund's withholding of the note until the end could suggest distrust: until he is absolutely certain that the Captain will comply, he will not release the paper. He is, after all, using a note in the first place, rather than an oral command, in order to cover himself: such business needed the seal of his partner and protector, Goneril. His hesitation now might be a gesture of self-protection. Or, secure in the knowledge that Goneril has endorsed his treachery, Edmund might flourish the note as he talks in order to tease—or torment—the Captain, who is not sure that Edmund will, finally, trust him with the task. The director may be using the piece of paper as a focal point for the Captain, who, out of awe or shame or surprise, cannot look Edmund in the eye. In short, if Edmund holds on to the note through part or all of the exchange, the note can contribute to the creation of either of the characters.

Edmund does have the option of passing the note at the point where the interpolated stage direction indicates the action. If he does give the paper to the Captain early, then the Captain faces the dilemma of whether or not to read it—and when. If he reads it, what is his response? Does he smile? Is he astonished? Does he make any attempt to get out of the situation, perhaps even turn to go? Does he try to give it back? Might his effort to give it back after having read it be the impetus for Edmund's persuasion speech? Whatever his reaction, how does an audience respond to the anonymous Captain, knowing that he knows precisely what his task will be? How does the Captain's knowledge contribute to his final expression of assent? —"If it be man's work, I'll do 't." Indeed, does the conditional "If it be" imply strongly that the Captain does *not* read the note? The Captain's final two lines, after all, might be a general statement, not so much a reference to the specific task, which he has already accepted, as the expression of a philosophy:

the Captain will do whatever is asked of him, which, by virtue of its having been requested by a superior, is "man's work."

Later on in the scene, the dying Edmund will confess that his "writ / Is on the life of Lear and on Cordelia." His "Nay, send in time" is completed by Albany's "Run, run, O, run!" (249–51). The urgency recalls Edmund's in sending off the Captain to that same prison, not to prevent the deed, as Albany here tries to do, but to accomplish it. Ironically, in the Quarto, it seems to be another Captain who rushes to the prison, this one doomed to fail in his mission.

Someone seeing *King Lear* for the first time, not having read the text, will know only now exactly what was in Edmund's note. But anyone familiar with the play has known what the note held since Edmund commanded the Captain to "go follow them to prison." For the knowledgeable audience especially, it makes a difference whether the Captain reads the note or not. For the horror of "man's work" is more unbearable if the Captain knows well what he is about.

The sequence, then, is a provocative one, for it offers a range of possibilities that must be addressed in production, where the audience is not left wondering whether Lear and Cordelia are still on stage when Edmund calls the Captain, whether the soldier has only on the instant been made a Captain, whether the Captain shows any hesitation in accepting the charge, or whether the Captain reads the note or not. Every production requires these decisions, and they are choices that become linked with others made elsewhere in the play. Such decisions were, of course, made in the mounting of the BBC *King Lear* and the Granada *King Lear,* and though together these two productions do not exhaust the possibilities, they represent suggestive interpretations that may profitably be compared.

Productions

BBC

Miller's Renaissance *mise-en-scène* for the BBC *King Lear* creates its own special decorum. There is always an ambience of "civilization" or refinement masking the elementary passions and routine cruelties of the dramatic world. So it is with the episode of the anonymous Captain.

In the aftermath of the battle, the scene is set in Edmund's

The Anonymous Captain. BBC Production. John Bird as Albany, Michael Kitchen as Edmund (immediately following the sequence). Courtesy of the British Broadcasting Corporation. Copyright © BBC.

spacious tent. Dressed casually in shirtsleeves, Edmund sits erect but comfortably at a table stage left, and Lear and Cordelia stand prisoners before him stage right. Since this is television, the camera determines what appears in the frame, and, throughout the earlier sequence, after an initial shot of Edmund, it remains fixed on father and daughter in this tender moment of defeat and triumph. This pattern is interrupted momentarily at Edmund's "Take them away," when the camera cuts to the speaker and we get our first look at the Captain, young and handsomely bearded in besashed battle dress, standing behind Edmund's right shoulder. The fact that this is television makes a difference as well in Lear and Cordelia's exit. When Lear pronounces his vigorous and resounding "Come," at once spoken to Cordelia in leading her off and flung as a challenge to his captors, the camera cuts to Edmund at the table and the Captain beginning an upstage cross, apparently intent on following the prisoners. At Edmund's "Come hither, captain," he turns as his rank is specified to face his superior. The expectant turn fills the pause before Edmund's "hark," but it is clear from the Captain's dress, his unruffled demeanor, and his secure position at Edmund's right hand that this is no on-the-spot promotion. Accustomed to doing Edmund's bidding, he stands poised and attentive, hat in hand. The camera thus frames the two of them, and it remains fixed throughout the encounter, changing only as the next sequence begins.

On "hark," Edmund picks up the note, already sealed, from the clutter of writing materials on the table, but he does not give it to the Captain. Throughout both his speeches, the confident Edmund holds on to the note, speaking rapidly and waving it slightly for emphasis. If Edmund is businesslike, the Captain is responsive but uncurious, keeping his eyes on his superior. He nods briefly on Edmund's mention of the note and the prisoners, and on Edmund's promise of "noble fortunes" he nods again and smiles slightly, even smugly. The sound of a trumpet in the background underscores Edmund's matter-of-fact admonitions about men at war and the relative importance of this assignment, all of which draws a quiet assent from the Captain. As Edmund briskly concludes his second speech, he passes the note into the Captain's gloved hand, which is waiting for it. The Captain gives Edmund the assurance he wants with scarcely a glance at the sealed order, though the officer does hold it up for his pronouncement on "man's work." Edmund, having given the note to the Captain, touches his moustache and his beard shrewdly, rising only to receive Albany, Goneril, and Regan. On his way out, the Captain stands aside for the arriving dignitaries and bows respectfully.

A genteel cynicism informs the episode. It might be an exchange between a corporate executive and a member of his staff. The Captain's delivery of his final two lines is especially telling. This officer is a gentleman in appearance, accent, and manner. The allusion to a condition of beastlike labor and privation has no reality for him, and he makes it with a complacent sense of his own superiority. He is merely trading aphorisms with Edmund, and he chooses one suitable to the occasion, expressing deference for a superior, ready acceptance of his proposition, and a shared understanding of the world. In short, the dramatic mode adopted by the director here is that of ironic understatement, and it may well be more chilling than some of the more obviously theatrical possibilities.

GRANADA

In the Granada production, Elliott evokes an era more ancient and more patently "barbarous." Recalling druidical times, the Stonehenge-like monoliths that provide the mythic setting at the beginning and at the end are associated obscurely in the minds of the audience with inscrutable gods and blood sacrifice. Yet, as we have remarked, Elliott avoids mere "primitivism" by presenting us with a society that is highly structured. The rules governing this pre-Christian world are well known by its inhabitants, and the violation of them registers all the more forcibly.

At the beginning of 5.3, Lear and Cordelia cling to each other, encircled by the swordpoints of Edmund's soldiers. An armed Edmund breaks into the circle and, removing his helmet to gaze steadily and grimly at the pair, gives the order to guard them well; then he turns upstage and moves away. The camera focuses in for a series of closeups on the white-haired old man and his blond daughter, both garbed in white, as they talk and touch. When Edmund in the background orders, "Take them away," the soldiers close in, and Lear raises his shackled hands over Cordelia's head to fold her in an embrace. The camera zooms back for this and then moves in even tighter on the two as Lear kisses and consoles Cordelia and finally releases her from the embrace, only to touch her face. After a last kiss, he murmurs his barely audible "Come" to her alone. Again

The Anonymous Captain. Granada Production. Robert Lindsay as Edmund. Courtesy of Granada Television. Copyright © Granada T.V.

the camera zooms back to admit into the frame the soldiers, who lead and follow father and daughter off. As the exodus occurs, Edmund, who is seen standing on a rock at the far left, directs his command to an unseen soldier, who breaks out of the ranks and into the frame from stage right; the audience first sees only his back and then, as he turns to Edmund, his shabby battle dress and unshaven face.

Edmund's first line to the Captain is changed here to accommodate the special blocking. Since he is picking someone out of a crowd, Edmund immediately identifies the man by rank: "Captain, come hither; hark." There is little chance of connecting his "come" with Lear's anyway, after the muted delivery of the first and after the time required to cover the exit. In effect, Edmund's line is treated as a new line of verse, with the pause coming before "hark" to allow the Captain traveling time and to give Edmund a moment to look around cautiously. On "hark," Edmund instantly hands him the note. Through the next line, the Captain opens the note and begins to read. In the given circumstances, this is not a battlefield commission. In fact, Edmund's "One step I have advanced thee" is omitted to create another pause and provide further opportunity for the Captain to read and react. Edmund's eyes, which looked away after he passed the note, now settle on the Captain, who looks up quickly. The camera cuts to a medium shot of the Captain, seen below Edmund's shoulder, as his face registers a startled, quizzical response, and then it cuts back to a closeup of Edmund, as he delivers his admonitions.

Physical appearance and blocking make the difference in station impressive. While the raw-boned Captain wears a simple egg-shaped helmet on his head and a sheepskin battle vest over his shirt, Edmund is accoutred in an elegant black coat armor with silver studs and trim, his visored helmet cradled in his arm. Similarly, standing on a slab of rock, Edmund towers over his subordinate. For the Captain, he is clearly the "image of authority."

With the camera close on his face, Edmund is persuasive as well as dominating, for he addresses someone who knows the enormity of the task he is imposing. Thus he speaks slowly and emphatically, punctuating promise and assurance. But the reference to "thy great employment" is gone. With a snarl, he concludes rapidly, as he presents his ultimatum. This is the end of Edmund's spoken discourse with the Captain in this production. Also cut are the Captain's initial assent and Edmund's second speech. Instead, there is a pause in which the camera rests on the Captain's upturned face. When he does speak, his mouth gapes and the accent is "working class." Unlike the gentleman Captain in the BBC production, this one knows whereof he speaks when he rejects the lot of an animal; the utterance is heartfelt. He is not merely resigned to do the "man's work" that Edmund demands of him; he is determined to do it. Knowing that it is villainy, he accepts the lot of the cutthroat, making himself a "serviceable villain."

On the Captain's last words, there are shouts in the background and the swelling strains of trumpets. As the Captain strides off upstage, a meditative Edmund lingers on his perch, looking downstage, his helmet in his right hand. It is probably at this point that one realizes the helmet precisely resembles a skull. Stepping off the rock, Edmund moves downstage, looking well satisfied, until he is almost on top of the camera. While so poised, as in a reverie, he is recalled to the moment by the entering Albany's praise: "Sir, you have show'd today your valiant strain, / And fortune led you well." The villain's expression reveals his own awareness of the irony in that praise.

The mode of line analysis we have employed in our approach to the anonymous Captain sequence may be applied wherever short or shared lines characterize the verse. For even in the structure of verse passages, Shakespeare has provided clues and cues to performance to which the alert reader may respond.

6

The Promised End: 5.3

In this play about seeing and mis-seeing, the final sequence, beginning with Lear's howls and ending with his death, may well compose the most powerful image of the play. The gratuitous death of Cordelia, who earlier exchanged love and forgiveness with her father, astonishes even an audience expecting a tragic ending, since Lear and Cordelia have become for us—as for Albany and the others—"Great thing of us forgot!" Diverted and preoccupied by the events unfolding on stage, we give little thought to the Captain sent off to do "man's work" or to Edmund's pending hope to do some good—prompted by Edgar's report of Gloucester's death, delayed by the reports of Kent entranced and Goneril and Regan dead, and activated only when Albany demands that he speak and Edmund, realizing he was "beloved," reacts. If we think of Lear and Cordelia at all in the welter of circumstances promising closure, we think of their solemn joy as they walk off to prison, Lear euphoric as he imagines their singing "like birds i' th' cage," Cordelia overwhelmed by pity and love. Or if stirred to uneasiness by the ambiguous exclamations of the Gentleman with the bloody knife—"Help, help, O, help! . . . O, she's dead!"—we are for the moment assuaged to learn he means Goneril. When father and daughter do reappear, Cordelia hanged, the shattering spectacle urges us to feel that if this is the "promise'd end"—of the world or of Lear and Cordelia—then there is no redeeming of sorrow and no hope of cosmic justice.

Never has the prevailing vision of Edgar, the primary spokesman of conventional consolations, seemed so shockingly inadequate to account for the action that the play presents. As an audience, if we grieve for the vulnerability of Lear and Cordelia, we also, as Stephen Booth suggests, grieve for "our own"[1] and await its explicit acknowledgment. When the acknowledgment comes, it is the more poignant that it comes from Edgar, with

the final lines of the play, in a voice chastened by the weight
of experience:

> The weight of this sad time we must obey,
> Speak what we feel, not what we ought to say.
> The oldest hath borne most; we that are young
> Shall never see so much, nor live so long.
>
> (328–31)

This concluding utterance seems a small concession and, surely,
a perfunctory comment on the meaning of this expansive and
enigmatic drama—James Calderwood calls it a "band-aid on a
gaping wound."[2] For Edgar, who has resisted the daunting les-
sons of experience throughout, the relinquishing of formulaic
expressions of a visionary ideal to insist on the sad validations
of a felt reality involves a basic change in perspective. Edgar
is the one character in the play who has lived through the
deepest agony of both Gloucester and Lear, serving as mad witness and spiritual guide on both the storm-beaten heath and
the Dover shore. If his heart seemed to break at what he saw,
it has also had to absorb the treachery, privation, and pain
he has himself known. Yet Edgar has repeatedly sought and
created compensations for the "worst," and in the immediate
aftermath of his victory over Edmund, with 150-odd lines left
in the play, he confidently proclaims, "The gods are just."

Other characters have made similar affirmations in circumstances that an audience, if not the character, recognizes as less
than validating. Albany, hearing of the heroic action of the servant who slew the brutal Cornwall, concludes, "This shows
you are above, / You justicers, that these our nether crimes /
So speedily can venge!" (4.2.79–81). But while Albany is pronouncing this judgment, Cornwall's partners in crime continue
to thrive and their victims to suffer—Lear is mad, Gloucester
is blind, and the servant is dead. Likewise, Gloucester, in response to Edgar's fraudulent miracle on Dover Cliff, believes
that the "clearest gods" have preserved him, even after his encounter with Lear in the same scene petitioning the "ever-gentle
gods" and invoking "The bounty and the benison of heaven"
(4.6.73, 218, 226). Now Edgar, having proved upon Edmund's
person the bastard's "heinous, manifest, and many treasons,"
seems legitimately to have vindicated the gods, and for the time
being the audience may concede, with the dying Edmund, "Th'
hast spoken right, 'tis true."

Events appear to be winding down; the redemptive process appears to be in force. Edgar tells of the joy and grief that burst his father's heart and of Kent's puissant sorrow. Edmund, moved to contrition, proposes to do some good. And the report of Goneril's suicide and Regan's poisoning prompts Albany to acknowledge the appropriate "judgment of the heavens." However, the salutary emotions and the fitting retribution that promise to mitigate past sufferings evaporate in an instant with Albany's "Great thing of us forgot!" The fate of the king and his loving daughter remains to be assimilated into Albany's sense of justice, Edgar's consoling creed, and the audience's vision of the play. The last line before Lear enters, Cordelia in his arms, contains Albany's desperate prayer: "The gods defend her!" But the gods do not deliver.

Nevertheless, even as he witnesses the distraught Lear's ministrations to his dead daughter, Albany attempts to offer the summation speech accorded the reigning dignitary of a Shakespearean tragedy:

> You lords and noble friends, now our intent.
> What comfort to this great decay may come
> Shall be applied. For us, we will resign,
> During the life of this old majesty,
> To him our absolute power. . . .
> . . . . All friends shall taste
> The wages of their virtue, and all foes
> The cup of their deservings.
>
> (301–9)

In this formal declaration, Albany means to restore comfort to Lear, order to the kingdom, and justice to the world of the play. It is what he "ought to say." But, as John Shaw points out in his essay on the final lines of King Lear, the declaration is not only premature but beside the point. Lear's death is yet to come, and Albany, "who has never been acutely perceptive," however well-meaning, remains an imperfect judge of the "events taking place before his eyes."[3] Notably, it is with the exclamation "O, see, see!" that he interrupts his concluding couplet and directs all eyes to the final agony of Lear.

Albany's next speech is in the accents of one who has seen Lear die. He speaks only to acknowledge "general woe" and the "gor'd state," relinquishing rule to Kent, who refuses it, and to Edgar, who speaks the last lines. Unlike Albany's premature declaration, Edgar's quiet reflection does not represent "what we ought to say": it presents no vision of virtue rewarded, vice punished, or order restored, resting rather in assurances that are essentially "negative and ambiguous." Though in itself inadequate as a comment on the disturbing substance of the play, however, Edgar's utterance may well stand as the playwright's comment on the play he has made. As Shaw puts it, in "defying the decorous pattern of the usual ending, Shakespeare is implying that any return to routine after the events of *this* tragedy would constitute an outrage to one's sense of moral justice as well as to one's sense of artistic rightness."[4]

Shaw suggests that the full impact of Edgar's speech lies not only in the failure of the cosmic and political order to assert itself but also in the refusal of the conventional artistic order to do so. This raises the question of Edgar as speaker of the lines, for the Quarto attributes them to Albany. The Folio, more cogently, gives them to Edgar. Having seen more than Albany and now having received what is left from him, Edgar has earned the privilege of speaking the speech. Again, as we have remarked, it seems that the reference to "what we ought to say" recognizes Edgar's own penchant for formulaic pronouncements—until this appalling end. Still, one would hope that if the moral content of these lines represented their primary reason for being, Edgar—and Shakespeare—could have said more.

If the speech is in effect a comment on the playwright's art, however, then for another reason it is appropriate for Edgar to speak it, and the lines offer a more satisfying, albeit ironic, conclusion. After all, Edgar has spent much of his energy playing roles and creating dramatic fictions. And it is Edgar who, at the final entrance of Lear, responds to the stunned Kent's question—"Is this the promis'd end?"—with another question—"Or image of that horror?" The exchange combines anticipations of the apocalypse with expectations concerning the tragic form. It reminds us, as the play so frequently does, that this is theater and that the promised end of tragedy is indeed an "image of that horror." However, if Edgar takes the initiative in recalling the tragic imperative as Lear enters, he resists it when Lear dies. The first to react to the king's passing, he misreads the event as a faint, urging his lord to "Look up," and requires Kent to identify death: "Vex not his ghost. O, let him pass!" Though a practicing artist who can claim some success in redefining perception and reshaping reality, Edgar is helpless here; he must yield to ineluctable death in both life and the tragic form. His reflexive allusion to the "image of that horror" may indeed suggest that Edgar is not quite sure whether he is a participant in life or, like Gloucester at Dover Cliff, a participant in a play. Now, having failed to affect the course of either, he will at least resist the artistic inevitability of decorous closure in his summary speech. Proposing we "Speak what we feel, not what we ought to say," he in fact says little of either. Instead, he replaces tragedy's conventional end, invoked ineffectually by Albany, with two couplets that leave no one—not nihilists, existentialists, moral optimistis, humanists, Christians, or Aristotelians—content.

King Lear is a play that deconstructs itself repeatedly, subverting one pattern of action and argument with the next in a teasing panorama of self-contradiction. If we are left with any moral certainty at the end of the drama, it is that life in its grand and its gritty dimensions is indeterminate, refusing to submit to the paradigms of justice that any of its characters propose. If there is any determinately present meaning to be found, it derives from Edgar's "Speak what we feel," a directive that settles attention on the imperfect authority of "unaccommodated man." If this too is searching for definition where there is none, then Edgar's final speech becomes the ultimate comment on the play, for, in refusing the promised end of tragedy, it dissolves the elements that are supposed to constitute the tragic vision. Stephen Booth, in "King Lear," "Macbeth," Indefinition, and Tragedy, is rigorous in his analysis of the irreconcilable paradoxes of the play but reassuring in his conclusion. Booth's thesis is that the "repeated evocation of a sense of indefiniteness generates a sense of pattern and thus of the wholeness, the identity of the play."[5] His comment on Albany's premature speech illustrates the point:

> The glory of King Lear as an experience for its audience is in the fact that the play presents its morally capricious universe in a play that, paradoxically, is formally capricious and also uses pattern to do exactly what pattern usually does: assert the presence of an encompassing order in the work (as opposed to the world it describes). Albany's restitution speech and the inadequacy it acknowledges when Albany breaks off and says,"O, see, see!" embody the paradox precisely: both in substance and kind Albany's speech proclaims a return to order and gratifies one's assumptions that the norms of society and the norms of plays can be counted on; both Albany and his speech fail of their promised ends, and yet the mere repetition of the two kinds of failure balances and qualifies the effect of one of them, the failure of form.[6]

Booth sees the last sixteen lines of *King Lear* as emblematic of the experience of the whole. Those final lines, like numerous other phenomena in the play, both disrupt our faith in artistic kinds and use our perception of kind "to compensate artistically for the intellectual terror that the same phenomena generate by illustrating the impossibility of definition."[7]

Booth's analysis of the coherent matrix in a play of indefinition reminds us of the related but more basic problem of definition that has been our primary concern: translating text into a series of stage images that produce a coherent whole. Albany's and Edgar's speeches are diegetic pronouncements, however imperfect, on the dramatic event. And that event—from Lear's anguished howls to his final "Look there, look there!" spoken just before he dies—is a cluster of textual ambiguities that seek definition on stage.

If readers of Shakespeare are both stimulated and vexed by the multiple possibilities inherent in the various sequences we have assessed, there is a special sense in which this final panel of *King Lear*, offering as it does the most potent image of the play, is indeed the promised end. For these seventy lines, when realized on the stage, create the image that endures beyond the life of Lear and beyond the life of the performance. The piercing resonance of Lear's pained and inarticulate howls conspires with the pietà-like emblem of human sacrifice and waste to usurp the language of the play.

Calderwood is among the many who notice the numerous references to seeing throughout the play and in particular in the final lines.[8] Anyone who has witnessed the sudden appearance of Lear carrying the dead Cordelia in his arms and heard his howls knows the stunning effect the king's entrance has on audiences both onstage and off. The sight transforms the stage onlookers, as Lear insists, into "men of stones," fixed in appalled, silent witness. Were Lear in their position, he would use his tongue and eyes "that heaven's vault should crack." Even as he delivers the narrative no one need speak, for it becomes apparent that Cordelia is dead, Lear seeks more definitive visual proof. Twice he mentions objects—actual properties? —that could supply the evidence his unbelieving eyes demand: "Lend me a looking glass; / If that her breath will mist or stain the stone, / Why, then she lives"; "This feather stirs; she lives!"

Remarking on Lear's casual response to the news of his eldest daughters' deaths, Albany observes, "He knows not what he says, and vain is it / That we present us to him." The line contains an interesting variant from the Quarto, which claims "He knowes not what he sees." "Says," of course, is more appropriate to the moment, but either is appropriate to the sequence, which is a gradual movement toward the verification of reality not through tongues but through eyes. The looking glass and the feather offer only theoretical potential: "If that her breath will mist or stain the stone"; "If it be so, / It is a chance which does redeem all sorrows / That ever I have felt." Nevertheless, at the moment of death, Lear insists on the visual as the paradoxical endorsement of both life and death: "Do you see this? Look on her; look, her lips, / Look there, look there!" The text does not reveal what Lear's "this" means: does Lear suppose that Cordelia's lips have moved as a sign of life, or does he point to their stillness as the seal of death? If he thinks her lips have moved, then the king indeed knows not what he sees. Nor do the others know. Yet, like Gertrude in the closet, though they see nothing, all that is there they see. Lear's directive, an invitation either to see life or to see death, secures ocular attention at the moment when the forming emblem becomes fixed. His monosyllabic last lines retain their ambiguity as language yields its authority to the visual image of the promised end.

Had Lear not insisted that all eyes rest on Cordelia, Albany's exclamation "O, see, see!" would have assured that attention was riveted on both father and daughter. Interrupting as it does his futile attempt to put a period to calamity and to shape rhetorically the conclusion of the play, Albany's directive signals the priority of sight over speech. Where language failed to sum up the experience of *King Lear*, the stage image to which Albany directs us says all.

In one respect, that image renders impotent even Edgar's final verbal assessment: "we that are young / Shall never see so much, nor live so long." The young, in fact, like all of us, in seeing the image have seen all—at least, all that the theater can offer. But in another respect, Edgar reasserts the value of language, for in directing us to "speak what we feel" he proposes the same validation that the stage image provides—not of justice, which is clearly capricious, but of the human bond. As Robert Egan describes the final image, "Cordelia is in Lear's arms, more his child now than ever, and Lear is massive with the dignity of his fatherhood."[9] The ties of sympathy that connect father and daughter and the human community surounding them, both onstage and off, are richly realized in this compelling image and cogently implied in Edgar's gloss.

Creating the promised end may well be the challenge of a mature actor's career, for Lear's death scene, played out over the body of his dead daughter and against the backdrop of so many other deaths shown, remembered, or anticipated, demands of "old majesty" staggering variety. In Walter Foreman's words, Lear in closing the play

> recapitulates the emotional responses to the world that he has exhibited throughout the earlier parts of the play. He is by turns imperious, accusing, hyperbolic, despairing, plain-spoken, revengeful, perceptive, accepting, deluded, hopeful. But the primary emotional pattern here is cyclic—despairing and hopeful according to whether Cordelia is dead or alive.[10]

Marvin Rosenberg, in *The Masks of "King Lear,"* also remarks on the enormous range of emotion involved in these final moments: "Rage, grief, desperate love, ego, pride, abstraction, stupefaction share in the dynamic that shunts Lear bewilderedly toward death."[11]

Despite the complexity of the promised end, however, Shakespeare gives no guidance concerning the emotional pattern of the sort that a G. B. Shaw might—no parenthetical notes or explanatory prefaces on how to play these final lines. Still, he does give clues of another sort. One of the more telling is the verbal frame that contains and expresses the sequence. The sequence begins with Lear's entrance howls, four in the Quarto, three in the Folio. Rosenberg, noticing the readings of a number of memorable Lears, suggests the histrionic changes that have been rung on this difficult half line. It has been sounded "in a full-bodied voice, like Gielgud's, or a high, cracked one, like Laughton's" and uttered as "an anguished cry (Karl Mantzius), a quiet sobbing, by a Japanese Lear, a deep baying (Redgrave), the wail of a wolf (Krauss), of a mourning dog (Cobb)."[12] Surely, the moment belongs to the actor and to theatrical history as one of the grand reentrances of the stage. Yet in what may be the greatest play by the greatest master of language, it is an inarticulate utterance, at once human and inhuman, that disturbs and defines the awful silence of the stage. Moved beyond language, the aching king begins the promised end with a howl. And in the Quarto, he ends the sequence with a similarly inarticulate utterance: "O, o, o, o."[13]

In conflating the early texts, editors have traditionally preferred the Folio ending to that of the Quarto. In the Folio, which omits the "O's," Lear's final words are the monosyllabic outcries "Do you see this? Looke on her? Looke her lips, / Looke there, looke there." The preference for the Folio ending is not surprising. Among other features that recommend it, in inviting both onstage and offstage audiences to see, it effectively seals the visual image. Moreover, it constructs a verbal frame for the death speech, balancing Lear's "Looke there, looke there" with Albany's introductory exclamation "O see see." Yet the Quarto, with its cryptic "O, o, o, o," may offer the more eloquent expression of the failure of language, balancing utterances to begin and to consummate Lear's ineffable experience.

The impression that Lear's experience is beyond words is reinforced by the iteration and intensification of negatives in his death speech. "No, no, no life!" he insists, suggesting at once that there is none in Cordelia and that there should be none without Cordelia—"Why should a dog, a horse, a rat have life, / And thou no breath at all?" The recognition that "Thou'lt come no more" provokes the impassioned climax of "nevers," three in the Quarto and, more astonishingly, five in the Folio. As G. K. Hunter remarks, the "action of the play has reached the final *nothing*. . . ."[14] Theatrically, the *something* that survives the *nothing* is again the visual image, a circumstance that Lear's last words in the Folio secure. While Lear struggles for sight as well as for utterance in the scene—"Had I your tongues and eyes" (262), "Mine eyes are not o' th' best" (283), "This is a dull sight" (286), "He knows not what he sees" (297 in the Quarto)—seeing finally does, as we have pointed out, preempt speech. Throughout the sequence, Lear's responses are informed by the presence of Cordelia's silent lips, the same lips that chose to "Love, and be silent" in act 1, scene 1. Though by Lear's measure in that scene Cordelia failed the test, now her silent lips speak to Lear's own understanding: he too is sure her "love's / More ponderous than [her] tongue."

Shakespeare gives another directive for playing the ending, one that implies his own awareness of the theatrical difficulty inherent in the sequence. Much has been said about the attenuation of the last scene of *King Lear*, which begins to end several times before it actually does so. After the battle of Dover, which might have concluded another play, Shakespeare repeatedly renews the drama. Booth, in discussing the delayed ending, notes how the focus shifts away from Lear and Cordelia after they are led off—to Albany, to the love-triangles (Edmund/Goneril/Regan, Edmund/Goneril/Albany), to Edmund, to the trial-by-combat and Edgar's victory over Edmund, to Edgar's narratives of Gloucester and of Kent, to the fates of Goneril and Regan, and, finally, to the "Great thing of us forgot":

> Even after the characters have remembered that the main business of the play is unfinished, the audience's travail continues. All the difficult plots and subplots have tumbled out on the stage at once, and the characters leap from focus to focus like the mad Lear of earlier scenes.[15]

As Booth puts it, "the play makes its audience suffer *as* audience; the fact that *King Lear* ends but does not stop is only the biggest of a succession of similar facts about the play."[16] When Lear reappears, the dead Cordelia in his arms, the audience must suddenly endure the culminating event it had deluded itself into thinking would not come. But if Shakespeare compels the audience to endure the emotional weight of Cordelia's and Lear's deaths, he also makes the burden bearable by means of a technical device. Here, as elsewhere in this extended scene, the shared verse line, which permits neither the luxury nor the pain of pause, regulates the pacing of the sequence.

The final panel, from Lear's entrance to his death, contains 54½ lines, 30½ of which are spoken by Lear in eleven segments. In seven of those segments, Lear shares a line with Kent, Edgar, or the Captain. Kent speaks a total of nine lines, with five of his seven short speeches involving a shared line. Albany, in addition to his premature summation speech, the first line of which he shares, delivers two and a half lines in two speeches, sharing lines in each. Edgar speaks three half lines, all shared; the Captain and the Messenger each speak a shared half line.

According to John Barton, whenever Shakespeare uses the shared verse line, the "second speaker is meant to pick up the cue at once," without pausing. Jane Lapotaire, commenting from an actress's perspective, notes that the shared line in effect means "think faster," a point Barton endorses by remarking that "It's no good if the richness and complexity of the verse leads one to think slowly and laboriously."[17] Thus, while the "promised end" mandates that the "audience suffer *as* audience," Shakespeare's choice of the shared-line strategy mitigates its pain. The attentuation of the agonizing spectacle is counterpointed by the rapid delivery of dialogue.

None of this is to suggest that the sequence in production should simply race from beginning to end unmodulated and unpunctuated. Any stretch of dialogue in Shakespeare is subject to various interpretive exigencies, such as blocking, movement, and gesture, that affect the delivery of lines. But if shared lines demand instantaneous pickup and incomplete lines indicate pauses, as Barton contends, then there are only two pauses inscribed in the text (only one in the Quarto), both of which occur in the recognition exchange with Kent. Any others in production are actors' or directors' interpolations. Such may indeed be warranted by particular circumstances and be supremely effective; Barton is speaking of "acting clues" and guidelines, not laws. In so intensely emotional a sequence, however, it behooves actors and directors to respect the inscribed signals rather than risk upsetting the strategically contrived equilibrium of the text.

There are, of course, additional clues to performance in this sequence, but many of them remain enigmatic as text. Only production can decide whether Lear directs his "O, you are men of stones!" to the assembled soldiers or to the principals, Albany, Kent, and Edgar, or whether he delivers the line as a general expression of despair, to no one in particular. Lear may address his "A plague upon you, murderers, traitors all!" to Kent, whom he has just dismissed with "Prithee away," or, like the first accusation, to any of those assembled. And he may direct his "Do you see this?" to one or more of the principal witnesses or to the crowd or, as in the 1985 Oregon Shakespearean Festival production, to the heavens in defiant reprimand. Or any of these lines may be delivered directly to the offstage audience, as Lear's "Do you see this?" was in Trevor Nunn's 1976 RSC production.[18]

Indeed, who is on stage is not fully prescribed by the text. Specified is the presence of Lear, with Cordelia in his arms, Kent, Edgar, Albany, and a Gentleman and a Messenger (in the Folio) or two Captains (in the Quarto), with the bodies of Goneril and Regan on display, their faces covered. While an exit for the dying Edmund is not recorded in a stage direction, Albany's order "Bear him hence awhile," together with the later report of his death indicates that he is not present. What remains unclear is how large a company of gentlemen attendants and soldiers witness the promised end. We may infer the presence of several on Shakespeare's stage from the concluding stage direction in the Folio, "Exeunt with a dead March," which calls for the ceremonial bearing off of four dead bodies. Though this mode of clearing the stage is not a practical necessity in modern production, the size and nature of the company of onlookers inevitably color the ending. Of critical importance is the position of Lear and Cordelia in relation to whoever else is on stage, since this serves to articulate the theatrical implication of the promised end, and it remains the prerogative of production.

Three properties are mentioned in the sequence that require production decisions of another sort. Lear twice refers to a validating property, which will establish whether Cordelia is alive or dead. Realistically, perhaps, there is little expectation that one of the witnesses will, on the moment, be able to accommodate his request for a *looking glass*. Yet, as John C. Meagher has suggested, one of Goneril's accoutrements may be a small hand-mirror hung from her girdle on a ribbon, a fashion enriched as an emblem of vanity in the iconography of Shakespeare's time, in which case the property might be readily produced.[19] The *feather* is more problematic, for Lear speaks as though he holds one in his hand: "This feather stirs; she lives!" Does he pluck a feather from his own or Cordelia's clothing or otherwise discover and produce one? Or does he hold merely an imaginary feather to her lips, even as he imagines that it stirs? Or does he, as Meagher proposes, hold up the mirror and call it a feather, showing that he is unable to distinguish which test for life he is actually employing?[20]

In the mock trial, Lear improvises evidence against his daughters and seizes upon a joint-stool to represent the absent Goneril. As in the mock trial, the relation of verbal images to actual stage images here is a direct reflection on the condition of Lear's mind. If all see the feather, he is in fact applying a reasonable test to determine whether Cordelia breathes. But if the feather does not exist or if Lear confounds one test with another, then he is both desperate and deranged as he wishes life into one whose life would "redeem all sorrows / That ever I have felt." Already a piteous sight, this father-daughter tableau becomes pitiful indeed.

The third property similarly may or may not be present, though in production it traditionally does appear. It is a costume property, the *button* that the dying Lear asks someone to undo. Usually taken to be a button at Lear's throat, suddenly constricted, the button may be Cordelia's and the implied stage business Lear's third effort to restore breath to the lifeless form. Philip C. McGuire devotes eight thoughtful pages of his *Speechless Dialect* to this property. He explores the alternatives, admitted by the Quarto and the Folio, of treating the button as Lear's or Cordelia's, Lear's request as specifically directed or generalized, and the respondent as either Kent, Edgar, Albany, or an anonymous soldier. McGuire shrewdly makes a case for either possibility of ownership and for at least eight possibilities in the undoing of the button, each appropriate to its premise and each shaping the meaning and effect of Lear's death. He even credits the button with contributing to the audience's reading of Lear's state of mind at the moment of death.

If the button is Lear's and the reading is that of the Quarto, he argues, then Lear in his final moments shifts his attention to his own death, wished for because he knows that Cordelia will "come no more": "He dies unwilling and unable to live without the company of his beloved daughter. . . ."[21] In the Folio reading, however, if the button is assumed to be Lear's, Lear turns his attention back to Cordelia, unable to accept his own assertion that she will "never" come again. He dies "believing that she lives."[22] Though McGuire may be attributing too much to this tiny property, for surely either reading of Lear's death is possible even without the button, this presentation of the permutations of undoing it is a model of how a production decision involving so small a thing can undo an assumed reading of text.

In reviewing the BBC and Granada productions, we shall be noticing the treatment of these properties and identifying the pattern involved in Lear's delivery of the several lines addressed to persons unspecified in the text, including his request that someone undo the button. But, most particularly, we shall be examining the ways in which each production accommodates the vision implicit in Kent's query—"Is this the promised end?"—and the theatrical implication of Edgar's provocative reply—"Or image of that horror?"

Productions

BBC

In Miller's BBC production, the setting is military, the British camp outside Edmund's tent, which stands as a barrier in the middle ground stage left; to the right stand ranks of soldiers, their lances upright, with Edgar and Albany posed before them facing the tent. The bodies of Goneril and Regan are not in view, and the dying Edmund is himself being carried into the interior of the tent when the first of Lear's four howls (as in

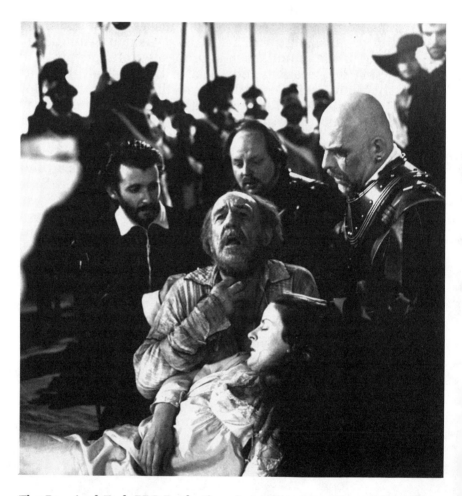

The Promised End. BBC Production. Anton Lesser as Edgar, John Bird as Albany, John Shrapnel as Kent, Michael Hordern as King Lear, Brenda Blethyn as Cordelia. Courtesy of the British Broadcasting Corporation. Copyright © BBC.

the Quarto) is heard offstage behind the tent. As everyone turns in the direction of the hoarse outcry, a vigorous Lear looms in the upstage frame, slightly off balance under the weight of the dead Cordelia. He is followed close on his left by a stunned and helpless Kent, in this production the one who rushes in vain to the prison. Lear shouts the rest of his howls in quick succession, angrily, looking first to the right and then to the left at no one in particular and yet at everyone. His eyes briefly meet those of the row of soldiers for the accusatory "O, you are men of stones!" but turn away before the line ends to stare downstage and then toward the face of Cordelia.

Coming up on either side of Lear, Edgar and Kent help "old majesty" to set his daughter and himself down. At this point, a tableau is formed that will remain essentially unchanged until the concluding blackout. Lear kneels downstage cradling Cordelia, pale as her smock except for the ugly rope burn on her neck. Her head lolls on his left arm, near Kent, who kneels close beside him; Edgar kneels behind his right shoulder. Upstage of Lear stands Albany, a captain on his left against the tent and behind and to his right the helmeted soldiers with their lances clustered in a semicircle. Later, when another captain emerges from the tent to announce Edmund's death—"a trifle here"—and become part of the assembly, Albany moves downstage to join the central group on the ground as he offers his aborted speech. The frame tightens slightly on the nearly motionless figures with Lear and Cordelia in their midst. The effect is one of audience (Edgar, Albany, Kent) within audience (the assembled soldiers) and, by extension, within the offstage audience as well.

Lear remains animated throughout the sequence. Cradling Cordelia, he busily attends to her, embracing and rocking her lifeless form, touching her face and neck, frantically slapping or pinching her cheeks, kissing her forehead and mouth, on "No, no, no life?" haplessly picking up and dropping her limp arm on the first two negatives. No one makes a move when he calls for a looking glass, nor does Lear show any sign of expecting to receive one in the hand he momentarily raises. He barely pauses in his stroking of Cordelia's cheeks to hold an imaginary feather to her lips. Lear's head is in constant motion, moving from one side to the next and looking downstage or down at his child as he addresses his lines to those surrounding him. Only once does he look directly at one of his comforters: "Who are you? . . . Are you not Kent?" Otherwise, because all the characters remain upstage of Lear, he makes direct eye contact only when he faces the downstage camera, the audience's surrogate eye. In this production, the placement of characters and camera identifies the offstage audience as part of the experience, for it is this audience that witnesses most persistently Lear's anguished expression.

Moreover, the assembled witnesses are actively engaged in the act of seeing, as though their presence were necessary to validate events too terrible to comprehend. Though Edgar and Kent become briefly meditative during Albany's summation speech, his "O, see, see!" serves only to refix all eyes on the spectacle they already behold. Lear himself grows meditative as he asks his unanswerable question and then, in a sign of defeat, begins his series of "never[s]." But he consummates only three of them (again, as in the Quarto). Gasping for breath, in the grip of a violent seizure, he screams out hysterically, "Do you see this?" and, cupping Cordelia's chin, "Look on her, look, her lips, / Look there, look there." In the intense excitement of his sudden belief that the lips have moved, Lear's flawed heart gives way, like Gloucester's, "'Twixt two extremes of passion, joy and grief."

All who witness Lear's anguish and his death share the responsibility and the sorrow. His accusation, "O, you are men of stones," is directed angrily at the soldiers. His "A plague upon you, murderers, traitors all!", delivered once he is fixed in the grouping, clearly implicates everyone, as Lear projects his angry voice into the stage-right space. In apologizing for this age—"I am old now, / And these same crosses spoil me"—he lifts his head toward the youthful Edgar, who, were he in Lear's place, might well "have saved her." And his gasping request that someone undo the button, literally gratuitous since there is not one on his open shirt, he offers to anyone who will oblige, a gesture that assures the shared experience of Lear's last breath.

In this production, it is Kent who responds on the instant, though Edgar also extends his hand and Albany leans forward. McGuire, speaking to the issue of who undoes the button, notes that the person who responds to Lear's plea will be "someone who feels more strongly than anyone else a desire or obligation to assist the king."[23] Kent's undoing of the button, he urges, "affirms the bond between master and servant by acting out again a love for and fidelity to Lear as exemplary as Cordelia's."[24] Kent's action thus also affirms the bond between child and father that finds its emblem in the final image. In act 1, scene 1, it was Kent who defended Cordelia, selflessly suffering Lear's wrath in an attempt to protect her. Like Lear's youngest daughter, Kent returned to serve the old king, in his case showing devotion in the disguise of Caius. Similarly, in refusing Albany's offer of a share of the kingdom, Kent recalls Cordelia's refusal to put her love in pawn. Here, in reacting without hesitation to Lear's plea, he seals the equation.

The BCC production reaffirms other bonds as well. Throughout the sequence, the three men closest to Lear respond to the king's terrible sorrow, understanding it as their own. As the father boasts of having killed the slave who hanged his daughter, knowing it was an empty act, Edgar lowers his head, bringing his hand to his face to conceal welling tears. He looks up again for the recognition between Lear and Kent, protectively placing his hand on Lear's arm. As Lear labors over the body of Cordelia, hoping to find life in the corpse, Edgar moves his hand to his mouth to stifle a sob, returning it to Lear's shoulder as Albany kneels behind the king. Similarly, Albany, whose business is "general woe," lets his head drop in tears as he redirects attention to Lear—"O, see, see!"—placing his hand on Edgar's shoulder. And Kent, who hovers over Lear throughout, responds to Lear's request to "undo this button" by pulling the fabric of his loose shirt away from his neck. The task accomplished, he rests one hand on each of Lear's shoulders, then lowers his face to his dead master's head, where he remains.

The emphasis on hands in the final tableau, continuing one of the production's dominant motifs, asserts and extends the bond of human connection begun in act 1, scene 1. In the BBC staging of that public test of filial love, the Fool (mute but present) placed his hands on Cordelia's shoulder as she pondered her dilemma—"What shall Cordelia speak? Love, and be silent. . . . Then poor Cordelia!"—and again as she witnessed Kent's defense and banishment; and Kent and Cordelia joined hands before they parted. Now in 5.3, hands connect in an emblem of shared sorrow and love: Albany's hand is on Edgar, Edgar's and Kent's hands are on Lear, and Lear's hand is on Cordelia.

Similarly, the emphasis on eyes—seeing, staring, or, like Gloucester's, sightless, their "precious stones new lost"—sustains and shares the horror: Cordelia's eyes are closed, as are Lear's, their "fringed curtains" pulled down by Kent; Albany's and Edgar's eyes are lowered upon Lear, and Kent's stare out into the distance, connecting with those not in the frame who share in the seeing. In act 1, scene 1, Cordelia stood downstage of Lear and the others, her back to the camera, reacting in silence and through asides to the expressions of love her sisters offered. Now the audience assumes Cordelia's downstage observation post, intending merely to witness the scene; but, just as Cordelia found herself a participant in the public event of the opening scene, so the BBC audience in 5.3 cannot remain outside the frame.

The viewers too become "men of stones," admonished by Lear for not railing against the heavens' injustice. For the offstage audience as for its onstage counterpart, Edgar's sober conclusion, spoken deliberately from within the grouping, is particularly telling, for it too repudiates Edgar's earlier dogmatism, which cannot accommodate this horror. Just as the audience witnessed a king's capriciousness in the ritual trial and "form of justice" of act 1, scene 1, so now we witness what seems the gods' caprice—if the gods are involved at all. As much as in the earlier scene, the BBC staging of 5.3 is a public event, and Lear's sad protests and fond ravings clearly have an audience, whose presence and whose responses are as much a part of the final panel as is Lear's own pain. The BBC audience, having publicly witnessed and communally participated in the event, knows that the final tableau of *King Lear* contains both Kent's suggestion—"Is this the promised end?"—and Edgar's—"Or *image* of that horror?" (our emphasis).

GRANADA

Quite a different stage image defines the promised end in Elliott's Granada *King Lear*. This is partly a function of the setting, which is not a camp, or military community, but an unlocalized arena, sandy ground relieved only by a slab of gray stone and surrounded by shadowy stone pillars and barriers; only at the end of the play does the audience perceive the setting to be the same as at the beginning, a druidical temple, a Stonehenge. Primarily, however, it is the work of the relentless closeup camera that creates the altered atmosphere and impact of the promised end in this production. Thus, of the twenty-four shots that compose the sequence up to the point of Lear's death, only four are long shots, three coming at the outset. The rest consist of a few medium shots and the many closeups, the focus of these being, of course, Lear and Cordelia or Lear alone.

The Promised End. Granada Production. Laurence Olivier as King Lear, Anna Calder-Marshall as Cordelia. Courtesy of Granada Television. Copyright © Granada T.V.

The effect of this strategy is to isolate the individual participants in the sequence and to engage the sympathies of the offstage audience without inviting it to take conscious part in a theatrical event.

The camera alternates shots for the opening of the sequence. In a long shot, Lear, in white robe, head thrown back, white hair flowing to his shoulders, enters from upstage center with Cordelia, tottering under her weight. He is literally howling, his high-pitched voice lengthening each successive exclamation. In closeup, we see his upturned face for the third howl and an anguished "O" that sounds much like a fourth, and then watch his head drop for "you are men of stones," directed at no one—only at the body of his daughter. When Lear sets his burden down on the stone slab, in a long shot, he does so without help, and when he insists that "She's gone for ever," the camera focuses on Lear alone to capture the agony in his countenance. In a third long shot, he hangs over the body, fussily pressing and pushing it, angrily and futilely exclaiming, "She's dead as earth." The camera then rests briefly on Cordelia's face and scarred neck. The only other figure the frame accommodates in this series is a Captain who advances a few paces to stand erect and motionless in the background.

When the camera acknowledges the presence of Kent or Edgar or Albany, it almost invariably cuts to the face of each just for the duration of his speech. When Lear extends his hand and asks in vain for a mirror, the camera moves quickly to Kent—"Is this the promised end?"—to Edgar—"Or image of that horror?"—to Albany—"Fall and cease!"—and back to Lear for "This feather stirs. . . ." Kent is admitted briefly into the frame with Lear for "O my good master!" only to be dismissed in favor of successive closeups of father and daughter. In the quick cut to the Captain, who confirms Lear's slaying of Cordelia's hangman—"'Tis true, my lords, he did"—the camera does not stay long enough for him to complete his line. For the recognition exchange between Kent and Lear, it momentarily allows Kent and Edgar into the margins of the frame before cutting to Kent's face; it spends little time on his hurried (and textually reduced) revelations, eager to return to Lear and his ironic gesture of welcome, not to the king's good graces but to this funereal occasion. Even when Lear pleads that someone undo the button at this throat, it is only Kent's arms that enter the frame rapidly to accomplish the task. Not until Lear is dead does the camera effectively bring into the picture, in two long shots, Edgar and Kent. Edgar, who drops to his knees upstage left, is unable to see Lear's face and hence thinks that he has fainted; Kent, kneeling downstage right of the stone slab, sees that Lear is dead. But the camera moves into the closeup mode again, focusing in turn on Kent and Edgar, then on Albany, Kent, and Edgar, as each speaks his final lines.

In its insistence on brief but probing closeups of the three men reacting to Lear, the camera particularizes their responses, permitting each a personalized expression of grief rather than representing that of an ensemble. Moreover, in prohibiting the trespass of others into the visual space containing Lear and Cordelia, the camera insists on Lear's own isolation. The enormity of grief occasioned by the death of his virtuous daughter and by the knowledge of his own part in causing it must be experienced by the king alone. Just as Lear acted independently in the opening scene to bring judgment on Cordelia and Kent, so is he alone in enduring the promised end.

But this Lear has no interest in judgment, either of others or of the heavens. Though the text provides several opportunities for accusatory railing or scorn, this Lear neutralizes each of them by fixing his eyes on Cordelia and, like the camera, hardly acknowledges anyone else. His "O, you are men of stones" involves no one on stage or above, no one but the dead Cordelia. The same is true for "Had I your tongues and eyes, I'd use them so / That heaven's vault should crack." This is no admonition to the men of stones but an expression of his own despair. Similarly, Lear's eyes are cast down upon Cordelia, with no one else in the frame, for "A plague upon you, murderers, traitors all!" The line is not so much his dismissal of Kent, who has just tried to reveal himself, as an expression of irritation that anyone has tried to disrupt his concentration on his lost child.

To sustain this intensely personal absorption in Cordelia, the Granada production dispatches Edmund earlier in the scene: he dies onstage, just before the entrance of Lear, not to be noticed again by the camera. It thus eliminates the messenger's interruption with the announcement of his death, which in the text occasions Albany's declaration of intent. It eliminates as well the bodies of Goneril and Regan, which remain offstage, and Kent's news to Lear that his elder daughters are dead. And, predictably, it omits Albany's aborted summation speech. The production moves from the sober "He knows not what he sees [as in the Quarto], and vain is it / That we present us to him" to the sighing "O, see, see!" As for Lear, he sees only Cordelia as he speaks more to himself than to an audience.

Olivier's portrayal of Lear powerfully manifests the design. He plays most of the sequence with his face only inches from Cordelia when it is not in fact touching her. When he tests the silent lips for breath, he bends over her face with an imaginary feather, looks up with a smile to proclaim "she lives!", and anxiously lowers his face to hers again hoping to "redeem all sorrows / That ever I have felt." After brushing Kent aside, now knowing "she's gone for ever," he kisses her lips, caresses her cheek, and speaks into her face, calling her by name. Suddenly heartened, he puts his ear to her lips, listens for her voice, chuckles, and raises his head only to celebrate the soft voice he hears or remembers hearing. The most extended single shot is reserved for the death speech, and it is fraught with such detail. Lifting the head of his "poor fool" to his own and then letting it drop back, he punctuates "No, no, no life!" by putting his cheek on her face, on her breast, and on her stomach. Then, looking into her face, he asks his anguished question. The first two "nevers" are spoken to her, the third is whispered above her, the fourth is uttered in full voice, with an emphatic nod, and the fifth is whispered to her again. After the undoing of the button, Lear's next words are not "Do you see this?", which is cut from the Granada production, but "Look upon her. Look, look there." Even here, the emotions are private. Kneeling upright for the moment as he gazes on her, Lear smiles and spreads his arms, proud of Cordelia, in awe of her beauty. On the more weakly and urgently uttered "Look, her lips," perhaps in tacit acknowledgment of the irony of his having once commanded them to speak of the love he did not—and may not now—understand. On the barely audible "Look there," he kisses her lips and neck, and, with his own lips now moving inaudibly, saying what no one can ever know, the father slides into the cradle of his daughter's breast and joins her in silence.

In the closing shot of the Granada production, the event finally becomes communal. After Edgar's last lines, the camera pauses over the dead pair. It then zooms out from the stone that is their bier, as the others, bearing torches, assemble in a circle about them and kneel, taking position as witnesses to the horror and as men of stones among the ancient monoliths of stone. The final shot invests the moment with ritual significance, recalling the ceremony of the opening scene. But because it appears as a postlude to a chamber piece of private grief, it neither repudiates the sequence as an intensely, even solipsistically personal one nor converts the promised end into the metatheatrical spectacle sustained in the BBC version.

In the production, Lear and the dead Cordelia may well present an image of doomsday, but nothing that follows Edgar's query offers any suggestion that Lear is an actor in a tragic world that is also a "great stage." For here, camera, stage business, and textual cuts, supplemented by the mellow tones of a cello, create an insularity that invites an intense empathetic response. But the emotional involvement of the audience is not coupled with an ocular strategy that prompts it into remembering it is watching a play. The psychological dynamic does not simultaneously admit the affective dimension of tragedy and the intellectual understanding that this is the promised end of the theatrical event. The burden of tragedy in the Granada production rests solely on a vicarious experiencing of the horror.

Conclusion

We began this book by referring to a would-be director who reacted to a proposed staging of the storm scene in *King Lear* by asking, "But does it read?" As we worked our way through possible readings of textual and performance cruces, we were constantly aware of how our interpretive ingenuity, or that of others, might disappear in production. A subtext as subtle and yet as particular as Lynda E. Boose's reading of act 1, scene 1, for example, like any other reading of the text, needs to be translated into stage images if it is to "read."

In choosing to propose an array of interpretations and then see how these might have been realized in only two productions, we knew we would leave unrealized most of what we proposed. However, we saw our inability to present theatrical evidence for all of our provisional readings not as a liability but as a strength, for we were making a navigational chart for many unexplored productions, both past and future, that have made or will have to make choices about these same cruces.

A study of this kind is much like an early rehearsal, in which directors and actors research and sound the text for possible meanings. But as every director or actor knows, production is a process that requires making choices and shaping the outcome into a single, seemingly inevitable reading. Janet Suzman, speaking of acting—though she might have been speaking more generally of performance—put it this way:

> Acting is a process of diminishing of choices. And then making those choices inevitable. That and only that is what the creature *must* do and say at that second. If a sort of encephalographic computer were attached to the brain lobes during a performance, the possible choices at each given moment would be myriad. I can perhaps make you aware of the choices open to me, but the *final* one I make must appear incontrovertible.[1]

The choices made by those involved in the BBC and Granada productions offer readings of *King Lear* that might not satisfy

158

every reader of Shakespeare imaginatively or intellectually. Nor can either—or any—production, whether on stage or on film, do more than guide its audience, at once complicit and resistant, into seeing *King Lear* in a particular way. But in assuming a place within this study of *Reading Shakespeare in Performance*, both productions have provided a testing ground for an approach that acknowledges—and celebrates—Shakespeare as a man of the theater.

Notes

Introduction

1. Maurice Charney, "*Hamlet* without Words," in *Shakespeare's More Than Words Can Witness: Essays on Visual and Non-verbal Enactment in the Plays,* ed. Sidney Homan (Lewisburg: Bucknell University Press, 1980), p. 24.

2. Michael Goldman, "Acting Values and Shakespearean Meaning: Some Suggestions," *Mosaic* 10, no. 3 (Spring 1977): 58.

3. Alan C. Dessen, "Discoveries in the Oregon Hills," *Shakespeare Bulletin* 3, no. 6 (1985): 7.

4. See, for example, Cleanth Brooks, "My Credo (continued): The Formalist Critics," *Kenyon Review* 13 (Winter 1951): 72–81; and Jonathan Culler, *Structuralist Poetics: Structuralism, Linguistics, and the Study of Literature* (Ithaca: Cornell University Press, 1975), pp. 123–24.

5. See, for example, Alan C. Dessen, *Elizabethan Drama and the Viewer's Eye* (Chapel Hill: University of North Carolina Press, 1977) and *Elizabethan Stage Conventions and Modern Interpreters* (Cambridge: Cambridge University Press, 1984); and David Bevington, *Action Is Eloquence: Shakespeare's Language of Gesture* (Cambridge: Harvard University Press, 1984).

6. We use the term *sequence* in the sense that Charles and Elaine Hallett use it in *Analyzing Shakespeare's Action* (Cambridge: Cambridge University Press, 1991), although not with the precision and rigor that the Halletts bring to their reconceptualizing of Shakespeare's organizing structures. For the Halletts, the characteristic unit of action in a Shakespeare play is the sequence, which contains an introduction, an intensification, and a conclusion. Unlike the scene, the sequence is not necessarily surrounded by a cleared stage. The Halletts point out that the scene is primarily a unit of place, not always tightly organized upon the traditional dramatic curve. In *King Lear* 2.3, for example, Edgar's twenty-one line soliloquy hardly contains a rising action, though it is a scene; at the opposite extreme, *King Lear* 1.1 contains three separate well-crafted and individually complete actions (lines 1–139, 139–87, 188–308). When a sequence is surrounded by a cleared stage, it will share its boundaries with a scene (in 1.7 of *Macbeth*, where Lady Macbeth exhibits her notorious persuasion, or in *King Lear* 3.7, where Cornwall and Regan blind Gloucester, sequence and scene run concurrently). But the typical dramatic curve associated with a unit of action is found repeatedly in segments of scenes as well. The sequence effecting Kent's banishment in 1.1, although it occupies only part of a scene, forms a complete action. Cf. also 4.6, where in one action Edgar places Gloucester at Dover Cliff (1–80) and in another kills Oswald (226–86), all within a single scene. Because one scene can contain

a number of independent actions, the Halletts distinguish between the unit of place, or scene, and the unit of action, or sequence. Cf. also *segments* in Bernard Beckerman, *Dynamics of Drama: Theory and Method of Analysis* (New York: Alfred A. Knopf, 1970), pp. 88–98; and *dialogue units* in Emrys Jones, *Scenic Form in Shakespeare* (Oxford: Clarendon Press, 1971), pp. 8–11.

7. Stanley Wells and Gary Taylor, eds., *William Shakespeare: The Complete Works*, The Oxford Shakespeare (Oxford: Clarendon Press, 1986), pp. 1025–98, together with *A Textual Companion* (Oxford: Clarendon Press, 1987). See also Gary Taylor and Michael Warren, eds. *The Division of the Kingdoms: Shakespeare's Two Versions of "King Lear"* (Oxford: Clarendon Press, 1983); and Steven Urkowitz, *Shakespeare's Revision of "King Lear"* (Princeton: Princeton University Press, 1980). For contrasting views, see Kenneth Muir, *Shakespeare: Contrasts and Controversies* (Norman: University of Oklahoma Press, 1985), pp. 51–66; and David Bevington, "Determining the Indeterminate: The Oxford Shakespeare," *Shakespeare Quarterly* 38 (Winter 1987): 501–19.

Chapter 1. Cordelia's Plight: 1.1

1. A. C. Bradley, *Shakespearean Tragedy: Lectures on "Hamlet," "Othello," "King Lear," "Macbeth"* (London: Macmillan, 1919), p. 249.

2. John Roland Dove and Peter Gamble, "'Our Darker Purpose': The Division Scene in *Lear*," *Neuphilologische Mitteilungen* 70 (1969): 312.

3. Bradley, *Shakespearean Tragedy*, p. 250.

4. Lynda E. Boose, "The Father and the Bride in Shakespeare," *PMLA* 97, no. 3 (May 1982): 325–47.

5. Ibid., p. 332.

6. Ibid., p. 333.

7. Ibid.

8. Ibid.

9. Ibid.

10. Ibid., p. 335.

11. Dove and Gamble, "'Our Darker Purpose,'" pp. 310–12.

12. Ibid., p. 315.

13. On line 104, which occurs in the Quarto only, see Gary Taylor, "Monopolies, Show Trials, Disaster, and Invasion: *King Lear* and Censorship," in Taylor and Warren, *The Division of the Kingdoms*, p. 87; and Bevington, "Determining the Indeterminate," p. 509.

14. Harry V. Jaffa, "The Limits of Politics: An Interpretation of *King Lear*, Act I, Scene 1," *American Political Science Review* 51 (1957): 405–27. (Now in Allan Bloom with Harry V. Jaffa, *Shakespeare's Politics* [Chicago: University of Chicago Press, 1986].)

15. Ibid., p. 414.

16. Ibid., p. 415.

17. Ibid.

18. The exception is Robert Fabyan's *New Chronicles* (1516). See Geoffrey Bullough, ed., *Narrative and Dramatic Sources of Shakespeare: Major Tragedies* (London: Routledge and Kegan Paul; New York: Columbia University Press, 1973), 7:273; and Wilfred Perrett, *The Story of King Lear from Geoffrey of Monmouth to Shakespeare* (Berlin: Mayer and Muller, 1904), p. 167.

19. Bullough, *Narrative and Dramatic Sources,* 7:312.

20. Ibid., p. 276.

21. Ibid., p. 339.

22. Ibid., p. 338.

23. Ibid.

24. Ibid.

25. Ibid., p. 339.

26. Dove and Gamble, "'Our Darker Purpose,'" pp. 315–16.

27. Boose, "The Father and the Bride in Shakespeare," p. 333.

28. See Samuel Johnson, *Johnson on Shakespeare,* ed. Bertrand H. Bronson with Jean M. O'Meara (New Haven: Yale University Press, 1986), p. 226; and Germaine Greer, *Shakespeare* (Oxford: Oxford University Press, 1986), p. 89. Helen Gardner, in *"King Lear": The John Coffin Memorial Lecture 1966* (London: The Athlone Press, 1967), may be taken as representative of the mainstream: "The action begins with a violent improbability, which the author does nothing to prepare for or mitigate" (p. 1).

29. Harley Granville-Barker, *Prefaces to Shakespeare: "King Lear," "Cymbeline," "Julius Caesar"* (Princeton: Princeton University Press, 1970), 2: 11–12.

30. G. B. Shand, "Lear's Coronet: Playing the Moment," *Shakespeare Quarterly* 38 (Spring 1987): 80.

31. Productions often introduce stage business involving a third property, Lear's sword, at 1.1.162–63, where the furious king reviles and seems to threaten Kent and where in the Folio Albany and Cornwall intervene. Such productions follow a stage direction not in the Quarto or Folio but in Rowe's edition of 1709, *"Laying his hand on his sword,"* a suggestion that many modern editions incorporate. If some gesture of physical violence is implied, Lear might also raise his hand to strike at Kent, or he might draw a knife or a dagger. Marvin Rosenberg, in *The Masks of "King Lear"* (Berkeley: University of California Press, 1972), notes that "Charles Kean seized a battle axe from an attendant for the attack" (p. 72).

32. Perrett, *The Story of King Lear,* p. 144.

33. John Russell Brown, ed., *Shakespeare in Performance: An Introduction through Six Major Plays* (New York: Harcourt Brace Jovanovich, 1976), p. 424n.

34. Marshall McLuhan, *The Gutenberg Galaxy* (Toronto: University of Toronto Press, 1962), p. 11.

35. Terence Hawkes, "'Love' in *King Lear*," in *Shakespeare: "King Lear,"* ed. Frank Kermode (Nashville: Aurora, 1970), pp. 179–80.

36. Shand, "Lear's Coronet," p. 79.

37. Cf. *Henry V* 2.Prol.10; and *The Tempest* 1.2.114.

38. See, for example, G. K. Hunter, "Flatcaps and Bluecoats: Visual Signals on the Elizabethan Stage," *Essays and Studies* 33 (1980): 16–47; and Fran Teague, "Headgear in *Coriolanus*," *Shakespeare Bulletin* 4, no. 4 (1986): 5–7.

39. Shand, "Lear's Coronet," pp. 79–80. On the coronet, see also Perrett, *The Story of King Lear,* pp. 151–54.

40. Rosenberg, *The Masks of "King Lear,"* p. 11.

41. Dove and Gamble, "'Our Darker Purpose,'" pp. 312–13.

42. Shand, "Lear's Coronet," p. 81.

43. Perrett, *The Story of King Lear,* p. 183.

44. See Dessen, *Elizabethan Stage Conventions and Modern Interpreters,* pp. 53–69.

45. Boose, "The Father and the Bride in Shakespeare," p. 334.

46. Bevington, *Action Is Eloquence*, p. xi.

47. Henry Fenwick, "The Production," in *"King Lear": The BBC TV Shakespeare*, ed. Peter Alexander et al. (London: British Broadcasting Corporation, 1983), pp. 24–28.

48. Possibly, Miller is taking a hint from the ambiguous speech attribution for this Folio-only line, *"Alb. Cor.,"* where *"Cor."* might conceivably mean Cordelia rather than Cornwall. For a defense of Cordelia as speaker, joined by Albany, see Beth Goldring, "*Cor.*'s Rescue of Kent," in Taylor and Warren, *The Division of the Kingdoms*, pp. 143–51.

49. Cf. Dove and Gamble, "'Our Darker Purpose,'" p. 318.

50. Peter Cowie, "Olivier, at 75, Returns to *Lear*," *New York Times*, 1 May 1983, sec. 2:25.

51. Jaffa, "The Limits of Politics," p. 405.

Chapter 2. The Wicked Sisters: 1.4 and 2.4

1. Peter Brook, *The Empty Space* (New York: Atheneum, 1968), pp. 13–14.

2. See Bullough, *Narrative and Dramatic Sources*, 7:339–42.

3. Rosenberg, *The Masks of "King Lear,"* pp. 49–50.

4. The speech attributions are reversed in the 1608 Quarto. Randall McLeod argues that Goneril is the more aggressive of the elder sisters in the Quarto, the more reserved in the Folio. See "*Gon.* No more, the text is foolish," in Taylor and Warren, *The Division of the Kingdoms*, pp. 166, 169.

5. Largely on the basis of these lines and Goneril's remark in her next speech—"I would breed from hence occasions, and I shall, / That I may speak" (1.3.26–27)—all missing from the Folio, McLeod, in "*Gon.* No more, the text is foolish," urges that "The Q Duchess . . . seems to have lost her grip on herself, and her Q-only vituperations seem to offer an inner glimpse of a woman so insecure about the 'authorities that hee hath giuen away' that she is impelled to force his hand by 'breed[ing] occasions.' When we contrast Q and F it seems that Gonerill the Bitch has yet to appear in *The Tragedie*; in *The Historie*, however, Gonorill is now taking on monstrous dimensions" (p. 175). In focusing on this character to argue the "purposeful differentiation" of the Quarto and the Folio, McLeod overstates his case. The lines are certainly signs of vexation but hardly of monstrosity. In both the Quarto and the Folio, the eldest sister makes the same complaints about the behavior of Lear and his "riotous" knights to Oswald and expresses her determination to force the issue with her father: "I'd have it come to [Q: in] question" (1.3.14).

6. Stephen Booth, *"King Lear," "Macbeth," Indefinition, and Tragedy* (New Haven: Yale University Press, 1983), pp. 50–51.

7. Ibid.

8. Ibid., p. 52.

9. Urkowitz, *Shakespeare's Revision of "King Lear,"* p. 45.

10. On the Folio-only lines, in addition to Urkowitz, see McLeod, "*Gon.* No more, the text is foolish," pp. 177–78; and Muir, *Shakespeare: Contrasts and Controversies*, pp. 58–59. While Urkowitz and McLeod assume that the lines represent a revision of the Quarto, Muir thinks it more likely that the passage involves "not a revision but a restoration."

11. Rosenberg, *The Masks of "King Lear,"* p. 148.

12. See Charlton Hinman, ed., *The Norton Facsimile: The First Folio of Shakespeare* (London: Paul Hamlyn, 1968), p. 802. Most modern editions locate Goneril's entrance two lines later, articulating it with Lear's "Who comes here?" In the Quarto, Goneril enters speaking a variant of Lear's line, "Who struck my servant, Regan. . . ." This would, of course, alter the stage situation. See Michael J. B. Allen and Kenneth Muir, eds., *Shakespeare's Plays in Quarto: A Facsimile Edition of Copies Primarily from the Henry E. Huntington Library* (Berkeley: University of California Press, 1981), p. 681; Urkowitz, *Shakespeare's Revision of "King Lear,"* pp. 36–38; and McLeod, "Gon. No more, the text is foolish," pp. 180–81.

13. Rosenberg, *The Masks of "King Lear,"* p. 173.

14. Brook, *The Empty Space,* p. 14.

Chapter 3. The Mock Trial: 3.6

1. Granville-Barker, *Prefaces to Shakespeare*, 2:33n. Granville-Barker later applies the phrase "technically 'daring'" to the episode (p. 71). See also J. L. Styan, *Shakespeare's Stagecraft* (Cambridge: Cambridge University Press, 1971), p. 216; and Robert Egan, *Drama Within Drama: Shakespeare's Sense of His Art in "King Lear," "The Winter's Tale," and "The Tempest"* (New York: Columbia University Press, 1975), p. 43.

2. Roger Warren, "The Folio Omission of the Mock Trial: Motives and Consequences," in Taylor and Warren, *The Division of the Kingdoms*, pp. 45–57, argues that, on the evidence of the Folio text, Shakespeare himself must have cut the mock trial segment as a result of difficulties with it in rehearsal or performance. Far from regarding it as "admirable on the stage," Warren sees it as filled with "eccentric individual detail" that distracts and confuses an audience. His argument remains speculative, and he himself admits to knowing of only one modern production that omitted the mock trial (Glen Byam Shaw's Stratford-upon-Avon production of 1959).

3. William Frost, "Shakespeare's Rituals and the Opening of *King Lear*," in *Shakespeare: The Tragedies,* ed. Clifford Leech (Chicago: University of Chicago Press, 1965), p. 192.

4. Granville-Barker, *Prefaces to Shakespeare*, 2:34.

5. Egan, *Drama Within Drama*, pp. 36–38.

6. Ibid., 42–43.

7. Victor Turner, *From Ritual to Theatre* (New York: Performing Arts Journal Publications, 1982), p. 106. For "rituals of affliction," see pp. 109–10.

8. Bevington, *Action Is Eloquence*, p. 172. On the "liminal" state, see pp. 3–5, 38 passim.

9. See Boose, "The Father and the Bride in Shakespeare," p. 330.

10. Egan, *Drama Within Drama*, p. 45.

11. *"King Lear": A New Variorum Edition of Shakespeare,* ed. H. H. Furness (New York: Dover, 1963), p. 207n.

Chapter 4. Dover Cliff: 4.6

1. John Barton, *Playing Shakespeare* (London and New York: Methuen, 1984), p. 13.

2. Dessen, *Elizabethan Drama and the Viewer's Eye*, p. 124.

3. Egan, *Drama Within Drama*, p. 25.

Chapter 5. The Anonymous Captain: 5.3

1. Barton, *Playing Shakespeare*, pp. 30–31.

2. Ibid., p. 32.

Chapter 6. The Promised End: 5.3

1. Booth, *"King Lear," "Macbeth," Indefinition, and Tragedy*, p. 11.

2. James L. Calderwood, "Creative Uncreation in *King Lear*," *Shakespeare Quarterly* 37 (Spring 1986): 18.

3. John Shaw, "*King Lear*: The Final Lines," *Essays in Criticism* 16, no. 3 (1966): 263–64.

4. Ibid., p. 266.

5. Booth, *"King Lear," "Macbeth," Indefinition, and Tragedy*, p. 21.

6. Ibid., pp. 27–28.

7. Ibid., p. 21.

8. Calderwood, "Creative Uncreation in *King Lear*," p. 16.

9. Egan, *Drama Within Drama*, p. 55.

10. Walter C. Foreman, Jr., *The Music of the Close: The Final Scenes of Shakespeare's Tragedies* (Lexington: University Press of Kentucky, 1978), p. 155.

11. Rosenberg, *The Masks of "King Lear,"* p. 313.

12. Ibid., p. 312.

13. The Quarto actually attributes one more line to Lear, which is Kent's in the Folio: "Breake heart, I prethe breake." The line sequence reads:

> *Lear*. . . . O, o, o, o.
> *Edgar*. Look up my Lord.
> *Lear*. Breake heart. I prethe breake.
> *Kent*. Vex not his ghost . . .

If this is not an error in attribution, then, presumably, Edgar's judgment is not incorrect: Lear does indeed faint but then recovers from the faint to pray that his heart (like Gloucester's) break—which it promptly does.

In the provocative reading offered by Boose ("The Father and the Bride in Shakespeare," pp. 325–47), Lear's reunion with Cordelia, though powerfully moving, endorses Lear's continuing attempt to subvert the marriage ritual and its effect; Lear goes to his death no closer to understanding the limits of father-daughter love than he did in act 1, scene 1.

14. G. K. Hunter, Introduction to *The New Penguin Shakespeare: "King Lear"* (New York: Viking Penguin, 1972), p. 26.

15. Booth, *"King Lear," "Macbeth," Indefinition, and Tragedy*, p. 10.

16. Ibid., p. 11.

17. Barton, *Playing Shakespeare*, p. 32.

18. See Philip C. McGuire, *Speechless Dialect: Shakespeare's Open Silences*. Berkeley: University of California Press, 1985, p. 100.

19. John C. Meagher, "Vanity, Lear's Feather, and the Pathology of Editorial Annotation," in *Shakespeare 1971: Proceedings of the World Shakespeare Congress, Vancouver, August 1971*, ed. Clifford Leech and J. M. R. Margeson (Toronto: University of Toronto Press, 1972), p. 253.

20. Ibid., p. 256.

21. McGuire, *Speechless Dialect*, p. 98.

22. Ibid., p. 99.

23. Ibid., p. 98.

24. Ibid., p. 103.

Conclusion

1. Janet Suzman, "*Hedda Gabler:* The Play in Performance," in *Ibsen and the Theatre*, ed. Errol Durbach (New York: New York University Press, 1980), p. 90.

Cast and Production Teams

BBC Television Production (1982)

Directed by Jonathan Miller
Designed by Colin Lowrey
Costumes by Raymond Hughes
Sound by Derek Miller-Timmins
Lighting by John Treays
Producer, Shaun Sutton

Cast

Lear:	Michael Hordern
Kent:	John Shrapnel
Gloucester:	Norman Rodway
Goneril:	Gillian Barge
Regan:	Penelope Wilton
Cordelia:	Brenda Blethyn
Albany:	John Bird
Cornwall:	Julian Curry
Edmund:	Michael Kitchen
Edgar:	Anton Lesser
Fool:	Frank Middlemass
Burgundy:	David Weston
France:	Harry Waters
Oswald:	John Grillo
Captain:	Tim Brown

Granada Television Production (1983)

Directed by Michael Elliott
Designed by Roy Stonehouse
Costumes by Tanya Moiseiwitsch
Music by Gordon Crosse
Executive Producer, David Plowright

Cast

Lear:	Laurence Olivier
Kent:	Colin Blakely
Gloucester:	Leo McKern
Goneril:	Dorothy Tutin
Regan:	Diana Rigg
Cordelia:	Anna Calder-Marshall
Albany:	Robert Lang
Cornwall:	Jeremy Kemp
Edmund:	Robert Lindsay
Edgar:	David Threlfall
Fool:	John Hurt
Burgundy:	Brian Cox
France:	Edward Petherbridge
Oswald:	Geoffrey Bateman
Captain:	Ian Ruskin

Works Cited

Allen, Michael J. B., and Kenneth Muir, eds. *Shakespeare's Plays in Quarto: A Facsimile Edition of Copies Primarily from the Henry E. Huntington Library.* Berkeley: University of California Press, 1981.

Barton, John. *Playing Shakespeare.* London and New York: Methuen, 1984.

Beckerman, Bernard. *Dynamics of Drama: Theory and Method of Analysis.* New York: Alfred A. Knopf, 1970.

Bevington, David. *Action Is Eloquence: Shakespeare's Language of Gesture.* Cambridge: Harvard University Press, 1984.

——————. "Determining the Indeterminate: The Oxford Shakespeare." *Shakespeare Quarterly* 38 (Winter 1987): 501–19.

——————, ed. *The Complete Works of Shakespeare.* 3d ed. Glenview, Ill.: Scott, Foresman, 1980.

Boose, Lynda E. "The Father and the Bride in Shakespeare." *PMLA* 97, no. 3 (May 1982): 325–47.

Booth, Stephen. *"King Lear," "Macbeth," Indefinition, and Tragedy.* New Haven: Yale University Press, 1983.

Bradley, A. C. *Shakespearean Tragedy: Lectures on "Hamlet," "Othello," "King Lear," "Macbeth."* London: Macmillan, 1919.

Brook, Peter. *The Empty Space.* New York: Atheneum, 1968.

Brooks, Cleanth. "My Credo (continued): The Formalist Critics." *Kenyon Review* 13 (Winter 1951): 72–81.

Brown, John Russell, ed. *Shakespeare in Performance: An Introduction through Six Major Plays.* New York: Harcourt Brace Jovanovich, 1976.

Bullough, Geoffrey, ed. *Narrative and Dramatic Sources of Shakespeare: Major Tragedies.* Vol. 7. London: Routledge and Kegan Paul; New York: Columbia University Press, 1973.

Calderwood, James L. "Creative Uncreation in *King Lear.*" *Shakespeare Quarterly* 37 (Spring 1986): 5–19.

Charney, Maurice. "*Hamlet* without Words." In *Shakespeare's More Than Words Can Witness: Essays on Visual and Nonverbal Enactment in the Plays,* edited by Sidney Homan, 23–42. Lewisburg: Bucknell University Press, 1980.

Cowie, Peter. "Olivier, at 75, Returns to *Lear.*" *New York Times,* 1 May 1983, Sec. 2, pp. 1, 25.

Culler, Jonathan. *Structuralist Poetics: Structuralism, Linguistics, and the Study of Literature.* Ithaca: Cornell University Press, 1975.

Dessen, Alan C. "Discoveries in the Oregon Hills." *Shakespeare Bulletin* 3, no. 6 (1985): 7–8.

169

_____. *Elizabethan Drama and the Viewer's Eye*. Chapel Hill: University of North Carolina Press, 1977.

_____. *Elizabethan Stage Conventions and Modern Interpreters*. Cambridge: Cambridge University Press, 1984.

Dove, John Roland, and Peter Gamble. "'Our Darker Purpose': The Division Scene in *Lear*." *Neuphilologische Mitteilungen* 70 (1969): 306–18.

Egan, Robert. *Drama Within Drama: Shakespeare's Sense of His Art in "King Lear," "The Winter's Tale," and "The Tempest."* New York: Columbia University Press, 1975.

Fenwick, Henry. "The Production." In *"King Lear": The BBC TV Shakespeare*, edited by Peter Alexander et al., 19–34. London: British Broadcasting Corporation, 1983.

Foreman, Walter C., Jr. *The Music of the Close: The Final Scenes of Shakespeare's Tragedies*. Lexington: University Press of Kentucky, 1978.

Frost, William. "Shakespeare's Rituals and the Opening of *King Lear*." In *Shakespeare: The Tragedies*, edited by Clifford Leech, 190–200. Chicago: University of Chicago Press, 1965.

Furness, H. H., ed. *"King Lear": A New Variorum Edition of Shakespeare*. New York: Dover, 1963.

Gardner, Helen. *"King Lear": The John Coffin Memorial Lecture 1966*. London: The Athlone Press, 1967.

Goldman, Michael. "Acting Values and Shakespearean Meaning: Some Suggestions." *Mosaic* 10, no. 3 (Spring 1977): 51–58.

Goldring, Beth. "Cor.'s Rescue of Kent." In *The Division of the Kingdoms: Shakespeare's Two Versions of "King Lear,"* edited by Gary Taylor and Michael Warren, 143–51. Oxford: Clarendon Press, 1983.

Granville-Barker, Harley. *Prefaces to Shakespeare: "King Lear," "Cymbeline," "Julius Caesar."* Vol. 2. Princeton: Princeton University Press, 1970.

Greer, Germaine. *Shakespeare*. Oxford: Oxford University Press, 1986.

Hallett, Charles, and Elaine Hallett. *Analyzing Shakespeare's Action* Cambridge: Cambridge University Press, 1991.

Hawkes, Terence. "'Love' in *King Lear*." In *Shakespeare: "King Lear,"* edited by Frank Kermode, 179–83. Nashville: Aurora, 1970.

Hinman, Charlton, ed. *The Norton Facsimile: The First Folio of Shakespeare*. London: Paul Hamlyn; New York: W. W. Norton, 1968.

Hunter, G. K. "Flatcaps and Bluecoats: Visual Signals on the Elizabethan Stage." *Essays and Studies* 33 (1980): 16–47.

_____. Introduction to *The New Penguin Shakespeare: "King Lear,"* by William Shakespeare, 7–52. New York: Viking Penguin, 1972.

Jaffa, Harry V. "The Limits of Politics: An Interpretation of *King Lear*, Act I, Scene 1." *American Political Science Review* 51 (1957): 405–27. (Now in Bloom, Allan, with Harry V. Jaffa. *Shakespeare's Politics*. Chicago: University of Chicago Press, 1986.)

Johnson, Samuel. *Johnson on Shakespeare*, edited by Bertrand H. Bronson with Jean M. O'Meara. New Haven: Yale University Press, 1986.

Jones, Emrys. *Scenic Form in Shakespeare*. Oxford: Clarendon Press, 1971.

Kott, Jan. *Shakespeare Our Contemporary*, translated by Boleslaw Taborski. Garden City: Doubleday, 1964.

McGuire, Philip C. *Speechless Dialect: Shakespeare's Open Silences*. Berkeley: University of California Press, 1985.

McLeod, Randall. "Gon. No more, the text is foolish." In *The Division of the Kingdoms: Shakespeare's Two Versions of "King Lear,"* edited by Gary Taylor and Michael Warren, 153–93. Oxford: Clarendon Press, 1983.

McLuhan, Marshall. *The Gutenberg Galaxy*. Toronto: University of Toronto Press, 1962.

Meagher, John C. "Vanity, Lear's Feather, and the Pathology of Editorial Annotation." In *Shakespeare 1971: Proceedings of the World Shakespeare Congress, Vancouver, August 1971*, edited by Clifford Leech and J. M. R. Margeson, 244–59. Toronto: University of Toronto Press, 1972.

Muir, Kenneth. *Shakespeare: Contrasts and Controversies*. Norman: University of Oklahoma Press, 1985.

Perrett, Wilfred. *The Story of King Lear from Geoffrey of Monmouth to Shakespeare*. Berlin: Mayer and Muller, 1904.

Rosenberg, Marvin. *The Masks of "King Lear."* Berkeley: University of California Press, 1972.

Shand, G. B. "Lear's Coronet: Playing the Moment." *Shakespeare Quarterly* 38 (Spring 1987): 78–82.

Shaw, John. "*King Lear*: The Final Lines." *Essays in Criticism* 16, no. 3 (1966): 261–67.

Styan, J. L. *Shakespeare's Stagecraft*. Cambridge: Cambridge University Press, 1971.

Suzman, Janet. "*Hedda Gabler*: The Play in Performance." In *Ibsen and the Theatre*, edited by Errol Durbach, 83–104. New York: New York University Press, 1980.

Taylor, Gary. "Monopolies, Show Trials, Disaster, and Invasion: *King Lear* and Censorship." In *The Division of the Kingdoms: Shakespeare's Two Versions of "King Lear,"* edited by Gary Taylor and Michael Warren, 75–119. Oxford: Clarendon Press, 1983.

Teague, Fran. "Headgear in *Coriolanus*." *Shakespeare Bulletin* 4, no. 4 (1986): 5–7.

Turner, Victor. *From Ritual to Theatre*. New York: Performing Arts Journal Publications, 1982.

Urkowitz, Steven. *Shakespeare's Revision of "King Lear."* Princeton: Princeton University Press, 1980.

Warren, Roger. "The Folio Omission of the Mock Trial: Motives and Consequences." In *The Division of the Kingdoms: Shakespeare's Two Versions of "King Lear,"* edited by Gary Taylor and Michael Warren, 45–57. Oxford: Clarendon Press, 1983.

Wells, Stanley, and Gary Taylor, eds. *William Shakespeare: The Complete Works*. The Oxford Shakespeare. Oxford: Clarendon Press, 1986; with John Jowett and William Montgomery. *A Textual Companion*. Oxford: Clarendon Press, 1987.

Appendix on the BBC and Granada Productions of *King Lear*: Production Commentary and a Select Bibliography of Reviews

Production Commentary and Critical Evaluations

THE PRODUCTION
Henry Fenwick

Jonathan Miller has directed *King Lear* twice before this current BBC production—once on stage at Nottingham, and then for BBC television in 1975 in a truncated version. He was anxious to do it this third time because, he says, "I was keen to record what I had done, and this seemed to be a very good opportunity to go back and rethink it slightly and change certain things. At the time I was offered an alternate play, which was *Love's Labour's Lost*, but I hadn't got any ideas about that at the moment and I've always been interested in *Lear*. It's such a complicated play, it's got such a complex symphonic structure that you can always find interesting new emphases in it which might not have been there in the previous version."

The cast for the new production is in certain key cases identical to the previous one. "There have been lots of substitutions, not because I disapproved of the previous performance but sometimes because the actor wasn't available, and in other cases simply because I wanted to ring the changes on it. About the character I feel very much the same; I haven't changed my ideas about that. I think there's very little one can change about that unless one starts off with the wrong idea, and I think I started off with the right one."

Henry Fenwick, "The Production," in *"King Lear": The BBC TV Shakespeare*, ed. Peter Alexander et al. (London: British Broadcasting Corporation, 1983), pp. 19–34.

In the earlier television production John Shrapnel, who now plays Kent, played Cornwall. Penelope Wilton repeats her performance as Regan. But the core of the production lies in the central casting of Lear and his fool: in each of the three Miller productions—the Nottingham stage presentation, the 1975 television version and this new production—Lear has been played by Michael Hordern and the Fool by Frank Middlemass. "There's such an intimate relationship between fool and king—as there is indeed between Middlemass and Hordern—so I was careful to preserve that," Miller explains. "I suppose there is something quite novel in having an old man play the Fool and I knew I wanted that fourteen years ago, when I first thought of doing the play. It had always struck me as a great literal-mindedness that, merely because Lear refers to him as 'boy' and the Fool refers to Lear as 'nuncle,' the relationship should be assumed to be indeed one of elderly man and young lad, when 'boy' is after all used by southern colonels when talking to their 60-year-old black body servants in the south, and the word 'garçon' does not necessarily refer to teenage waiters! I think it's very hard to understand the wisdom and the reproving peevishness of the fool in someone young. I know there's a great traditional theory that the fool was played by the same person who played Cordelia and that it therefore has to be a boy. Regardless of that, I think that something much more interesting happens if you really do make it into an old man. Then you suddenly get this extraordinary sense of parity, that here are two people exactly the same age who experience the same amount; you have a common base line which enables you to judge the wisdom of the fool and the folly of the king."

Perhaps because Middlemass and Hordern are of the same generation, perhaps because this is the third time they have played in tandem together in these roles, there is an intimacy in their scenes which is not only supremely right for the play but rarely achieved by any actors in any circumstances. "The relationship between Lear and the Fool is a sort of haunting thing," says Middlemass. "It stays with you, and particularly playing with someone like Michael, of whom I'm extremely fond; and coming back to it I think perhaps you do get a fresh eye, you do get a new insight, because there's a background there in you, subconscious, and you're meeting it again and you do find new things. To that extent I do hope it's deepened and better. And it doesn't really make sense that a little capering boy would get away with the sorts of things he does. It's such bitter stuff. He doesn't pull his punches with the old boy at all. We see the fool getting away with murder with the king, which nobody else does. Other people are banished and threatened with death when they say things to the king but he gets away with it because of the depth of their relationship and one does feel . . . that, of course, is one of the great advantages and joys of playing it about the same age, because you feel that this relationship is so long established, that they grew up together as boys, you know, and played around the court. Their relationship is so deep that he can say anything to him and he's threatened, yes, but not very seriously, ever, and he says to the king . . . he tells him the truth! In fact, he's a sort of—he's the wisdom of the king. One sees him almost as a reflection of the king, like the king's conscience or the king's common sense, and significantly, of course, when the king loses his marbles the fool disappears. When the brain goes, the fool goes! That," he adds, with an actor's momentary self-interest, "might be an excuse for bringing him back at the end—which of course they don't!"

There has been one slight but significant change in this performance from previous ones. "I think right from the start it had a little more edge this time," says Middlemass. "But then when we had the first real run-through and Jonathan was obviously hearing the whole thing in sequence with a new ear, the following day he came in and said, 'You know, I've suddenly realised this: be even tougher with him because the fool really is very, very bitter. He's getting at Lear all the time, so do more of it.' I think it's right. It's a sort of whipping of the king, the fool really does lay into him through all those early scenes."

Miller recalls this shift of emphasis as being typical of the way in which, when directing a play again, lines take on a new significance. "Certain lines which perhaps had been inaudible when you rehearsed them the first time suddenly become very, very important. There's a very strange line which the Fool says which made me restyle Frank's performance slightly, a little line in the scene when Goneril is reproving the king for his bad behaviour. Just before she comes in the Fool says: 'Thou hadst little wit in thy bald crown when thou gav'st thy golden one away.' Then he says, 'If I speak like myself in this, let him be whipp'd that first finds it so.' The very fact that he emphasises that he's speaking in his own voice implies to me—or it suddenly for the first time seemed to imply—that the fool had been so outraged, in much the same way that Kent was, by Lear's folly and cruelty that he was now speaking in his own voice and not as the Fool. It enabled me to see that he was playing it very much as the man himself behind the mask, saying, 'You are a silly fool and you shouldn't be behaving like this!' It led me to ask Frank to play it much more firmly, almost bullyingly, with a reproving, angry, cold emphasis to the lines, which had seemed previously nothing more than conundrums—albeit moralistic conundrums. Behind the public office of Fool one saw the infuriated and outraged face of the private person whose name we never know."

One of the most marked differences between Miller's last televised *Lear* and this one is in the staging of the first scene, when Lear divides his kingdom between his daughters. Last time this was staged quietly, statically, the family and close advisers seated round a long table. This time the scene is much more mobile, with more of the court apparently in attendance, including the silent figure of the Fool. "A marvellous idea of Jonathan's, I think," says Middlemass, "to put the Fool in the first scene, where he doesn't in fact belong, to establish that marvellous relationship, the love and protection between him and Cordelia. It makes *good sense*. When Cordelia addresses her asides to him it's an alliance. It ranges him right away agin' the other two. It lends great weight to when the gentleman says later that the Fool has been all to pieces since Cordelia went into exile, and Lear says, 'I know all about that, shut up, I don't want to hear about that!' It's a sort of nanny relationship with Cordelia and a very nanny relationship with Lear: The Fool is like a very strict nanny telling the king he's made an absolute idiot of himself."

The restaging of the first scene had another motive. "I was taken to task," Hordern remembers, "for unregality. One does see now—and I suppose I saw then really, but it's been emphasised getting to know the play again—that the only chance the actor has of really showing himself a king, which he's got to live with for the rest of the three and a half hours, is that first scene. So one's got to bring some weight, power and regality to it, which I didn't do before, and which before was very much more domestic, almost like the reading of the will the day after the funeral, you know, with the three daughters grouped round the table. I find it difficult to wear a crown, metaphorically speaking, as an actor and I have persuaded myself to see Lear much more as a family man—although a very bad one—than a king, so I was happy to go along with a rather more domestic opening to the play, which is wrong, I think. To that extent we've changed it a bit."

Miller takes the criticism of lack of regality much less seriously than Hordern: "I think on the whole that sort of criticism is largely irrelevant, it's usually a demand on the part, I think, of rather lower-middle-class critics that people be more aristocratic than they can possibly be. After all, the subject of the play is *absence* of regality; it's not a drawback of the production, it's a topic of the play. On the other hand, I felt there was something worth emphasising at least in the regality of the office, if not of the man—to show in fact that here was a person rattling around inside an office which was much too large for him. We hear very early on, albeit from two people who are not altogether reliable witnesses, i.e. his two daughters, that 'the best . . . of his time hath been but rash' and that 'he hath ever but slenderly known himself,' and I think that, although this comes from two girls who turn out not to be altogether well inclined towards him, it is curiously accurate. One has got the evidence of his behaviour towards Cordelia to show that he is rash and impulsive and foolish and vain. But I did feel that it was worth emphasising the panoply of kingship in order to emphasise the inadequacy of the king.

"I think that Shakespeare is always interested in the idea of the disparity between the office and the officer, the magnitude of the office and the inadequacy of the incumbent. You get it in *Richard II*, of course. And there are other things I've changed my mind about—or rather, not that I've changed my mind, but I've seen greater complexities than I had previously recognised. The more you see the more you become aware of the fantastically elaborate symphonic interplay of themes: the theme of nothingness, the theme of clothes, the theme of loss and growth through loss, and of redemption through suffering. The theme of recognition I hadn't been quite so aware of—the theme of recognising and failing to recognise: people appear in disguise and are not recognised, and this is often regarded as a drawback of Shakespeare's plotting but actually it is a topic of the play again. The implausibility of people failing to recognise their oldest companions or their sons or their daughters or whatever is actually what the play's about. They're metaphors of how much people see: the fact that Kent can present himself to Lear within a week of leaving him, albeit in a very thin disguise, and not be recognised, or that Gloucester can fail to recognise his son by hearing his voice, or fail to see before he loses his eyes that Edmund is wicked and Edgar good, and that the king fails to recognise that Cordelia is the good daughter and that the elder ones are bad. And then there's the recovery of sight, often at the expense of losing your physical sight. Shakespeare plays with these themes in a very complicated way and, though of course I was always aware of them in a very general way, I think the more you come to terms with the play in performance the more very specifically aware of them you become."

Probably the most important difference between the earlier television production and this present one is that while the previous production was cut drastically to prune the play to a two-hour running time, very little has been cut from this production. Both Middlemass and Hordern remarked on this fact as affecting their characterisations and it is a point that Miller reiterates. It is only with a complete text, he says, that the full symphonic structure of the play becomes apparent. "You can see all these themes being deployed over the full length of the movements of the symphony. It was very seriously distorted by having to cut it down to two hours but it wasn't my choice. In the previous production I had to cut out Oswald's attempted murder of Gloucester, which left Oswald's character hanging in the air. It's very important that you see this awful creep shifting, changing sides: he's really like that dreadful man John Dean in Watergate and you really have to see him come to grief—not just simply to see him have his come-uppance because the audience would otherwise be left unsatisfied, but because it's a rather marvellous moral point that someone who is capable of such shifting, such deceit, is actually caught out by the much more transparent deceit of Edgar, and it's lovely to see deceit caught by its own tail."

Designing this production took quite some time, despite the fact that, or perhaps because of the fact that, Colin Lowrey had already worked with Miller on such previous productions as *Antony and Cleopatra*, *The Taming of the Shrew*, *Othello* and *Troilus and Cressida*. "You start working with Jonathan so early," Lowrey laughs. Design after design was produced—they went through four models of the possible set—"but it came out looking like *Troilus and Cressida Mark II*, which was exactly what Jonathan didn't want." The final solution was of ultimate simplicity. "At an early stage we were thinking of another austere set," Miller recalls, "but it turned out to be a little too elaborate, and since we were in a smaller studio this time I really felt there was no point in spending thousands of pounds on an elaborate piece of carpentry, when all the same effects could be produced by hanging up a piece of cloth and lighting it. Then my son happened to bring back from the States this volume of Irving Penn photographs, *Worlds in a Small Room*, in which Penn took around a little box studio, then just hung drapes of cloth behind people, and that seemed to me to be a splendid foil against which to play elaborate costumes." Eight box-like columns stand round a stark central space, floored first with pieces of sectional dance floor, then with a rough wooden platform built on top of that. "The set is so minimal," says Lowrey, "we agreed that it would be a good idea to spend the minimum amount of money on the set and the money we saved could go on costumes. As for the floor, we just gave the carpenters a bundle of sawn wood and left them to it. It also meant that we could afford to make a lot of the props ourselves. For the entire first scene every prop was a piece of built furniture, which is very unusual. It's got an even feel to it. Everything's monochrome so it was easier to make our own furniture and stain it black rather than get anything with the merest hint of color in it. That throne over there we had made for *Troilus and Cressida*, so we stained it black. Every piece of furniture was monochrome and very, very simple—take a look at those tables, for instance." He points out an antique table which is not being used and one in black standing by it which looks rather like its shadow—the same basic shape but slightly larger, dark, undecorated, starker. "I redesigned that table—the original is used on television time after time—you lose count of the number of productions you see it in. What I've done is taken the basic elements and reproduced them there."

There is an improvised quality about much of the set—Christo, whose habit of wrapping up museums and coast lines and such has made him into an international figure in the art world, has been the inspiration for the exteriors. Exteriors in the studio are always a problem and in this case the original stumbling block had been to find a style that would marry with the extreme simplicity of the dark interiors. Canvas cloths are put heavily into use. "We've got a pile of cloths six foot high everybody's chucked out," says Lowrey proudly; "the girls were saving them for us." The columns were wrapped in canvas, huge barrels were draped and swathed in canvas, canvas is

stretched over flats to form lean-tos and outhouses. "Our original intention was to leave these floorboards down—well, they're coming up
tomorrow before we shoot the exteriors," Lowrey points out, showing
me round the studio, "because of the sound. It's smashing for the
interiors but for the exteriors! We're going to put canvas down, then
camouflage netting—we used that on the floor for the camp in *Troilus
and Cressida*, an idea I pinched from David Myerscough-Jones on
Dream. Just now I've been up to Jonathan to finalise what we're doing
tomorrow. We're going to put a gauze, right away round, graduated
from white at the bottom to grey at the top, and eventually we're
going to introduce a massive grey ceiling-piece as well."

There is an excitement, an extra adrenalin, to working quickly, off
the cuff, but there are also drawbacks. Working late in erecting the
set the crew run out of black paint and have to use floor paint to
cover the upper reaches of the columns. Later, when storm and rain
begin to lash the set, strange and sinister-looking black spots begin
to appear on John Shrapnel's shaved head as he, playing Kent, shelters
with Lear from the storm. The floor paint wasn't waterproof and some
hasty cleaning up and readjustment has to be done.

Such extreme simplicity in the set puts a great deal of responsibility
on the lighting designer—in this case John Treays, who had also
worked with Miller, Lowrey and costume designer Raymond Hughes
on *Othello* (as well as with Lowrey and Miller on *The Taming of
The Shrew*). "Jonathan's design concept," he remarks, "was an abstract
form with no details but one would create the illusion of situations
by lighting and all you've got at your disposal are the sources of
illumination. In the way you use them, the intensity and the colour
and with various combinations, you can portray different aspects of
things." At times in such a design frame the lighting can be traditional.
"The first scene we did when Lear divides up the kingdom was a
day interior and one assumed a certain direction of light from a win-
dow. But when one came to a scene like the blinding of Gloucester,
which was set in some sort of situation within the castle and at night,
but with no sources of illumination apparent, one can just let the
imagination run riot. One went for effective pictures. The direction
of light was changing throughout the scene—we were going for effect
and to get a balance within the scene. You can create mood and atmosphere by abnormal angling of light, you would never see people
normally lit from such directions.

"Where one runs into difficulty is matching the abstract interiors
to daylight exteriors. I have the impression that Jonathan is much
more happy in night abstract situations. When one gets into daylight
it's very difficult to use the same rules—he'd always like to run an
exterior on house lights, he's always searching for that soft quality
of light which is created in the eye by the working lights in the studio.
It's a soft light with weird shadows cast by all the gear, but it's very
difficult to emulate at a level of light sufficient for cameras to expose

it. Probably if you're doing an exterior within the studio it's better to go for the unreal, to create a token distant horizon, then have the actors in a basic all-round lit condition. When you're in long shot it's reasonably easy to create the abstract feeling, but then when you go into close-up it becomes very difficult to preserve it because you're almost into normal face-lit conditions." What, then, is the solution to this recurring problem of style? He laughs. "I wish I knew, actually! The credibility of it is that you do get the occasional long shot which puts it back into perspective."

In shooting, Treays and Miller decided to desaturate the picture of colour far more than would normally be done. "We're averaging about 30% desaturation. It gives a cold feel and it does emphasise the style." Even for a normal drama Treays likes to desaturate slightly. "I would generally have taken off 10%, just the edge taken off the colour, because I think it gives everybody a much greater chance to go for some sort of realism. It is difficult to create a grotty atmosphere on television with normal saturation—everything tends to come up far too colourful. If you put a limited amount of desaturation in to start with, it takes that awful newness off everything. Certainly with tragedy the less colour the better."

The monochromatic approach to the production was also carried on from sets and lighting into the costumes. If Raymond Hughes was able to spend more lavishly than usual because of the share of the set budget he inherited, he wasn't able to spend it on creating a riot of colour. In the costume room in the basement below the studio the walls are hung with beautiful designs (Hughes is famous in the BBC for the quality of his artwork), all in tints and shades of black and grey and white. The room seems full of blacks, with a short row of tan tunics looking almost intrusive in one corner. "It was a great rod for my back to design twenty-two principals, each with changes, and all with black on black on black. The only bit of colour there is the English army and that's buff. *Othello* was very muted but there was *some* colour in it. In *Lear* the very first bit of colour you see is the coxcomb on the Fool's hat and the last bit of meaningful colour is the red cross on Edgar's costume. One colour to open the play and one to close it. I like it, I find it very pleasing, but I wouldn't like to do it again. It was a horrendous effort."

The directive was to go for a late-Renaissance look and to soften the silhouette, so Hughes drew for his initial inspiration on a book of German line-drawings from the latter part of the Renaissance. Then, to soften the silhouette further, he pushed the period a few years on, "early Cromwellian," he says, "so you get a softer look to the legs, the jackets are tighter and you get smaller ruffs—an El Grecoish look. The play is in fact written as though it was pre-Christian, God knows when, 1500 BC maybe, and it's often done Stonehengian, so this is a very different approach. Obviously the plays in Shakespeare's own time were done with people wearing their own dress, there was no such thing as a costumiers, and they merely added accoutrements—a helmet, a crown—to offset their everyday gear. I felt that this had a feeling of what it might have been like, though we've gone about ten years past Shakespeare's death. Jonathan felt that what was needed was a soft, understated elegance, with no decoration. Well, there is decoration: one has to have a certain amount of something. A flat front with a couple of plain sleeves and a pair of trousers isn't going to last four hours, and I find it difficult to characterise anyway even in colour, let alone in black and white, so the decoration was needed."

It also proves, on close examination, exquisite. Hughes has not only smuggled in ornament; in some cases a hint of colour has also crept in, a matter of depth rather than anything else. The King of France, for example, Hughes points out, is in a fabric which was originally "a light navy blue which was covered in a black dye and eventually we got this wonderful grey, sandy-bluey colour." The material is also lightened with silver bullion embroidery. "It is a classic example of how to make things look different with colour—though it became grey, the blue was nevertheless a nuance." One of Regan's dresses, he points out with pleasure, has a bodice which is made up from an old Worth dress. "It had gone home, unfortunately, so I pulled it apart and used it here. It's a signed Worth piece, early twenties, gold bullion embroidery on silk velvet." The same dress has a striking ruff which had taken the light remarkably in the scene of Gloucester's blinding, the light shining through it and bouncing back to backlight Penelope Wilton's head, while an elaborate shadow was cast across her face by the embroidered lace. It is one of a set of beautiful ruffs made of very early lace—"about 1800," says Hughes, "not as early as the production but very attractive stuff and *almost* too good to use. But such a lot of it was going home again I felt it had to live beautifully and courageously once more, so we mounted it on muslins and gauzes and they really have made up into something quite beautiful. They frame the faces so wonderfully it's almost like the proud head on a platter, and there's all this wonderful blackness below and just this modicum of interest every now and again."

The decoration, as Hughes points out, is to characterise as well as to please the eye: Cornwall's jacket is magnificent in slatey grey, with monkey fur looking spikily dangerous at the shoulders and pieces of metal decoration giving a warlike, armorial look. Edgar in disguise has a monklike habit. The wicked sisters have gowns and head-dresses that have an architectural strength and a sinister quality in their beauty. "Certain lines like 'Gouge his eyes out' can't be delivered from a pretty little frock," says Hughes pragmatically. The play is heavily imbued with Christian imagery "and Jonathan did say if we could get as much as possible of the imagery coming through—not obviously, we don't want the point to be thrust in the audience's faces, but delicately." The image of Cordelia is of almost nun-like simplicity:

"she's not in church but she's virtually married to Christ, there's an overall feeling of the religious about her." That feeling is carried through in her head-dresses—in the first scene, in contrast to her sisters' elaborate headpieces, Cordelia is wearing a wimple-like cap; later her coronet looks like a stylised crown of thorns. Goneril and Regan have bodies embroidered in stump work, "a sort of exploded embroidery, the sort of thing you see on altar frontals. We had images of Adam and Eve, rather naughty images, floating about, and poison ivy leaves, which to the uninitiated would seem just rather nice and highly decorative."

Miller himself is well pleased with the overall visual style achieved. It is, he feels, a culmination of the way his productions have been leading. "I think you could do a large number of the tragedies like this. I think what we've shown is that you only need foils in order to give break-ups of space and shafts of light, and there really isn't much more necessary. You can produce an effect of grandeur without in fact having to be grandly expensive. There's an awful waste of time and money and I think there's vulgarity behind building enormous, elaborate sets. You just hang up lots of bits of cloth and the wonderful thing is how sumptuous filthy cloth looks when you light it from various unexpected angles. And it gave Raymond Hughes a chance to go quite over the top with the costumes. You get the silhouettes of grand furred gowns against something really quite austere."

Important throughout the play are the themes of clothes and of disguise. The disguise theme is first sounded when Kent presents himself as a serving man to Lear rather than go into exile. "Kent is a fairly blameless man," says John Shrapnel. "His fault, if anything, is that he questions the authority of the king, which an Elizabethan audience would perhaps see as a crucial error. But I think they would primarily have recognised him as a long-time family friend and generally good man; and I think his main function in the play is early on, designing a situation in which Lear should see where everything is going wrong. He adopts the disguise of a serving man, about whose real life he would presumably know nothing at all—that's another major theme in the play, that people realise with new vision parts of the world and parts of society which they didn't understand before. When he gets put in the stocks I believe he *wants* to get put in the stocks. He knows how Oswald and Cornwall will react to his behaviour. It's an insult to Lear to have his man abused in this way and Kent had actually forced this in order to make Lear see how he is capable of being abused by his own family."

Kent, Shrapnel points out, is there through all the phases of Lear's recovery, merely in attendance, commenting on it, finally apparently to die after the action of the play is over, rather as Horatio threatens to do after Hamlet's death. "I was talking to an academic," says Shrapnel, "who said it was plausible that Kent came on in the final scene so wounded from the battle that he can't live long. That would be a totally tenable reading but I think you lose a bit of magic in it. His lines are so mystical:

> I have a journey, sir, shortly to go.
> My master calls me; I must not say no.

It's my guess that Kent comes in having fought in the battle, thus making the battle more real to the audience—and because it's difficult not to make Kent kind of soggy at the point of Lear's death I want to strengthen him with some wounds. But when he says 'I have a journey,' although it means that Kent is suggesting that he hasn't long to live, I don't think it means that he's losing blood. I think it means that he's dying of a broken heart."

If the theme of disguise is first sounded by Kent, it is most repeatedly in evidence in the character of Edgar, Gloucester's good son. He moves throughout the play, once he has been forced into flight by the plots of his wicked brother Edmund, from disguise to disguise. Doesn't this, I asked Anton Lesser, present problems for the actor in finding the character of the real Edgar? "In a way the problem isn't finding Edgar but allowing Edgar to *become* each successive disguise," he says. "The part was very personally interesting to me because the way Jonathan had seen it is as a spiritual journey. Through political necessity Edgar has to assume a disguise but that external pressure, that situation, actually gives him an opportunity to pursue a journey I feel he wants to take anyway. He starts off as the academic, clerical, diplomatic part of the brother relationship—I think we've hinted in the first scene that he's not at all inclined to be the hero or the warrior. I think he can handle himself, but it's just not his nature. The journey he takes is that of somebody bringing out of himself qualities of his character which, in the way we live our lives in habitual responses, we would not develop. His first disguise is as the lowest of the low, Poor Tom, then each disguise is a stepping stone until he becomes at the end, I suppose, a Christlike warrior. His first emergence is as the next king. Each disguise is a different facet which he must either shed or live through in order to find, as we all have to find, some sort of core or real self.

"Jonathan's idea of this spiritual journey was totally consonant with my own and I felt totally happy with it right up to the point where he disarms and then kills Oswald. I said, 'Now, hang on; in the text it says *Edgar interposes . . . they fight . . . Oswald dies*,' and I thought that would be totally admissible in spiritual terms if one was acting in self-defence and he was taking a life in saving Gloucester's life. But the way we have staged it I've disarmed Oswald and therefore have removed the threat, but go on wilfully, consciously to kill Oswald, and I said, 'That is going one step too far in the way we have seen it,' and Jonathan said, 'Yes, I can see that, but I want him not only to be the defender but the avenging angel, the actual bringer of retribution.' I had a little bit of a problem reconciling that. That is where my own philosophy departs from my portrayal of Edgar. From that point on I just throw myself into what Jonathan sees. It's not denying everything that's gone before—my own feelings about him have informed Edgar up to that point quite reasonably. I see it as going along a spiritual path on the ground in turmoil and then at that point when he becomes this strange figure in a crusader's outfit with a crimson cross he sort of takes off, leaves the ground and becomes a symbol, a big spiritual flag instead of a person taking a journey."

He pauses, then begins to smile. "But you know, talking about it now, I think I *can* reconcile the thing. Talking to you now on the last day of shooting I finally figured out what it's about. Have you read the *Bhagavad Gita*? The main scenario is the battle which becomes a symbol of the inner battle between man and his lower self, which he must slay remorselessly from day to day in every situation to find his higher self in his relationship to God or the absolute or whatever. The slaying of Oswald I can reconcile on my terms as Edgar; having gone through the renunciate, mendicant, priest, ascetic, the final step is the killing—the complete annihilation, not just the denial from day to day of bad habits but the actual complete slaying—of his lower self, symbolised by Oswald and then finally by Edmund, the dark side of the brothers." He smiles happily. "But that's really putting all the emphasis on Edgar and I wouldn't for a moment say that is the point of the play. The main point of the play is Lear and fatherhood and fathers and children."

As Lesser points out, *King Lear* is at least partly a morality play in which many of the figures acquire a half mythic stature, paralleling, counterpointing or underlining the moral status of Lear and the spiritual movement of the plot. In a curious way much of the moral energy is shared by the subplot, in which Gloucester is betrayed by one son and protected by the other. "We're deliberately mirror images of the same thing," says Norman Rodway, who plays Gloucester. "It's a play about the generation gap to some extent. One of the through lines of the part seems to me to be in Lear's mad scene, when he meets the blinded Gloucester. Gloucester asks him right at the beginning: 'Dost thou know me?' And then, just before Lear recognises him, the king says: 'Get thee glass eyes, / And, like a scurvy politician, seem / To see the things thou dost not.' That's what Gloucester has been—a scurvy politician, a first secretary, a civil servant. His first statement in the play is equivocal: Kent says, 'I was very surprised . . . ,' but Gloucester is very prudent, he says: 'That's exactly what I thought, yes, but a perfect compromise has been reached . . .' I think that's what he is, a man who preserves the status quo, a manipulator, a politician, everything is smooth and nice and the establishment is always very nicely there. Because his values are all based on compromise and manipulation he has to go through a similar journey to what Lear goes through, guided by Edgar. When this appalling thing happens to him he actually begins to understand what it is all about. 'I stumbled when I saw' is absolutely true.

"He's very psychologically clear to me—whether I've made him clear I don't know. The problem was the technical one of being blind. There were eight hours in the studio when I couldn't see anything and I didn't know where I was. To begin with you're very clear and after a while you're disoriented. I didn't know where I was or where the camera was or where the other actors were. Jonathan kept saying in rehearsal that blind people never look to where the sound is coming from, you listen with one ear or the other to where the sound is. I felt my mind had been interfered with in some odd way—though it does wonders for your concentration. There's no danger of your drying—I stumbled when I saw is right there too!"

Gloucester's bastard son, Edmund, is a glamorous figure, a person of conscious evil, as frank in his own admissions to the audience as Richard III or Iago, and with a sexual aura that those two lack. "Edmund never gives a very long account of himself," Miller points out. "He's somewhat perfunctorily sketched in as a character, but some of the speeches Shakespeare does give him are very close to those of Iago. They're ones which deny the authority of official positions in society and deny all the official superstitions of society. He pours cold water on his father's astrological beliefs in much the same way that Iago pours cold water on the peculiarly conventional views Cassio has about reputation. In both cases you have people who are mischievous tricksters, jokers in the pack. Edmund is prepared to overthrow the old in favour of the young, to change sides wherever it is convenient, and just simply to calculate. In Shakespeare's imagination calculation is a sort of sin: to weigh odds, to see things in terms of what is expedient and what is profitable as opposed to accepting the traditional morality. He sees what dangers that can lead people into. It's interesting that another villain in Shakespeare has the same sort of contempt for astrological predictions, and that's Cassius in *Julius Caesar*: 'The fault, dear Brutus, is not in our stars . . .' These, of course, are Shakespeare's new men, the new men of the sixteenth century who are struggling out of a world which is based on status and moving towards an equally legitimate world which will eventually be based on contract: but at a time before rank and status had been questioned thoroughly and contract had not been given its formal constitution. Cassius and Iago and Edmund are in fact dangerous disturbers of the peace. I think Shakespeare himself probably found them attractive to some extent; he was very equivocal about them. The fact that he gives them such amusing lines to speak means to some extent that he sympathises with people who are able to question the official and the inherited and the traditional—but at the same time he was enough of a creature of his time to know that such men are dangerous, attractive and intolerable."

But the core of the play, its depth, its range, of course is in Lear himself. "He's a dreadful old man," says Hordern practically. "Let's face it, he's a bloody awful father and he's just not used to being crossed either as a father or as a king. I don't think he even listens to Cordelia when she gives those extremely good excuses in the first scene. 'Why should I love my father all?'—absolutely sensible stuff but I don't think by then Lear is listening to what she's saying at all. He's full of disappointment and shock. It's only later by his own awful experiences that he begins to realise how dreadful that moment was when he ought to have listened to her."

It is a part that has been called impossible to play, because of the scale of the emotions, and Hordern, a modest man, wouldn't argue with the description. "I think it is awfully hard to dredge up from your own experience anything comparable that you can use to convey what the author is after—and just as well! The human part is *almost* within one's compass—one may not have experienced the depth of it but one does know what goes on in families and one does know how old men react. And I think that the enormous size of it is made easier by the fact that you are speaking such tremendous words, such colossal poetry."

FOCUS: THEATER ON VIDEO, *KING LEAR*
Ronn Smith

A realistic *King Lear*, circa 800? Shot entirely in a studio? Preposterous. "Oh, yes," says Roy Stonehouse, production designer of the upcoming Granada production, "quite mad. But unlike anything you've seen in the BBC series.

"Television traditionally approaches the Bard in one of two ways: either in a very stylized manner, with black drapes and furniture pieces, or in a very realistic way. The latter, however, is usually shot on location and ends up looking rather ordinary. It's very hard to suggest period on location—a green field always looks like a green field. Had we filmed *King Lear* on location, the finished product would have been judged as a film. It would also have been compared to other films of Shakespeare's plays. As it is, this production will be judged on whether it succeeds as Shakespeare-in-a-studio."

"This production," with Sir Laurence Olivier in the title role, was directed by Michael Elliott. David Plowright and Olivier were, respectively, executive producer and producer. The costumes were designed by Tanya Moiseiwitsch and the makeup by Lois Richardson. The lighting supervisor was Chris White; Ron Greenhalgh was the technical supervisor. Production designer Roy Stonehouse, who joined Granada in 1958 and became head of its design department in 1975, is best

---

Ronn Smith, "Focus: Theatre on Video, *King Lear*," *Theatre Crafts*, April 1983, p. 12.

known in this country for his design work on the dramatization of Charles Dickens' *Hard Times*. Among his other credits he includes *Country Matters, Invasion, Three Days in Sczecin*, and *Strike*.

"The obvious problem," Stonehouse explains in describing the production, "was what to do about the storm. If it's a problem in the theatre, it's an even bigger problem in a television studio where everything is live, covered with electrics. Someone suggested we use a rain loop in front of the camera, but we didn't want to do that. No one would have noticed the use of the loop in the distant shots, but we wanted real rain on a real set. There's a certain authenticity gained in the close-ups when you can see the rain bouncing off the actors. So I had made the largest shower curtain ever. It was 28' high and 230' long, and hung around the entire periphery of the set.

"The set itself was tiered like a cake and stood in a large, plastic-lined tank. To remove the steps and give it a gradual, hillock appearance, it was covered with 3,500 sand bags and 200 yds. of turf. This allowed the rain to soak through rather than just run off."

This set, with its moor, heath, hovel, beach, copse, and stream, was the first of four composite sets used in *King Lear*'s 3½ week shooting schedule. The other sets, changed in elaborate overnight turnarounds, included (1) the Duke of Albany's palace, Gloucester's palace and courtyard; (2) Stonehenge and a section of a campsite; and (3) the French camp, the English camp, and a battlefield. Each scene was shot with four cameras.

For a designer who likes to base his work on documented research, the *King Lear* concept presented a particular challenge for Stonehouse. "There are no records of what England was like in 800," he says, "none at all. Archeologists have made some rough sketches of what they think things might have been like, but there's no documented proof. Many designers would have been excited by that, for it would have given them a certain degree of freedom. But I need a starting point. You say you want a French tent? Okay. That's simple enough, you think, but where do I start? What color was it? Did it have flaps? Was there a ridge pole? Guide ropes? Was the tent made of hide? There was nothing I could look at. Yes, the situation does offer freedom, but I didn't want it to look like a circus.

"What we did, finally, was look at photographs. Photographs of Stonehenge and bogs and mists—general atmospheric photographs—for the basic feel of the production. What we have, then, is an impression of what England must have been like in 800.

"As you can imagine, the furniture was a problem, too—and for the same reason. No one knows for sure what it looked like. For any other television production you could go to stock and pull the pieces you need. But there was nothing for 800. It all had to be designed from scratch. I remembered looking at several pieces of Saxon jewelry in the British Museum several years ago when I designed *Ceremony of Innocence.* The jewelry was part of the Sutton Hoo ship burial and came from about the same period we were using for *Lear.* So I copied bits and pieces of the jewelry for the furniture details.

A major element in the look of *King Lear* is the perpetual—or what seems to be perpetual—fog. Fog was used to erase the sharp delineation between the ground and the sky which, in turn, tricks the eye into thinking that there is more distance in the set than there actually is. "Six feet in front of the eye," explains Stonehouse, "I suspended a mid-grey gauze. The space between the eye and the gauze was filled with fog. Additional fog was pumped onto the set. While the fog between the eye and the gauze stayed fairly dense, I had a certain movement in the fog in front of the gauze. While this gave us much more control over the fog, it also gives an illusion of distance.

"One thing that is awfully difficult to do on television—and which is absolutely essential to this project—is to make anything look old. Television lighting enhances colors, and the high quality camera makes everything look beautiful. So it is hard to get ten years of wear and tear into a set. We therefore took particular pains to stress and age the *Lear* sets. This, too, gives a certain authenticity to the realism we were after. I say 'realism,' but what I should say is stylized 'realism.' It isn't real in the sense that it can be documented. It's more like an impression of what we *think* was real."

In conclusion Stonehouse adds: "What we tried to do was to give each scene as much production value and depth as we could. For me, that meant bringing the actors out from the background as far as possible. This in turn allowed for more control over the background lighting, making the picture more interesting. It gives the picture depth. When you place people too close to the background, it tends to creep forward and distract the viewer. Knowing this, knowing that we were going to pull the actors away from the background, I concentrated on silhouettes and outlines instead of on hard-lined, solidly built pieces. This is particularly true in the interiors. It is these silhouettes and outlines that suggest the period of *King Lear.*"

IN THE PICTURE: THE OLIVIER LEAR
Peter Cowie

In the plush suites of American TV moguls, serried monitors wink at the visitor with a rude succession of clips from current packaged shows. But in the plain, functional office of David Plowright, head of Granada TV in Manchester, a single monitor relays scenes actually being rehearsed or shot in the studios several storeys below. As he

Peter Cowie, "In the Picture: The Olivier Lear," *Sight and Sound* 52 (Spring 1983): 78.

holds forth on the solid virtues of British television, Mr. Plowright can thus keep one eye cocked on Jeremy Kemp and Diana Rigg running through part of the *King Lear* that may yet bring Granada more kudos than *Brideshead Revisited* did a year or so back.

David Plowright finds an enjoyable logic in shooting the week's next episode of *Coronation Street* on a stage adjacent to that dominated by the Olivier *Lear*. He is proud of the serial's enduring popularity, and delighted at the freedom it gives Granada to tackle such peaks as Shakespeare's most obdurate tragedy, not forgetting the lavish adaptation of Paul Scott's Indian tetralogy, *The Jewel in the Crown*.

Why, one asks, when a majority of American TV amounts to what even Fred Silverman concedes is "good trash," does its British equivalent remain so superior, and in the commercial sector too? "There's not so much competition for advertising revenue," responds David Plowright. "There are only two channels carrying ads, and here in the northwest someone wishing to advertise on TV must choose Granada; there is no alternative. While one does not want to take advantage of that, it does make a public service broadcasting system that much easier to run, in that you are not constantly looking for ratings, not dominated by audience size for everything you do. We can take more risks."

Quite fortuitously, Mr. Plowright happens to be brother-in-law to Lord Olivier, and had worked with him on a series of dramas for Granada TV during the mid-70s, among them *Cat on a Hot Tin Roof*, *Come Back, Little Sheba* and *The Collection*. But *Lear* remained a dream until, at a family gathering at Christmas 1981, David Plowright noted "a stubble of beard and a gleam in Larry's eye" that indicated the time was ripe.

Olivier has played Lear only once before, at the Old Vic in 1946. "When you're 39, you're full of spunk and vinegar and the toughness of the role doesn't upset you very much," he says. "But the age comes naturally now. If you're 75, which I am, it's damned hard to find roles and Lear—well, it sounds terribly boastful, but there's nothing to it. He's just a selfish, irascible old bastard—so am I. It's a straight part for me. Absolutely straight. My family would agree with that: no wonder he's all right, they would say, he's just himself, he's got just that sort of ridiculous temper, those sulks. Absolutely mad as a hatter sometimes."

This Granada *Lear* looks very much a collaborative effort. Michael Elliott, the stage director known recently for his brilliant work at Manchester's Royal Exchange, discussed with Olivier and the designer, Roy Stonehouse, an abridged and visually persuasive version of the play that could grip the attention of TV viewers and be mounted within a reasonable budget. A.D. 800 has been chosen as the focal point from a design point of view, a phase of English history that leaves a costume designer much latitude, as there is no art to contradict his speculations. Tanya Moiseiwitsch has opted for tunics and robes, and everyone

loves the surrogate Stonehenge that figures prominently in the production. "There were sixty henges in England at that time," declares Olivier. "There were sacrificial altars, and whether it was human or cat
or cow or what, you can only guess, and the luridly romantic side
of your nature hopes that it was human—virgins and stuff like that!"

Much of the taping proved arduous. Technicians emptied 900 gallons
of water over Olivier in the storm sequence. "The only trouble," he
recalls, "was that it poured down so strongly that I could hardly
open my eyes, and in that scene one wants them to blaze, you know."
Olivier, whose health remains frail, was left pretty much in peace
during the morning run-throughs. Then, at precisely 2:30 p.m. on
the day of one's visit, he makes a leonine entrance through a pair
of rough-hewn gates, to light on Kent imprisoned in the stocks. "Ha!"
he exclaims, "Mak'st thou this shame thy pastime?" A trim white
beard softens his imperious stance; he seems to lean upon the air,
mouth agape in piteous concern, before indulging in a smart patter
of repartee with Colin Blakely's Kent. When he blows a line, he puts
his hand to his head in frustration and apology, compensating on
the next take with an altogether new reading. "I must be a director's
notion of hell where TV's concerned," he tells one later, "for I cannot
do anything the same way twice."

The cast glitters. Dorothy Tutin as Goneril, Diana Rigg as Regan
(replacing Faye Dunaway, who had to opt for Michael Winner's remake
of The Wicked Lady instead), Anna Calder-Marshall as Cordelia, John
Hurt as a mercurial Fool. Now being broadcast over Easter in Britain,
and with world distribution to follow, this Lear does not suffer from
the disadvantage of Olivier's Othello in being a mere replica of a
stage performance. Instead it is a wholly fresh interpretation of a
classic part, closing a circle that began as long ago as 1938, when
the young Laurence Olivier made his TV debut as Macbeth.

OLIVIER, AT 75, RETURNS TO *LEAR*
Peter Cowie

Tethered horses, awaiting their cue, chomp nervously on straw. "Sir's
coming," whispers a technician. Red lights on four mobile cameras
wink on and off, and a clapper-boy stands ready. It is 2:30 P.M. in
the Granada Television studio in Manchester, and "Sir" is the affectionate, respectful greeting accorded Sir Laurence (now actually Lord)
Olivier, about to make his first appearance of the day on set as King
Lear.

Retainers strain to draw back a pair of creaking gates, and Mr. Olivier

---

Peter Cowie, "Olivier, at 75, Returns to Lear," New York Times, 1 May 1983,
sec. 2, pp. 1, 25.

emerges to be hailed by his faithful Kent, who has been consigned to the stocks by the King's vindictive daughter, Regan. "Ha!" exclaims the King, "Mak'st thou this shame thy pastime?" The trim white beard softens his imperious stance. Tall, gentle, Mr. Olivier stands beside the stocks, full of piteous concern, mouth agape as though gasping for relief at the sight of such treachery.

On each take, he delivers his speech with a different emphasis, as though reliving the role anew. "I must be a director's notion of hell where TV's concerned, for I cannot do anything the same way twice," the actor comments to a visitor on the set.

The final videotaping of the $2 million Olivier *Lear* took place last fall. It will have its official American premiere Tuesday evening at an invitational screening to be held at the Ford Foundation in New York, with its celebrated star in attendance; Wednesday afternoon at 2:30, its first American public screening will be given at the Museum of [Broad]casting on East 53d Street.

This *King Lear* was televised in Britain earlier this spring; when American viewers will have the opportunity remains undetermined. Negotiations for a U.S. broadcast outlet are still in progress. Meanwhile, special screenings of the production have been arranged for a few Americans, including President and Mrs. Reagan, who entertained Mr. Olivier at a private White House dinner party for 36 this past Tuesday. The 75-year-old actor was in the United States for the Film Society of Lincoln Center's tribute to him the night before.

*

Granada's is by no means the first *King Lear* on large or small screen. The BBC has already released a version, with Michael Hordern as the King, which was telecast in the United States last October as part of public television's "Shakespeare's Plays." And there have been cinema productions by Peter Brook (in 1969, with Paul Scofield in the lead) and by the late Grigor Kozintsev, the Soviet director, in 1971, based on a screenplay by Boris Pasternak.

But for those to whom Mr. Olivier in Shakespeare represents the pinnacle of dramatic experience, this *King Lear* should come as a notable event, even if not all the critics in Britain were ecstatic about the production. The most vivid appraisal came from the Observer's Robert Cushman: "Laurence Olivier as King Lear made me cry. . . . He seemed on more intimate terms with this drama than any other in which I have seen him. . . . And he was every inch a king."

Mr. Olivier did, in fact, make the very first television production of the Bard—a *Macbeth*—as far back as 1938, and his film versions of *Henry V, Hamlet* and *Richard III* are benchmarks of the genre. He has played Lear only once before, at the Old Vic in 1948. And so, having tackled most of the great Shakespearean characters on film, he regards this Lear as the capstone of his career.

*

Has his interpretation of the role altered over the years? "Not at all, as far as I can see. The age comes naturally now," Mr. Olivier says with a chuckle. "It's just a little less archangelic, by virtue of his not having this long hair and beard all the time—save in the mad scenes, where Lear's out in the wilderness and you're not sure how long he's been there. So, we shot those at the beginning, when the beard was at full length. Of course, when you're 38 [the actor's age in 1946], you're full of spunk and vinegar, and the toughness of a role doesn't upset you very much."

At his present age, Mr. Olivier takes cautious care of himself. A lion in winter, he moves warily both on set and off. A stool is found by some thoughtful assistant as the makeup woman fusses around his features. When he blows his lines, he puts his hand to his head in frustration and apology.

Michael Elliott, a British stage director who has done some thirty television productions, scarcely appears on set. Instead, as is the mode in videotaped productions today, he sits in a distant eyrie, communicating with his crew on the set via headphones, switching from closeup to midshot at the press of a button, editing as he goes along, as it were, and descending between takes for a quiet word with Mr. Olivier. Together they have trimmed the play down to a little over two hours ("I don't think the medium will hold the interest any longer," comments Mr. Olivier), and while Mr. Elliott will have the right of the initial editing, Mr. Olivier, as producer and general catalyst, will, by his own cheerful admission, "come whanging in, messing around, killing it stone dead!"

The setting of *King Lear* poased, as always, a challenge. "In spite of some sophisticated lines and inferences," says Mr. Olivier, "the feel of it is pretty remote. Nobody knows anything about what costumes were like circa 800 A.D. There's no art to show us. To the Romans, the English were barbarians, hardly clothed, probably wearing kilts of some kind."

Granada's research department was able to provide designer Roy Stonehouse with enough Anglo-Saxon detail to create a series of credible sets—farmyard huts roofed with wattle and clumps of turf, a circle of awesome stones, that evoke Stonehenge. "There were sixty henges in England at that time," Mr. Olivier explains. "They were sacrificial altars, and whether it was human or cat or cow or what, you can only guess. And the luridly romantic side of your nature hopes that it was human—virgins and stuff like that."

Mr. Stonehouse also had four cowhides stitched together to form the huge map of the English boundaries used in the opening scene to show the division of Lear's kingdom. "They had no cartographers of any distinction at that period, everything had to be guessed at," muses Mr. Olivier.

He extols a cast that includes Leo McKern as Gloucester ("He's on screen longer actually than Lear"), John Hurt as the Fool, Dorothy

Tutin as Goneril, Anna Calder-Marshall as Cordelia, Colin Blakely as Kent, Jeremy Kemp as Cornwall, David Threlfall as Edgar, and Diana Rigg as Regan.

Speaking of Lear's daughters, who drive him to his eventual undoing, Mr. Olivier cautions against describing them as inhuman. "Two of them are horrid girls. The other's very, very nice. But they all start off all right, and you must sympathize with them. Of course," he adds with a sly grin, "Goneril and Regan slip into bed with anyone they take a shine to," referring to the lecherous glances given by both women to Robert Lindsay as Edmund.

Mr. Olivier speculates on the British facility for turning out first-rate players: "It's a funny thing, because acting is out of key with the English character. We're so reserved, tight upper lip and all that, and I suppose that we're in some degree liberated when acting. But we do have a repertory system, a better training for stage actors than they do in America."

What is it that makes *King Lear* the Mount Everest among serious actors' roles? "It's the only star part for an old man in dramatic literature that I know of," replies Mr. Olivier. "Nobody ever wrote a play about Methuselah. If you're 75, which I am, it's damned hard to find parts. If you're the right age for King Lear . . . ," he pauses, then continues with candor, "It sounds terribly boastful, but there's nothing to it. He's just a selfish, irascible old bastard—so am I. It's a straight part for me. Absolutely straight. I'm not asking for compliments. It is so. My family would agree with that statement. No wonder he's all right, they'd say, he's just himself, he's got just that sort of ridiculous temper, those sulks. Absolutely mad as a hatter sometimes.

"Yet often," he adds, "if you're too much akin with the part, in common with the character, it doesn't work. When you're younger, though, Lear doesn't feel real. You're searching for a reality."

*

Heading Granada is David Plowright, Mr. Olivier's brother-in-law (in 1961, Joan Plowright, the actress, became the actor's third wife). Some five years ago, he and Mr. Olivier considered doing *King Lear* on the stage and simply transferring it to television. But Mr. Olivier has had to combat a fearsome battery of serious illnesses, including cancer, and while he has beaten them off, he has become increasingly wary of the physical strain a role may impose. So, it was deemed easier to mount the whole of *King Lear* in the studio, using video techniques.

"The final signal that he was prepared to have a go," recalls Mr. Plowright, "was the appearance of a stubble of beard around Christmas '81, and after that I put him together with Michael Elliott. So, it's a joint concept of theirs, together with our designer, Roy Stonehouse.

"We've tried to bleach out backgrounds and give a more impressionistic look to the picture," Mr. Plowright adds, glancing at the monitor in his office that shows the scene being shot at that moment in the studios downstairs. "On the heath scene, for instance, we used real grass and rain, and by judicious use of gauze and bits of fog, we gave a look of infinity to the studio, which suggests the real struggle being waged between Lear and the elements." Some nine hundred gallons of water were deluged over the King as he stands foursquare upon a rock. "The only trouble," says Mr. Olivier, "was that it poured down so strongly that I could hardly open my eyes."

Mr. Olivier was no stranger to Granada's studios, having directed there two of his favorite plays, *Cat on a Hot Tin Roof* and *Come Back, Little Sheba*, both made in the mid-1970s in conjunction with NTC-TV (and rather poorly received when telecast in the United States), as well as other twentieth-century pieces.

The talk strays to earlier acting triumphs. John Osborne's *The Entertainer*, for example. "What a part!" exclaims Mr. Olivier. "It's the most superb bit of writing I've ever come across. I think it's a great play, underrated in the late 50s. The critics had raved over Osborne for *Look Back in Anger*, and they weren't going to be hoodwinked so easily again. So, they decided that if it hadn't been for the performances and the casting, there would have been very little to say about it. In New York, too, they just refused to believe it was a good play. But all my American theater friends said of the critics, 'They're mad. This is a great play, a fantastic play.' It was a study of England, a sort of modern *Heartbreak House*, and the fall of Archie Rice is the fall of Great Britain."

Any more stage work? "I don't know," he replies. "It's getting harder and harder to face up to. At my time of life, I infinitely prefer the other two media, and I don't see much difference between television and film, except that you do the television work in about a tenth of the time."

Mr. Olivier must travel across town to listen to the original music Gordon Grosse has composed for *King Lear*. As he dons his coat and scarf he tells a little anecdote about his Richard III: "I knew I had to have a special tone, a special inflection, so I based his voice on what people had told me of Sir Henry Irving's." And in a fleeting phrase he is once again that hectoring, guileful monarch, eyes rolled up, head cocked askance, before venturing out into a winter's day, every inch one's image of the courteous English gentleman, full both of sweetness and tribulation.

A KING LEAR NOTEBOOK: OLIVIER'S FIRST
SHAKESPEARE EXCLUSIVELY FOR TELEVISION
Si Isenberg

Laurence Olivier plays the title role in the British production by Granada Television of Shakespeare's *King Lear*. This is the first time Olivier has appeared in a Shakespeare play made exclusively for television. The production is being shown to an invited audience in New York as part of the "Britain Salutes New York" celebrations, in conjunction with the Museum of Broadcasting. When it was screened on British television (Channel 4) it won wide praise from the critics. . . .

Olivier has played the title role in Shakespeare's tragedy on one previous occasion. That was in his own production with the Old Vic Company at the New Theatre, London, in 1946 when he was 39. The cast then included Alec Guinness as the Fool, Margaret Leighton as Regan and Harry Andrews as the Duke of Cornwall. The following year Laurence Olivier was knighted, and in 1970 was created Baron Olivier for services to the theatre. He has previously appeared in television productions of Shakespeare, playing the title role in a 1938 screening of *Macbeth*, based on the previous year's production at the Old Vic and in an ITV production of *The Merchant of Venice*, in which he played Shylock opposite Joan Plowright as Portia, based on Jonathan Miller's 1970 National Theatre staging. This was the last time that Laurence Olivier appeared in Shakespeare.

A Television Lear

Olivier, now 75, last worked as a producer at Granada five years ago on a series of plays representing his personal choice of the best plays of this century. "We have been talking about a television version of *Lear* ever since," says David Plowright, Granada's managing director and Olivier's brother-in-law. "Larry had been plagued by some debilitating illnesses since then, and we were both acutely aware of the physical strength needed to cope with the part. I got the unspoken signal that he was ready when we met for Christmas in 1981. There was mischief in his eye. He stroked the beard he'd begun to grow, patted his pocket edition of *Lear* and said he was ready to have a go."

A Book About Stonehenge

Since January 1982, director Michael Elliott has worked on Granada's production of *King Lear* with Olivier and production designer Roy

Si Isenberg, "A King Lear Notebook: Olivier's First Shakespeare Exclusively for Television," *Bulletin of the New York Shakespeare Society* 1, no. 12 (June 1983): 1–3.

Stonehouse, apart from taking time out to direct two plays at Manchester's Royal Exchange Theatre, where he is a founder artistic director. But he had worked on his concept of *King Lear* since Plowright suggested the partnership with Olivier a year earlier. It was a book of photographs of Stonehenge, which he discovered while on holiday in Wiltshire in August 1981, that helped his search for the way in which he was to visualise *Lear* on the television screen.

"The pictures of Stonehenge taken at various times of the day led Roy and me to agree that we wanted nothing to be abstract but that we had to get away from total realism by misting everything out. We agreed to set our *Lear* in the ninth century. It is a primeval time, a world of mists and fogs."

But why then did Granada not film *King Lear* on location?

"The film camera on location insists on literal naturalism," says Michael. "But Shakespeare is not primarily concerned with the surface of things. The storm is in Lear's mind. In the studio, under controlled conditions, you can let the performances speak for themselves without being drowned by film exteriors. In the studio I tried to capture the scale of *Lear* with long shots. For the depth of performance from the sort of cast I had, I used lots of close-ups. So although you always know where you are with the setting, I had to have the courage not to dwell on Roy's sets. *King Lear* is the story of a society passing from one epoch to another, from the rule of a divine tyrant king into a democratic era. Lear learns what it is to become an ordinary mortal."

For Elliott, this is the first time in a distinguished career in the theatre and television that he has tackled Shakespeare's great tragedy, though he remembers being taken as a 15-year-old schoolboy to see Olivier's previous stage production. "You have to have a special reason for doing a play like this. I would say that Larry's is the best *Lear* I have ever seen. Most *Lears* evade the part. With him it is straight down the middle—no tricks, no effects."

Ilkley Moor in Manchester

Roy Stonehouse is the man who almost drowned Britain's greatest actor—who brought parts of Ilkley Moor into Granada's studios and ordered the largest shower curtain in the world. As production designer of Granada Television's *King Lear* he was responsible for creating 14 settings for the three-week taping at the Manchester TV Centre. His shopping list for the production reads like that of an over-ambitious pre-Conquest landowner: 2000 clumps of heather from the moors outside Ilkley. 3500 sandbags. One oak tree weighing four tons. The bed of a Yorkshire stream.

For the opening and final scenes of the play, set in a circle of stones or "henge" similar to that at Stonehenge, Roy has 24 huge stones made from polystyrene and covered in five tons of plaster. For the buildings belonging to the Earl of Gloucester and the Duke of Albany, he bought 120 wattle fence panels from a man in Devon: "He was convinced we were starting a sheep farm," Roy recalls. And for the heath onto which Lear flees after rejection by his two eldest daughters, he used 150 sacks of earth, his Yorkshire heather and the sandbags.

But his triumph came when he drenched Olivier during the storm scene on the heath with 900 gallons of cold water, which rained down from 40 sprinklers connected to a van of water parked outside Granada's studios. Six hours of continuous rain spread over three days poured into the studio, whipped into stormy weather by two large fans. The camera crew wore protective wet-weather gear. Roy's shower curtain—230 feet in length and 34 feet high—protected the studio's electronics from the deluge.

Other, drier extras for *King Lear* included 12 butterflies used in quieter moments on the heath.

Costume designer for *King Lear* is Tanya Moiseiwitsch, and the music is specially written by Gordon Crosse. Among the instruments used for the music were the gemshorn—an obsolete medieval type of flute— a medieval fiddle, a set of medieval bells and the cimbalom.

THE MAKING OF *KING LEAR*
Marion Perret

On 4 May 1983 the Museum of Broadcasting in NYC offered a public preview of Granada Television's *King Lear*, starring Laurence Olivier (reviewed in *SFNL*, Dec. '83). The screening was followed by two hours of comments and discussion by Michael Elliott, the director, and Roy Stonehouse, the set designer.

Elliott spoke of the privilege and opportunity of working with Olivier on what all involved felt was an "historic event." Olivier, he explained, was the dominant force in the production: because at 75 Olivier felt he *was* Lear and knew what he wanted to achieve with the part, Elliott gave him little direction, although Olivier worked closely with Elliott in the early stages of production. They were able to draw a strong cast, all experienced in working before cameras, because the actors wanted to work with Olivier on this play.

Designed as a tv film rather than as a movie, the play was photographed mainly in closeup. There turned out to be advantages to this. Olivier, frail, missed ten days of the five week rehearsal period. For all the scenes in which he appeared, one camera focused on Olivier, another on the reactions of others to him. If he had a moment of weakness, the reaction shot could be used.

Marion Perret, "The Making of *King Lear*," *Shakespeare on Film Newsletter* 8, no. 2 (April 1984): 1, 7.

Despite the intimacy of the medium, Olivier wanted the ensemble to achieve the passion of a stage performance; he insisted that inner feeling not be reduced to the level of domestic conversation. To achieve this, the usual moving in to focus on emotion was sometimes reversed (as in his *Henry V*): where Shakespeare builds, the camera moves back. On the whole, though, closeups were many and long shots few.

The whole production, as Stonehouse explained, was shot in the limited space of studio twelve in Manchester, which became ninth-century Britain. They strove to recreate the feeling of Stonehenge, which appears in the first and last scenes, aiming for impression rather than accuracy. The fairly realistic sets were seldom clearly visible because almost every scene was enveloped in mist, which with the cyclorama solved the problem of how to get a sense of horizon, of infinity, in an acting space much limited because it had to leave room for five cameras and a grid of forty sprinklers.

During the three weeks of shooting there were four major resets, all composite: heath, countryside, and hovel; courtyards and palaces; Stonehenge; and camps. The scenery shopping list contained some odd items: a 230-foot shower curtain, a five-ton oak tree, twelve hawthorne bushes, four cowhides, and a dozen butterflies.

The life of the play, Elliott stressed, was more important than huge visual effects. Olivier's conception of Shakespeare's was quite clear. The play is obsessed with violence. Lear is a virile old man, and we are to feel not pathos but a heroic overcoming of difficulty. Lear dies happy, believing that Cordelia is alive—the text was shaped slightly to enforce this interpretation. (There was also much cutting of the Fool's part, and Lear's retainers were combined into one character, the king's knight.)

Permitted the luxury of being more concerned with artistry than finances when making this tv film, Elliott noted that the company had two overriding priorities: to preserve Olivier's Lear and to serve William Shakespeare. Those who see this production will surely agree that the filmmakers have met both standards well.

TWO LEARS FOR TELEVISION: AN EXPLORATION OF TELEVISUAL STRATEGIES
Hardy M. Cook

The fifth season of *The Shakespeare Plays* opened in America on October 18, 1982, with the last play that Jonathan Miller directed for the series. The result is a provocative version of *King Lear* that marked the third time that Miller had cast Michael Hordern in the role of the foolish old king.[1] Fifteen months later, on January 26,

Hardy M. Cook, "Two Lears for Television: An Exploration of Televisual Strategies," *Literature/Film Quarterly* 14, no. 4 (1986): 179–86.

1984, Americans finally got to see the much heralded Laurence Olivier's *King Lear*. This version, taped earlier in England for Granada Television, was directed by Michael Elliott and produced by David Plowright. These two productions of the play differ radically, each with instructive strengths and weaknesses. Having these two recent productions of the same play to compare and contrast provides us with a valuable opportunity to assess the possibilities for "translating" *King Lear* to television.

The acting styles in these two *Lears* differ in many significant ways. Michael Elliott conceived of his *Lear* as existing in a mythic world with characters who appear somewhat larger than life. Naturally following from this is his emphasis on individual performances. There is little doubt that the casting of Olivier in the title role was the principal reason for the production, but Olivier had a splendid cast to back him up, and the members of that cast turned in some memorable, indeed unforgettable, performances. The *mise en scène* and editing of this production call attention to these individual performances with a preponderance of closely framed one-shots and rapid cutting—the effects of which are to accentuate the faces of the actors and the slightest nuances of expression that flicker across them. I shall consider in a moment what this strategy denies us on television.

In Jonathan Miller's production, the emphasis is exactly the opposite. Miller's actors perform in ensemble, consistent with his view that in *Lear* the family is a metaphor for the state. Michael Hordern graciously defers to the other members of the cast, who all give subdued performances consistent with Miller's beliefs about how Shakespeare should be acted for television. Miller uses a relatively static camera, which records fairly long takes of the actors generally in medium two-shots, three-shots, and four-shots, as opposed to Elliott's shorter takes and dominating one-shots.

Both of these productions of *King Lear* last approximately three hours. However, because each makes different aesthetic assumptions about the play, each reveals much about the possibilities available for producing Shakespeare for television. Miller's version is faster-paced than Elliott's. This pace is established in several ways—through transitions between scenes, the illusion of cross-cutting, the deletion of one scene, and the shortening of others. The pace of Elliott's *Lear* is slower because Elliott chose to take a more "cinematic" and less "televisual" approach in his production. Elliott, like Miller, gives the impression of cross-cutting between II.iv and III.ii–vi, but Elliott cuts more of the text. Three complete scenes are excised—III.i, IV.iii, and IV.iv (as opposed to Miller's one—IV.iii), and some speeches and scenes are noticeably shortened. As a result, Elliott has additional screen time that enables him to create new scenes which emphasize visual elements over verbal ones.

These new scenes call attention to the lavishness of his production. I.ii opens with Edmund's soliloquy on the now-deserted Stonehenge

set. After it, Gloucester enters, and the two discuss the letter suppos-
edly from Edgar. Rather than continuing the scene as the text does,
Elliott creates a new scene at the stables of Gloucester's castle. Edgar
rides in on a horse, followed by Edmund, also riding. After they dis-
mount, the textual scene continues. A similar expansion happens at
the end of I.v. After Lear and his retinue leave Albany's castle, a
brief new scene, without dialogue, is added in which Lear and the
Fool on the lead horse are followed by Lear's train. This expansion
sets up another one that opens II.iv when, still on horseback, Lear
and his men ride through the heath. The first few lines are delivered,
and then a new scene begins after they enter the gates of Gloucester's
compound. The most noticeable expansion occurs in IV.vi. After
Gloucester vows to "bear affliction," he and Edgar walk off in a dissolve
to Lear washing his rags in a stream. Lear snares a rabbit, opens
it with a knife, eats its entrails, and drinks from the stream. There
is a cut to Lear making and wearing chains of wildflowers before
he says, "No, they cannot touch me for coining. I am the king himself."
Lear recites a few more lines and sings a song that is not in the
text. Only then does he run into Gloucester and Edgar, the dialogue
of the scene continuing with Edgar's "Sweet marjoram." These changes
reveal Elliott's more "cinematic" approach to the play, as he creates
visual equivalents to the spoken word. We know from the text that
Lear has gone mad—in Elliott's version we *see* much of the madness
that we would normally *hear* more about; consequently, Elliott has
no need for IV.iv, in which Cordelia discusses her father's condition
with the Doctor.

Elliott, then, employs a more "cinematic" and less "televisual" approach than Miller does. His choices emphasize editing and visual
equivalents as opposed to techniques that allow Shakespeare's language to carry a greater weight than is usual in cinematic versions
of the plays. Since this distinction mimics a controversy that dominated film theory and film production up to the theoretical revolution
of the mid-1960s, it will be useful to examine some of the theories
of André Bazin, who in the 1950s distinguished between directors
"who put their faith in the image and those who put their faith in
reality."[2] Bazin sets the techniques of *montage* against those of *depth
of field*. He first differentiates between two orders of montage: (1)
images joined according to some abstract principle (a technique associated primarily with the silent cinema) and (2) images joined according
to psychological montage whereby an event is broken down into those
fragments which resemble the changes of attention we might naturally
experience were we physically present at the event (a technique associated with the coming of sound). In opposition to these, Bazin sets
depth of field techniques which permit an action to develop over
a long time on several spatial planes, constructing dramatic interrelationships *within* the frame rather than *between* frames.[3] Although contemporary theoreticians convincingly call into question the use of

the term "realism" by Bazin and others,[4] much of what Bazin has to say about depth of field techniques relates to the distinction that I am making between "cinematic" versus "televisual" approaches to Shakespeare on television.

Bazin explains that with depth of field techniques, dramatic effects which had formerly relied on montage can be created out of the movements of actors within a fixed framework where whole scenes are covered in one take with the camera remaining motionless.[5] With this approach, montage is partially replaced by frequent panning shots and entrances, based on "a respect for the continuity of dramatic space and, of course, of its duration."[6] From Bazin's theories, we may conveniently label those televisual strategies that are similar to Elliott's *montage technique* and those that are similar to Miller's *depth of field* technique. These two techniques rarely appear in unadulterated form, yet they describe the two major approaches that have been employed to translate Shakespeare's plays to television.

. . . Elliott's use of montage technique establishes interrelationships primarily by cuts between frames. Miller's use of depth of field technique establishes relationships within the frame. There are many accompanying differences between these two techniques. Elliott's takes are short; Miller's are long. Elliott frequently uses reaction shots; Miller uses them selectively. Elliott uses a highly fluid camera; Miller's camera is largely static—he moves his actors within the frame, and therefore blocking is extremely important. Elliott uses tightly framed one-shots; Miller uses looser, generally medium, ensemble shots.

I contend that Miller's televisual approach is ultimately more effective for realizing Shakespeare on television than Elliott's, which depends more upon cutting and visual equivalents. . . . Realizing Shakespeare for television alters the dynamics of television as a cinematic subgenre because the density of Shakespeare's language must of necessity be sacrificed in more "cinematic," montage approaches. In a highly visual medium like film, images can often be in competition with Shakespeare's language. Roger Manvell notes that "there can be little doubt that the full-scale spoken poetry of Shakespeare's stage and the continuous visual imagery of the cinema can be oil and water."[7] Charles Marowitz, an assistant to Peter Brook during the filming of Brook's 1970 *King Lear*, makes a similar observation:

> When we came to consider how the words should actually be treated on the screen, we realised that the power of Shakespeare's writing—particularly its evocative power—is so enormous that although one can find images which may seem appropriate, images become unnecessary or even unwanted—they can actually get between the audience and the power of the words.[8]

Because of the differences in image quality and the relation of the audience to the screen, in television the spoken word carries more weight than it does in the cinema. This is an especially important difference when dealing with a Shakespeare play in which language is paramount. As Sheldon P. Zitner points out, "Since its spoken words loom larger in the total sensory input, television can go further than film towards restoring the Elizabethan Theatre's primacy of words."[9] Therefore, my contention is not that Miller's televisual approach is more "realistic" than Elliott's, but that it better establishes a relationship between the spectator and the object on the television screen, replicating an experience with Shakespeare's plays that is similar to the theatrical one. To illustrate this contention, I now propose to examine Elliott's and Miller's televisual choices in I.i.

Elliott opens his *King Lear* with ominous background music. The first shot, which establishes the scene, is a high-angle, long-shot of the enormous Stonehenge-like set as the sun rises behind it in the mists of the morning. Characters are seen moving to the inside of the circle of stones as the camera cranes down. It continues moving to set up a two-shot of Gloucester and Kent on the outside perimeter of the stone circle. As Kent begins speaking, the camera continues to move in to frame a much tighter two-shot. At Kent's "Is not this your son, my lord," Elliott cuts abruptly to a three-shot that now includes Edmund, viewed from the back. As Gloucester says, "His breeding, sir, hath been at my charge," there is another abrupt cut to a closely framed reaction shot of Edmund in which we see a slight raising of his left eyelid in response to his father's statement. This shot is held during Kent's "I cannot conceive you," at which time Elliott cuts back to the two-shot of Kent and Gloucester. After Gloucester's ". . . ere she had a husband for her bed," we are given another very quick reaction shot of Edmund before returning to the three-shot. At Gloucester's "But I have a son, by order of law . . . ," Elliott returns to the two-shot of Kent and Gloucester. When Gloucester says ". . . who yet is no dearer," Elliott has Gloucester move toward Edmund with the camera following in a pan that sets up a two-shot of Gloucester and Edmund. Gloucester moves back to reform the two-shot with Kent and says, "Though this knave came somewhat saucily to the world before he was sent for." At "there was good sport at his making," the camera tightens the two-shot; then Elliott cuts back to the three-shot and continues with it until Edmund's "My services to your lordship," which is delivered in a close one-shot. Next, there is a cut back to the three-shot for Kent's response, a cut to a one-shot of Edmund's reply, and then a return to the three-shot. After Gloucester's "He hath been out nine years," Elliott cuts to a reaction of Edmund at "and away he shall again" and then cuts back to the three-shot for "The King is coming." At this point, Kent and Gloucester turn to enter the circle of stones as Gloucester signals to Edmund not to follow.

What I have just described takes less than a minute and a half of screen time. In that time, Elliott cuts thirteen times, with some of the takes (especially Edmund's reactions) lasting only a second or two. In many respects, this opening is a perfect example of the montage strategy. Rather than showing the reactions of the characters within the frame, Elliott presents them to us in reaction shots through cuts between the frames. The cuts isolate individual performances in these reaction shots, such as the one featuring Edmund's raised eyelid; further, they replicate psychological changes in attention. However, they are completely under the control of the director. They give spectators little choice about where to direct their attention. This to me is a major shortcoming of using the montage technique for presenting Shakespeare on television.

Miller's version of these same opening lines also takes about a minute and a half, but there is not a single cut during that time. Miller opens his scene with a long-shot of the darkly lit, relatively artificial interior of Lear's palace. Kent and Gloucester enter the set from the extreme right in deep field and walk to the front and center of the frame. Even before Kent begins to speak, Edmund, who had been sitting with several other courtiers on a bench to the right in deep field, rises and walks into the mid-field between the two Earls, creating the first of innumerable triangular blocking patterns in this scene. Edmund's body language suggests that he is trying to overhear what the two Earls are saying. Kent and Gloucester speak in hushed voices as if they do not wish to be overheard by the others present in the room. Kent looks over his shoulder, and Edmund's attitude implies that he is attempting to act casual, hiding his real purpose. The exchange between Kent and Gloucester continues, and Kent once again looks over his shoulder and asks, "Is not this your son, my lord?" Edmund's and Kent's eyes meet. As Gloucester responds, Edmund moves behind his father to the right, establishing another triangular pattern. Sometimes this movement is only the slight turn of the body or the head. Gloucester, for example, in the middle of this threesome, directs his remarks to Kent and then turns to look at Edmund's reactions. When Gloucester announces, "The King is coming," the three move out of the way to let Lear enter from the right front. Rather than cutting, Miller has his actors move *within the frame:* we see all three all the time.

Miller, therefore, directs this same portion of scene one quite differently from the way Elliott does. Miller establishes relationships within the frame rather than between frames. We still have the reactions of Kent, Gloucester, and Edmund to what is being discussed, but we may choose how we wish to direct our attention during these interactions. With this strategy, the emphasis is less upon individual performances and more upon the interrelationships among the characters. This is just what the montage strategy denies us.

I want to make a few other points about the differences between these two versions of I.i before drawing some conclusions. After Gloucester and Kent enter the stone circle, Elliott continues the scene at a leisurely pace with music and the ceremonial entrances of Goneril and Albany, Regan and Cornwall, and Lear and Cordelia. After these entrances, Elliott moves in for a close one-shot of Lear, to an overhead shot of the interior of the circle, to another quick one-shot of Lear, to another overhead shot, and then to a shot of Lear on his throne. These cuts at times create the impression of a slide show; they are obtrusive and are not, in my view, as seamless as they should be. Throughout this production, Elliott cuts between frames to establish relationships. When Lear explains his intention of dividing his king-dom and retiring from active rule of it, Elliott cuts between one-shots of Lear and two-shots of Regan and Cornwall, two-shots of Goneril and Albany and one-shots of Cordelia. This montage strategy denies us the simultaneous impact of Shakespeare's language upon all the major characters in the frame (their collective reactions to what is happening) and the choice of where to direct our attention during those interactions.

The depth of field technique allows viewers to exercise more control over what they see. In this approach, blocking within the ensemble shots is extremely important, as it is in the theatre. Miller's blocking in this scene is a visual essay on the shifting relationships among the characters, and it is appropriate to consider some of these triangles and their effects.

The first triangular pattern, after Lear enters the frame, occurs when Lear, in the center of the foreground, examines the map, while in deep-field to the left are Regan and Cornwall and to the right are Goneril and Albany. After Lear's "while we / Unburden'd crawl toward death," Miller makes his first cut to a close one-shot of Lear. The camera then dollies back, setting up another triangle: the elder sisters and their spouses remain in deep-field in the same positions as the last triangle; at the apex of this new triangle in the center foreground is Cordelia; Lear sits on his throne slightly in front of Goneril and Regan and almost in the middle of the three points. Goneril declares her love for her father to the right of a triangle formed by Cornwall, Albany, and Lear. Cordelia's reaction to her eldest sister's remarks is addressed to the Fool in another triangle: the Fool to the left in the foreground, Cordelia to the right, with Lear at the apex in deep-field. Regan declares her love in a triangle composed of herself, Corn-wall, and Lear, and Cordelia's reaction is presented in the same pattern as before. When Lear asks Cordelia "what can you say," Goneril and Regan are together at the apex of a triangle with Lear and Cordelia on either side in the foreground. As Cordelia explains her reply of "Nothing," Kent moves into the apex, replacing Goneril and Regan. As Lear's anger increases, he steps to the right and blocks out Kent. As Kent bids goodbye, he does so in another triangular pattern: Lear is at the apex in deep-field; Cordelia and the Fool are together at the left foreground, while Kent is at the right. When Burgundy and France enter, they too form a triangle with Lear at the apex. The camera then dollies and pans to set up a triangle with the Fool and Cordelia at the apex and Burgundy and Lear at the other points in the foreground. When Cordelia pleads, "I yet beseech your Majesty," she does so in a triangle composed of herself, Lear, and France. During France's "My Lord of Burgundy," France, Cordelia, and Burgundy are blocked in yet another triangular pattern, while a triangle during France's "Fairest Cordelia" is composed of France, Lear, and Cordelia. When Cordelia bids her sisters farewell, they form another triangle, and the scene concludes with a triangle formed by Goneril, Regan, and Edmund. Most of these triangles are created within the frame primarily by the movement of the actors, with some movement of the camera, usually slow and gentle.

Miller's blocking thus replicates the shifting relationships among the characters. It also enables viewers to shift their attention among those characters. Miller's blocking places his characters in the dramatic space that we observe, and in that respect it controls emphasis as a director in the theatre does. However, with this technique, we have more freedom to direct our attention where we wish than we do with montage technique, and this strategy restores to Shakespeare's language the primacy that it loses with montage technique. There is no denying the power of the performances in Elliott's *Lear*. The difficulty is that the viewer is not permitted to observe a large portion of those performances because the camera often excludes from our sight many of the actors who are present. With Miller's strategy, we see most of the actors present in a scene most of the time. In this ensemble performance, we see more of the simultaneous effects that language has on the characters. With depth of field technique, the language is not as much in competition with the visuals, and thus a greater emphasis is given to the spoken word.

. . . Miller's version creates a televisual analogue to the theatrical experience—one in which Shakespeare's language is not sacrificed to the images. Montage can create competition between the visual and the verbal elements in a production. Those who direct Shakespeare's plays for cinema generally accept that this competition exists and substitute visual equivalents, paring down the verbal texts—often by as much as one half, as in the Reinhardt and Dieterle *A Midsummer Night's Dream* and the Olivier *Henry V* and *Hamlet*. Further, theatrical versions of Shakespeare's plays in cinema, such as Stuart Burge's *Othello* with Laurence Olivier, do not work well for the very reason that the visuals are uninteresting. This does not mean that one cannot have a satisfying experience with a filmed version of a Shakespeare play. Quite the contrary, many Shakespeare films are true to the spirit of the plays from which they were derived; but the importance of Shakespeare's language alters the dynamics of television as a cinematic subgenre. Therefore, a more "cinematic" approach to Shakespeare on television is not as effective a use of the medium as the depth of field technique.

Miller's televisual strategies enable viewers to watch Shakespeare on television in a manner that is similar to the theatrical experience. As H. R. Coursen notes, "The best TV productions gradually erase our concentration on technique and draw us into that attentiveness similar to what happens to us in the theater."[10] This, I contend, is what Jonathan Miller's production of *King Lear* does and what Michael Elliott's does not do. Miller's style accomplishes this through a greater, uninterrupted continuity of dramatic space and time, a more active relationship between the spectator and the object, more choice about where and how to direct one's attention while viewing a production, and a greater weight given to the spoken word.

Notes

1. Production credit was given to Shaun Sutton, who took over the reins of series producer from Miller.
2. André Bazin, *What Is Cinema?*, vol. 1, trans. Hugh Gray (Berkeley: University of California Press, 1967), p. 24.
3. Cf. Dudley Andrew, *The Major Film Theories* (New York: Oxford University Press, 1976), pp. 156–57.
4. Dudley Andrew, *Concepts in Film Theory* (New York: Oxford University Press, 1984), p. 48.
5. Bazin, *What Is Cinema?*, p. 33.
6. Bazin, *What Is Cinema?*, p. 34.
7. Roger Manvell, *Shakespeare and the Film* (New York: Praeger, 1971), p. 15; cf. p. 107.
8. Ibid., p. 138.
9. Sheldon P. Zitner, "Wooden O's in Plastic Boxes: Shakespeare and Television," *University of Toronto Quarterly* 51 (Fall 1981): 6.
10. H. R. Coursen, "Shakespeare and Television: The BBC-TV *Hamlet*," in *Shakespeare and the Arts*, ed. Cecile W. Cary and Henry S. Limouze (Washington, D.C.: University Press of America, 1982), p. 127.

HUSBANDED WITH MODESTY: SHAKESPEARE ON TV
Barbara Millard

> Most of the BBC Shakespeare Plays were dismal at full length. Here, chopped up in pieces and used to discuss specific themes, they're even worse. Don't settle for bites of the Bard; avoid "The Shakespeare Leftovers," and wait for new and better video renditions of Shakespeare's works.
>
> David Bianculli
> *The Philadelphia Inquirer*
> January 25, 1986

Barbara Millard, "Husbanded with Modesty: Shakespeare on TV," *Shakespeare Bulletin* 4, no. 3 (May/June 1986): 19–22.

Too harsh, perhaps, this summary dismissal of an effort to reach a greater television audience for this series by repackaging it, but not easily discounted. A more perspicacious critic than most of the locals, Bianculli has ample precedent for his condemnatory remarks.[1] Since "The Shakespeare Hour" has been badly slotted in this area for Saturday mornings at ten, between "Sesame Street" and "Living with Animals," it would appear that the local PBS station agrees with him. As valuable as the BBC/Time-Life Shakespeare Plays have been and promise to be as teaching materials and, of course, as public television rebroadcasts, Bianculli's "review" points to more than one reality: that "dismal" is an apt description for too many of the productions; that the series has not presented us with definitive productions; and, most importantly, that whatever Shakespeare does appear on this medium in the future will be measured, especially with a viewing public with a quick trigger-finger on the remote control, according to the standards of good "video."

As this truncated word suggests, television is becoming, at least in its entertainment programming, an increasingly visual medium. In television drama, even that which pretends to substance as a "TV movie" or "epic mini-series," the plot lines are thin, the narrative straight and easily interrupted, the dialogue brief, simplistic, and colloquial. Television producers and directors like Lee Grant, who made an auspicious directorial debut with "Tell Me a Riddle" (1980) and who has made several documentaries and docu-dramas since, insist that the line between TV and movies is blurring as television movies become more cinematic.[2] Meanwhile, the advent of rock-videos, with their chromatic aberrations and surrealistic effects, has helped challenge realism as the necessary mode of television production.

Rather than cater to the perceived limitations of the small, two-dimensional screen, as the producers of the BBC series did all too often, creative Shakespearean productions should seek bolder, more imaginative use of a developing medium. Give the ever-growing power of television to reach millions, Shakespeare's plays must continue to be broadcast from this medium to the people as "free" Shakespeare, not only for the education of the masses but also for the reason *Bleak House* or the New York City Ballet performance of *Swan Lake* must be broadcast—to generate larger audiences for the original medium. To the devotee of the Metropolitan Opera, viewing a videotape of Zeffirelli's film version of *La Traviata* might prove less than aesthetically fulfilling (as it did for a friend privileged with season tickets), but the film and the tape have made converts among those who have never experienced opera in professional performance. With their historical and mythic contexts, complicated plots, lengthy poetic speeches, archaic idiom, erudite analogies, soliloquies and asides, Shakespeare's plays require techniques for television production that go beyond those adequate either for traditional TV fare or for the

more easily adapted classic fictions like those on "Masterpiece Theatre."

With their "mingled yarn" of successes and failures, the BBC plays
offer themselves as a base for critical discussion of what Shakespeare
should or could be on television. The purpose of the series, as stated
by both Cedric Messina and Shaun Sutton (originator of the series
and head of the BBC television group, respectively), was to make
the plays accessible to a popular audience as "entertainment."[3] I would
argue that an American audience requires not a simple Shakespeare
nor a merely entertaining one, and probably not a gimmicky one,
but rather an *emphatic* one, that is, a compelling dramatic experience
with all the excitement, delight, and vividness which Messina had
hoped to achieve but which, in fact, only a few of the productions—
long on quiet conversation and short on energy—could sustain. With
a popular audience, Shakespeare's legend works both for and against
the experience of his art. Some viewers will never attempt to view
a play, having been cowed forever by the myth of difficulty and the
dullness universally attributed to the "classics." But many others want
to be seduced into going on a journey of imagination and spirit and
prodded to understand. Such is the audience our regional Shakespeare
festivals woo so successfully, and such productions work very hard,
as any television production should, to achieve the comprehension
that leads to delight.

For Shakespeare on television, as for Shakespeare on the stage, the
major challenge to delight is the language of the plays, which requires
interpretation through the medium. Precisely because Shakespeare's
language creates context, and because Americans increasingly are hard-
put to comprehend this language at first-hearing, this language must
be interpreted and supported by the visual context, special effects,
and a dramatic cinematography which further expand the limits of
the medium. In 1974, Alistair Cooke pinpointed the challenge to classi-
cal programming on American television:

> The most striking thing to me is that television has produced a generation
> of children who have a declining grasp of the English language but who
> also have a visual sophistication that was denied to their parents. They
> learn so much about the world that appeals immediately to their emotions,
> but I'm not sure it involves their intelligence, their judgment.[4]

Despite the avowed goal to reach a popular audience, the BBC productions made little, if any, accommodation for American audiences
regarding the barriers that Shakespeare's language presents. The
"fast-paced action" that Messina promised is more often in the actors'
delivery of their speeches than in their languid movements, relaxed
postures, or the interminable close-up shots.

Frequently in these British productions the pace of delivered lines quickens or slows in accordance with scene activity or the lack of it to produce the extremes of incomprehensible passion at one end or tedium at the other. When, in *Richard II* (2.1), tension builds after Richard makes his response to Gaunt's death and York finally confronts the king, Jacobi seeks to avoid the message by sidestepping and turning his back on the old man. Although constrained by space, the actors achieve a moment rich in portent and texture: as the magnificent apparel of the figures contrasts insolently with the sobriety of the occasion, the agile king seeks to elude the elder man's words of warning by ducking into the circle of his followers. But it is York's words, central to plot and theme, which all too easily elude the unaccustomed ear, as they rush out in a harshly whispered cascade from Charles Grey. I have seen students who have studied the text drop their eyes from the screen at this point to seek the words they cannot distinguish. For them the moment is diminished; for an unprepared audience it may be lost entirely. So too, in *A Midsummer Night's Dream*, Puck's energy is short-circuited by a static camera much of the time, while his wit is obscured by an impenetrable accent all of the time. Speeches riddled with topical jokes, arcane conceits, difficult puns, and unfamiliar idioms jeopardize Shakespeare's comic scenes enough without the complication of regional accents. Whatever nuances of class such realism provides hardly compensates for lost sense and hilarity.

At the other extreme, in an attempt to exploit the intimacy afforded by the small screen, the longer lyric speeches and soliloquies have been delivered slowly and carefully as lifeless set pieces shot in unrelieved close-up. While a few actors, like John Cleese or Bob Hoskins, could dominate the camera to bring the audience into complicity with Petruchio or Iago, most, like Michael Hordern, underplayed their parts to the point of boredom. As Maurice Charney observes in his review of the second season of the plays, we come to know the actors' faces very well, "down to the last wart," but the characters too often remain "a shadowy presence."[5]

Granted that one cannot expect to experience the electricity of a theatre performance on the television screen, one should not settle for Shakespeare presented on television in the mode of a drawing room conversation. The success of some of the BBC productions, like *Measure for Measure*, suggests that the limitations in filming Shakespeare for television are not always in the medium but in the use made of it. Are Shakespeare's most provocative or beautiful lines best rendered by actors seated around tables or slouching in armchairs? Does a nineteen-inch screen mandate so many static scenes? The fault is not always in the technology; it is sometimes in the direction.

In the BBC production of *A Midsummer Night's Dream*, one of the most visually handsome scenes is that in which Theseus discourses on imagination, poets, lovers, and madmen to Hippolyta. Both are seated at table in a splendid seventeenth-century library, the set filled with richly bound volumes, carved furniture, and elegant appointments. As Theseus explains his analogy in the most detached manner, a clock is assertively ticking, and the camera slowly moves in closer to the figures to capture a large leather globe situated in the background and now visible between them. Together the globe and the ticking sound steal the scene. Rather than clarify or enhance the matter of the speech, these details interfere with our apprehension of it. Perhaps if Theseus (Nigel Davenport) had interacted with the mise en scene, had left his chair, as he surely would on stage, to spin or search the globe, ponder the clock, embrace Hippolyta, or even fondle a book, the establishment of such a contexture would, at the least, have secured our attention; at best it might have knit word to detail, bonded concept to sign. The risks in substituting such pictures for dramatic action have been noted by Stanley Wells:

> It is not enough to do justice simply to the "tableaux." The very word suggests a freezing of the action which is a denial of drama. A successful visual style would be one that is effective when the play is moving fast as well as when it is moving slowly.[6]

Television as a medium does not preclude many of the more effective tactics of the theatre. Production devices can be employed to direct the audience's reaction to the play, and production styles can illuminate the text. While I would not argue that the filmed stage play is a match for the real thing, it is true that such presentations of first-rate performances have provided excellent TV viewing and have drawn large audiences. Olivier's Merchant is a case in point, as are the many superb productions regularly broadcast on the Arts and Entertainment Cable Network, such as Bus Stop or Absurd Person Singular. Length of a play need not spell defeat, as the recent success of Nicholas Nickleby demonstrates.

These successes also challenge the notion that realism must attend television production. When viewing two filmed stage productions of A Midsummer Night's Dream (Papp/New York Festival) and The Taming of the Shrew (CBC/Stratford Festival Theatre), my students have been fascinated by the actors' use of the unrealistic and minimal stage sets but more so by the exhilarating energy of actors on stage in front of live audiences: the broader gestures, the projected, clearly inflected delivery, the thumping and banging and noise of stage action, even the mechanics of entrance (Oberon rising from the "floor" of the forest) and exit (Kate stomping up the theatre aisle) were compelling features.

Lacking the third dimension and radically reduced in size on the television screen, these actors of varying talent nevertheless create a compelling dynamic on tape for a popular and student audience. Neither of these productions is more intelligent than their counterparts in the BBC series, and the production values of the latter are superior. But both of these theatrical performances worked harder to support the written word, create the illusion of spontaneity, and evoke a sense of wonder, values too often missing from the more subtle if more lyrical BBC comedies.

In broadcasting the Stratford Festival *Shrew* (1982) as part of the "Stage" series, the programmers of the Arts and Entertainment Network appear to have been sensitive to their mission in reaching a broad subscription audience. More than theatre or film, television offers attractive formats in which to educate people regarding what they are about to see, a point lately realized in the repackaging of the BBC series, which now features an "introduction" by Walter Matthau. As host for the Stratford Festival productions, Tony Roberts illustrates his lucid synopsis of the plot and incidentally comments on the play's artifice while handling props and costume articles in a dressing room. His lively introduction is followed by a trumpet fanfare announcing stills of the major characters identified by superimposed credits. This simple ploy not only helps the inexperienced audience but serves surprisingly well to heighten anticipation. Unlike the BBC version, this *Shrew*, starring Len Cariou and Sharry Flett and directed by Peter Dews (Norman Campbell produced and directed for TV), retained and lightly completed the Christopher Sly "frame," clearly suggesting to its audience that the play, albeit a male fantasy, transcends gender issues to establish a complex relation between Sly's and Kate's imaginative experiences. Tapes of live performances on stage like this one have been criticized for their obvious inclusion of a live audience and its laughter, on the grounds that such a "sound track," like the declassé tactic of sitcoms, insults us by dictating our response.[7] But I would propose that the laughter of those visibly responding to the performance is a valuable catalyst for the general viewer and, for the neophyte, a cue to catch up with the joke that might otherwise be missed. So too, the ceremony of bow-taking and applause is an appropriate form of closure for a play, as the epilogues remind us.

Another alternative to the "television drama" format for the production of the Shakespeare plays is the cinematic. The launching of the BBC series in 1978 coincided with two of the most important developments in television viewing and marketing: the advent of cable television in communities across the country (except Philadelphia) and the "video revolution" sparked by the affordable and irresistible VCR. Both of these systems are accustomizing us to the "small" movie, will we, nill we. Moreover, the phenomenon of mini-series productions and made-for-cable movies has demonstrated that television producers have learned that the public wants not only the richness of production detail but also the visual depth, larger effects, and sweeping scale of feature films. Such elaborate production is not incompatible with literary richness.

In the production of a Shakespeare play for television, what is wanted is not a big budget extravaganza but the employment of those cinematic effects which aid comprehension of the language, enhance viewing pleasure, and secure attention. When Malvolio appears "cross-garter'd" before Olivia, the camera should encompass the whole tortured and ridiculous figure, instead of the close-up and bust shots employed in the BBC version (except for one quick shot of the lower legs to prove that he was indeed cross-gartered). In David Giles' *1 Henry IV*, why are there no heraldic banners behind Falstaff to provide the context for the soliloquy maintaining that "Honor is a mere scutcheon"? That blank space behind Anthony Quayle does nothing to support his intelligent communication of Falstaff's ironic conception of himself. Although filming *As You Like It* on location turned the clever artifice of this exploration of pastoral into "barnyard realism," according to James Bulman, there is much to be said for shooting on location those scenes that are topographically and historically meaningful.[8] At the very least, imaginary gardens should have real toads in them, and Prospero's island should not be devoid, as John Gorrie's was, of wonderful noises, nimble marmosets, and clustering filberts.

A recent production for television that illustrates the potential of this medium for Shakespeare plays is the *King Lear* produced by Laurence Olivier and directed by Michael Elliott for Granada TV (1983). When the news releases announced that this film was in the making, the production details were sought-after material. Presumably, anticipation ran high because of Olivier's reputation not only as legendary actor and director in the theatre but also as a film director whose Shakespeare films are benchmarks in the genre. A veteran of television Shakespeare as well, dating from his *Macbeth* in 1938, Olivier was well-teamed with Elliott, a British stage director who had done over fifty television productions. Together they were able to combine filmic and stage effects to harmonious purpose in this television production, which had to be shot in a Manchester studio using video techniques because of Olivier's fragile health. The result is a visually persuasive version of the play that grips the attention of the television viewer.

It is not my purpose to argue here with the concept behind the production, which was deliberately straightforward and, like every other I have seen, a partial vision. Rather, I would concentrate on the efficacy of the production in presenting the play as vividly alive as an expert production crew, a first-rate cast, and two million dollar budget could make it. Olivier and Elliott began by trimming the text of the play down to a little over two hours, Olivier remarking, "I don't think the medium will hold the interest any longer."[9] Unlike the BBC *Lear,* whose localized setting in a Jacobean court dispels the mythic aura of the play, this *Lear* emerges from the hazy dawn of Stonehenge ritual and concludes in the sunset circle of sacrifice.

In between, this production eschews stifling enclosures for expansive sets. Selecting 800 A.D. as a focal point, designer Roy Stonehouse was able to create credible Anglo-Saxon sets out of plank, wattle, clumps of turf, and, of course, a wonderfully evocative circle of mighty "stones." The effect belies the limitations of four cameras and an enclosed studio. Even indoor scenes take place in seemingly cavernous halls. Outdoor scenes, Stonehouse explained, were expanded by bleaching out backgrounds to give a more impressionistic look to the picture: "On the heath scene, for instance, we used real grass and rain, and by judicious use of gauze and bits of fog, we gave a look of infinity to the studio, which suggests the real struggle being waged between Lear and the elements."[10] The use of the Stonehenge set to simulate the on-location filming precluded by Olivier's frailty works extraordinarily well and proves that, in extending our eye into visual depth on television, the camera does not necessarily lose dramatic depth. There is also intelligent use of overhead shots—of Lear arriving on horseback with his retinue in Gloucester's courtyard (and heralded by the appropriate noise and confusion) or of Gloucester's "leap," which involves a sizeable arc to render him prone and upside-down on the slope of a hill (and upside-down on the television screen as well). Such shots provide a sense of scope and a dramatic excitement worthy of Shakespeare's play, in defiance of the perceived limitation of the medium.[11]

As the effects are large, so are the visual details meaningful in terms of the script. The wheel of fire that comes full circle is visible in the huge sun rising and setting behind Stonehenge; in the circular configuration of the courtiers prostrate in obeisance to Lear; in the circle of stones forming the henge; in the circle motif used in the embroidery of the costumes, brooches, torques, and head bands; in the crown itself which Lear holds up to his face, peers through, and finally sends rolling over the map toward Goneril and Regan; in the circling movement (shot from overhead) of troops closing in with pointed swords around the captured Lear and Cordelia; and at last in the round embrace Lear makes with his manacled arms to "catch" Cordelia for all eternity. A deliberate Olivier touch is the telling use of physical embrace, hand holding, clasping, grasping, kissing—with which the characters identify their alignments: the villainous characters close the circle of conspiracy in the first half of the play, their movement balanced by the reunion of the good characters in the second half, all culminating in Lear's final embrace of Cordelia upon the sacrificial stone in the henge to which the action has returned. Literally alive in detail, this Lear shows a hunted king, desperate to survive, snaring a live rabbit; a newly gentled old man, forgiving sinners while playing with a mouse and real butterflies; a madman stripped of the illusion of pomp, making chains of wildflowers for his adornment. The production is attentive to every gesture that might illuminate the poetry.

In this production, music serves for dramatic heightening. With the exception of the healing music called for in the French camp, music is not presented in a realistic mode, as part of the environment of the scene. Admittedly jarring at first, and thoroughly despised by some, the "thrilling" music and zoom shot announcing, say, the entrance of Goneril in 1.4 to chastise her father is at least a cue for those unfamiliar with the play that a confrontation is about to ensue. It is also an interesting way to vary pace and underscore tone in a lengthy, demanding performance. Such background music, used often in Masterpiece Theatre productions, effects needed transition and supplies a tension lost on a television screen. In fact, this production uses this device to establish a startling analogue by casting both Edmund's and Edgar's soliloquies in the same context of Stonehenge, with the same background of soft music. The effect for the viewer is an unexpected tension between the confidences of both characters. It is precisely because television induces passivity in the viewer that technology must be brought to bear to quicken our engagement with what is presented on the screen.

One would hope that those who work to bring Shakespeare to the television screen would demand more of the technology than is usually demanded of it for regular programming. Is the persistent employment of the close-up for long periods of monologue a necessary approach? Since its signal advantage is to let us see more of the inner movement of the drama than the long shot does, should it not be used dramatically for that purpose rather than as a cliché (together with the reaction shot) to the diminution of larger effects? Because of Olivier's condition, Elliott too relies heavily on closeup shots of Lear. But the battle scenes, so dreaded by the production crews of the BBC plays, were superbly handled by Elliott, who surrealistically superimposed shots of burning buildings and embattled men over blind Gloucester's listening head. Beyond solving a technical problem the ploy presents a powerful image of Gloucester seeing "feelingly" the chaos of war and the incipient catastrophe.

Whatever its flaws, the Olivier *Lear* lived up to its promise and the challenge of being broadcast on commercial television in this country. It earned both respect and enthusiasm, and it demonstrated that televised Shakespeare need not consist of constricted movement, small effects, dark interior scenes, and incomprehensible dialogue—need not be "dismal."

Throughout this essay, I have discussed the success and potential of Shakespeare on television in terms of the popular audience to whom the medium addresses itself. As the latest budgetary news from Washington makes clear, federal funding for PBS may soon evaporate. If Shakespeare is to be broadcast on television, it will have to be on commercial and cable networks as well as on the educational network. While the sophisticated audience of Shakespeare scholars, students, and devotees will keep the plays alive in the theatre, a popular audience must keep them alive on television.

Lest this essay appear to be another exercise in BBC-bashing, I would assert that this series was a crucial first step in securing that audience. To have access to taped performances of every play is to be possessed of an invaluable resource. Rather than discourage future television and film production, the series might well encourage it, as the Granada

Lear perhaps demonstrates. One unlooked for benefit of the series is that it has led us to reevaluate prior television broadcasts of Shakespeare. With 20/20 hindsight, one could say that the attempt to provide the "complete works" was bound to give us what we received, not definitive productions but eminently useful ones.[12]

If it takes legendary actors and larger budgets underwritten by cable and commercial networks to have better television Shakespeare, so be it. Canadian and American resources and artists are ample for such projects and more attuned to the audiences they would reach. It is up to those of us who profess Shakespeare studies to support such efforts and to be wary, lest as a critical establishment we stifle the initiative by condemning the medium. Those of us who cut our teeth on Shakespeare in the theatre may never be satisfied with a television production, but we may be fast approaching an era when that will be all that is wanted or at least understood. By combining the most effective techniques of stage and film with its own technology and capacity for intimacy, television might yet produce a fulfilling sense of Shakespeare's dramatic power. As the Lord observes in the Induction of *The Taming of the Shrew*, if one creates the illusion "kindly . . . / It will be pastime passing excellent."

Notes

1. Michael Mullen documents some early blasts in "Shakespeare USA: The BBC Plays and American Education," *SQ* 35 (1984): 534n.

2. Cited in an interview by Morgan Gendel, *Los Angeles Times*, 3 February 1986.

3. Quoted in a preface to the BBC edition of *As You Like It* (New York: Mayflower Books, 1978), p. 9.

4. *U.S. News and World Report*, 5 April 1974. Reprinted in *Mass Media and the Popular Arts*, ed. Fredric Ressover and David C. Birch (New York: McGraw-Hill, 1977), p. 272.

5. "Shakespearean Anglophilia: The BBC-TV Series and American Audiences," *SQ* 31 (1980): 289.

6. "Television Shakespeare," *SQ* 33 (1982): 268.

7. "A Video *Taming of the Shrew*," *SFNL* 1.1 (December 1976): 1.

8. "The BBC Shakespeare and 'House Style,'" *SQ* 35 (1984): 573.

9. *New York Times*, 1 May 1983, p. 25.

10. Ibid.

11. Compare this "leap" of Gloucester's with his counterpart's in the BBC version, in which the camera cuts from Gloucester, just as he is about to jump, to a close-up of Edgar for a reaction.

12. Although Mullen details an elaborate program for the distribution of materials to schools and viewers across the country, I have yet to hear of anyone who has received any of this material (See "Shakespeare USA," 586–87). Twenty English teachers from Philadelphia schools participated in a four-week Shakespeare Institute which I directed last summer, and none of them had access to either the BBC tapes or the materials in their high schools. They lost no opportunity, however, to enjoy and study them during the Institute, often sacrificing lunch and dinner hours to do so.

THE STONE AND THE OAK:
OLIVIER'S TV FILM OF *KING LEAR*
Tucker Orbison

According to Charles Marowitz, Peter Brook once described *King Lear* as "a mountain whose summit has never been reached. On the way up one found the shattered bodies of other climbers strewn on every side."[1] Directors and actors have yet to achieve anything more than a partial view of this most mysterious play—at once, as T. R. Henn has written, "the most profound, intimate, and 'public' of the great tragedies [of Shakespeare]."[2] Two recent examples: Brook's own film rendered the cosmic, existential, cruel side; Grigori Kozintsev's film the personal, social, and more optimistic side.[3] In earlier days the great Shakespearean actors captured only one aspect or another of the central character. Thus, Macready missed "the brooding, mythic, almost apocalyptic hints and intimations" in the play, and Irving played Lear as a "doddering lunatic."[4] Actors of our own time, according to Maynard Mack, have fared no better. In certain critics' eyes, Charles Laughton was a "'funny old Father Christmas,'" and Paul Scofield "'a Stalin . . . a gutteral upstart whose behavior is . . . arbitrary and graceless.'" With Scofield, concludes the reviewer Alan Brien, "'another aspect of Lear is erased. As well as the King, we have lost the High Priest.'"[5] Jonathan Miller's recent television film points to another problem: if the action is too localized—here Jacobean England—the mythic element in the play disappears and the events are so distanced that the audience can escape emotional involvement in the brutality and terror, the sorrow and pity. The film directed by Michael Elliott, with Laurence Olivier as Lear, is a partial view like all the others, but it does avoid many of the usual crevasses. It has its limitations, but it shuns the two sentimental extremes of comforting reassurance (as may be found in a recent Royal Shakespeare Company production[6]) and cynical despair (Brook's film, for example). The ruthlessness and bestiality, the compassion and courage of Renaissance tragedy coalesce in this film to produce an affecting catharsis.

Olivier's film opens in a Stonehenge-like setting, localized but distanced in time to the age of legend and myth. It ends in the same spot: the camera retreats from a close-up of the dead Lear and Cordelia to a long shot of the circle of mourners within the circle of stones. In both scenes the moon, partially veiled by mists, glows sullenly in the distance. This structural envelope establishes an aura of mystery, transporting us to the epoch of the druids,[7] when the Celts believed in enigmatic, unfathomable gods,[8] who might be kind and just as Albany and Cordelia think they are, or cruel and sadistic as Gloucester

Tucker Orbison, "The Stone and the Oak: Olivier's TV Film of *King Lear*," *CEA Critic* 47, nos. 1–2 (1984): 67–77.

at one point believes. According to Geoffrey of Monmouth, Merlin said of these monoliths, "In these stones is a mystery, and a healing virtue against many ailments."[9] The setting's portentous aspect may recall as well the age of sacrificial rituals. In his book on Stonehenge, Hawkins refers to the long tradition of belief from Julius Caesar at least through John Aubrey that Stonehenge was the site of druidical sacrifices.[10] Though unscientific, so strong has been this conviction that to this day one of the flat monoliths (outside the circle) is called the slaughter stone. Another, situated near the center of the inner circle, is named the altar stone. It is here that Lear lays the dead Cordelia. Between these framing scenes takes place the tragedy of Lear and his alter ego Gloucester, as well as the sacrifice of Cordelia. At the center stands Lear, facing what Richard Sewall terms "the first (and last) of all questions, the question of existence: What does it mean to be?"[11] Olivier takes him from a state of childish innocence, so protected has he been by his position of authority (a dog's obeyed in office), through a dark night of evil, disorientation, and madness, and into an understanding of the need for compassion, an acceptance of his mortality, and a personal revolt against the absurd nature of an irrational universe, in which a horse, a rat can have life, Cordelia no life at all. The setting of Stonehenge and the film as a whole lead us to ponder the mystery of our existence.

The Elliott-Olivier film does not, be it noted, maintain, between the first scene and the last, this aura of cosmic mystery. To an extent the reviewer for *Punch* was right when he wrote, "*King Lear* is one of those big plays which will not be squeezed into a small box. Reduced, as it must be by television, to spacial bankruptcy, it cannot meet its emotional commitments. . . ."[12] The way the storm is presented, for example, gives little sense of unleashed titanic forces, because Olivier is filmed mainly in close-up throughout. Brook's film, by way of contrast, uses at one point the long shot to show Lear a tiny figure struggling across vast, storm-beaten stretches of waste. Is the persistent employment of the close-up a necessary concomitant of the television screen? At all events, both television films (Olivier's and Miller's) utilize it relentlessly, to the diminution of some of the large effects. Its signal advantage, on the other hand, is to let us see more of the inner movement of the drama than the long shot does. Thus, for example, we can perceive the unconscious struggle in Lear's mind, rising, muffled, to the surface, as he mutters, "I did her wrong."[13] Except for the broadening and deepening effects of the first and last scenes, Elliott's direction focuses on Lear's journey of mind and spirit, in much the same way that the *Hippolytus* of Euripides puts dramatic emphasis on the human struggle taking place between two scenes that reveal the irrationality of the gods. Unlike Miller and Brook, Elliott invites us into the action, in order to awaken our sensibilities.

The first scenes of the film make clear that neither Lear nor Gloucester has cared to concern himself with the problems and difficulties of others. No sense of compassion troubles Leo McKern's Gloucester in the little ante-scene before Lear's arrival. His craggy, coarse face echoes the unyielding, dense monoliths that form the backdrop to his insensitive description of his pleasure at Edmund's making. This vulgar way of talking about Edmund, within his hearing, reveals the kind of obtuse sensibility that Lear evinces in the scene that follows. Edmund's face betrays no sign of annoyance at his father's manner, not even when Gloucester, upon telling Kent that Edmund "hath been out nine years, and away he shall / again" (1.1.32–33), shakes his admonitory finger at Edmund. Gloucester well earns the contempt that Edmund later expresses.

After Goneril and Regan, with their husbands, arrive, somber in manner and dress, Lear enters, lovingly supported by Cordelia garbed in white and smiling expectantly. The Court prostrates itself as Lear approaches his throne. He seats himself and for a moment gazes around complacently to insure that all have shown the proper obeisance. Only then does he order Gloucester to fetch France and Burgundy, who long "have made their amorous sojourn" (1.1.47) and whom Cordelia awaits. He fully expects to have his way in all things. Yes, he is old: his need for support and his flowing white hair reveal this; but his face is round, uncreased—almost, as one reviewer put it, a baby's face.[14] He may well wish to shuffle off "all cares and business," as he says, but they have left no mark on him. After he casually announces that he will divide his kingdom, Lear, with a puckish glint in his eye, springs his surprise—the love test. Goneril (Dorothy Tutin) kneels and is about to kiss his hand, but Lear imperiously gestures to the ground. She must act the submissive subject again—this after her father has asked for an expression of love. Her fulsome speech Lear accepts with satisfaction. Diana Rigg's Regan is clever, sharp: she is about to kiss the royal hand, but with an ingratiating smile first bows to the ground; and if an even more fulsome profession of love will garner a larger chunk of land, she will outdo her sister, who makes a wry face at Regan's "I find she names my very deed of love; / Only she comes too short." Lear's childishness becomes all too apparent at "too short," when he emits a pleased chortle and glances gleefully around him.

After each of her sisters' speeches Cordelia turns to the camera and *sotto voce* indicates her dismay. We immediately take her point of view. Why would a sensitive young girl thinking of her forthcoming marriage say she will love her father all? When she says, "Nothing," Lear thinks she, like him, is playing a game.[15] "Nothing?" he asks with a half-smile, hand cupped over his ear. Surely he did not hear aright. "Nothing." The heart begins to harden: "Nothing will come of nothing." After her subsequent response Lear's pain begins: "But goes thy heart with this?"—plaintive, uncomprehending. Finally, with anger and severity, "Let it be so; thy truth then be thy dower." Stonehenge has found its way into his heart. He will cruelly sacrifice his own daughter to his pride and childish self-love. So distraught does Lear become that, contrary to his words "This coronet part between you" (addressed to Goneril and Regan), he takes off his own crown and tosses it carelessly down onto the map, where it rolls haphazardly. Whereas his intention was to invest Cordelia with a coronet, he throws away the symbol of the very things he wishes to keep: "The name and all th' addition to a king." He is petty and foolish here, not towering and tyrannical as some may think he ought to be. He cannot forgive Cordelia's spoiling his game, just as he cannot forgive Kent, who immediately steps to Cordelia's side and encircles her with a protecting arm. When Kent attempts to thwart his will, Lear loses all control, drawing a huge sword that he can hardly lift. It is the rage of a weak king. After banishing Kent, he indulges himself in vindictiveness toward Cordelia, sneering at her when he tells Burgundy, "Now her price has fallen," lashing the daughter he loved best with the pauses between each word of "We / Have no such daughter." This long opening sequence, then, gives us a Lear who is foolish, proud, petulant, human. Not for Olivier the arrogant tyrant of Paul Scofield in Brook's film. True, Olivier's Lear *looks* grand, with his handsome face, flowing beard, and golden crown; he *seems* authoritative, because all pay deference to him. But this Lear is more human than grand, more flawed than noble, more peevish than overbearing. In short, Olivier provides a Lear with whom the audience can identify and sympathize. Rather than watch the fall of a god-like Oedipus, we will partake in the suffering of a human Job. With his folly of dividing the kingdom, his hardness of heart, and his inability to be contradicted, Lear has opened an abyss and, like Gloucester, he "must stand the course" (3.7.53).

The treatment of Gloucester parallels and supports the dramatic impression made by Lear. After the Court scene, he wanders into camera view looking stunned. He is absolutely befuddled by Lear's behavior. Given this failure to understand anything of human nature, one sees how he can become such a gullible dupe in Edmund's hands. Of course, he has no way of knowing Edmund's Machiavellian character, for not only is Edmund personable and apparently straightforward, but also he has been away from home for nine years past. Also true, Edmund's intrigue with the letter is clever. But as Robert Lindsay handles the stage business, Edmund's attempt to hide the letter from his father is so obvious that Gloucester ought to suspect something. Gloucester is so emotionally obtuse that he believes the son whom he does not know, rather than trust the noble son he does know. Like Lear, he becomes enraged when crossed. The text is slightly reordered her so that the dialogue builds to Gloucester's shouted "Give me the letter!" Within minutes, he believes Edgar an "Unnatural, detested, brutish villain!" Both Gloucester and Lear give themselves blindly into the hands of the very offspring who will betray them.

The camera cuts to Goneril's hall, where we see another side of

Lear, now living a life without crown and without responsibility. He
is kind, likeable, charming—the last a quality, as Stanley Wells suggests, "not often associated with Lear" (p. 353). His knights follow
him not because he lets them run riot but because they like him.
They laugh at his jokes and run to obey his orders. His treatment
of Kent-as-Caius is generous, and when the Fool enters, Lear hugs
him. We even see Lear feeding his horse sugar. As the scene develops,
it becomes clear that Lear commands affection and allegiance. Kent
and the Fool, in particular, are loyalty itself. As Kent, Colin Blakely's
square-faced honesty breathes out of him, and the furrowed expressions of John Hurt's Fool show that he is not trying to punish Lear
for rejecting Cordelia, as Frank Middlemass's Fool seems to be doing
in Miller's film, but gently bringing Lear to an understanding of the
consequences of his actions. Much of the Fool's part has been cut,
but enough remains to develop his caring attitude and the motif of
Lear's growing self-knowledge. The Fool's line "thou hadst little wit
in thy / bald crown when thou gav'st thy golden one / away" reminds
us of Lear's earlier act of self-deposition. This scene, in its general
effect, recalls the Lear we first saw, supported by the loving Cordelia.
As the Fool reveals to Lear his folly in giving his crown to Goneril
and Regan, and as Lear understands the depth of Goneril's betrayal,
Lear's natural goodness reasserts itself over his hardened heart: thinking of Cordelia, he mutters, "I did her wrong." As the scene ends,
Lear's fearful curse on Goneril draws from her a hardened, lined look
of hatred. She will be unrelenting in her attempt to reduce him to
nothing. What is the cause in nature that makes these hard hearts?

This question, cut from the film but posed in the action, focuses
one of the central themes of the play. In a world that values the
natural bonds between parent and child, ruler and subject, gods and
men, why does success attend those who break these bonds and why
do men allow evil to invade their hearts and turn them to stone?
Olivier's Lear returns again and again to the paradoxes of justice and
injustice that inhabit the film's innermost regions. Unlike Peter Brook,
for whom "'King Lear is not a play about justice, but about movement,'"[16] Elliott and Olivier concentrate on the tragic arc of Lear's
folly, confrontation with evil, and *anagnorisis*, with the resulting catharsis. In the opening scenes evil has an agreeable face: the direct
gaze of Goneril, the charming smile of Regan, the smooth brow of
Edmund. Indeed, one of the reviewers' complaints has been that this
Edmund is too "bland" (Wells's word). Yet up to a point the "sense
of ancient evil," as Sewall terms it (p. 6), came through. The last
scene excepted, the film points to man himself as the source of violence
and terror. With the division of the kingdom the "monsters of the
deep" rise to the surface. To enforce her dictatorial control, Goneril,
for example, humiliates her own father, who does not deserve her
rebuke. Rather than committing what Goneril calls "gross crimes,"
Lear rides his horse sedately into the hall, calls for dinner, and refuses

to let Oswald and his sarcastic smile insult him. The knights are under control; even at Lear's departure, they leave quietly (Brook's knights trashed the hall). As the action develops, Goneril becomes ever more contemptuous of Albany and lustful for Edmund, finally breaking the marital as well as the filial bond. That other monster Regan is all acquiescence, coyness, and affection with her father in the Court scene, but alone with Goneril after Lear has left, a sardonic, crooked smile accompanies her "He hath ever but slenderly known himself" (1.1.293–94). Later, at Gloucester's castle, she like her sister deliberately undercuts Lear's self-esteem: "I pray you, father, being weak, seem so" (2.4.203). Goneril arrives, and as each daughter reduces the number of retainers she is willing to house, Lear stands between them looking from one to the other as though seeking to find some way to escape an ambush. Wearing her snake-like necklace, Regan pitilessly concludes, "What need one?" Then, when Gloucester is about to be blinded, Regan spits in his face, rips hair from his beard. Her monstrousness becomes more clear when the wounded Cornwall, unable to lift himself off the floor, begs her to help him. Unmoved and unmoving, she communicates in an instant with a Gorgon stare her hatred of the man who stands between her and her lust for Edmund.

Until the moment of his death, when he realizes that Regan has betrayed him, Jeremy Kemp's Cornwall conveys the clearest possible sense of the implacability of evil. One will hardly encounter a more baleful expression than his when he is contemplating his revenges on Gloucester and when he observes Regan kissing Edmund goodbye: the dead eyes show no spark of feeling, the mouth is hard and sour. He is the very man—or demon—to perform the drama's single most grotesque act, and as he gouges out Gloucester's second eye, his face contorts with hideous pleasure. It is the only point in the action when he comes to life. This Cornwall is the earthly embodiment of the gods who kill us for their sport. The scene as a whole—the feral Regan urging, "Hang him instantly," the vicious Goneril exhorting, "Pluck out his eyes," the sadistic Cornwall exulting, "Out, vile jelly!"—concentrates part of Olivier's conception that "the play is obsessed with violence,"[17] but why men prey upon one another like this remains a mystery. And, though crass of sensibility and bumbling of mind, does Gloucester deserve such punishment?

If in Cornwall evil shows its face most directly, in Robert Lindsay's Edmund evil appears at its most deceptive. His soliloquies, addressed for the most part straight into the camera, reveal his scornful attitude toward the gods, his contempt for his father and brother, and his general cynicism, but he does not appear to be revengeful or malevolent. His is the coldest heart in the film. When Gloucester is about to go to Lear's aid, for example, he describes for Edmund the way Goneril and Regan have treated Lear. Edmund replies, "Most savage and unnatural!" (3.3.7), but his voice, absolutely composed even when he could have put on an act before his father, carries no exclamation point. Nothing brings him to life. He preys upon others but virtually without emotion. Until his death-bed repentance he is the epitome of the unfeeling egotist who perceives everything but understands nothing. Pursued by the lubricious Goneril and Regan, he fulfills Gloucester's description of the "lust-dieted man . . . that will not see / Because he does not feel" (4.1.67–69). His diabolical *sang-froid* permits his final act of cold cruelty, the execution of Lear and Cordelia: "To be tender-minded / Does not become a sword" (5.3.32–33). The final, most devastatingly brutal action results not at the hands of the pitiless gods, except insofar as they are within us. The main thrust of the film's vision of evil, then, does not include, except by implication in the last scene, a conception of some kind of cosmic, metaphysical evil. It is Edmund's frozen heart that ordains "the promis'd end" (5.3.263). He does feel compassion at Edgar's description of their father's death (he is human, after all), but it comes too late to save Lear and Cordelia. His change of heart enacts in little the massive transformation of Lear himself.

In Brook's film Paul Scofield was a Lear "more sinning than sinned against," as Richard Proudfoot puts the matter (p. 165), and in Miller's television film, "The real interest throughout the play," one reviewer wrote, "seems to be not in Lear's suffering, but in the character of his enemies."[18] Elliott and Olivier reverse these tendencies. The blinding of Gloucester does receive emphasis, it is true, but the film focuses on the pathos of Lear's suffering and subsequent change in attitude and understanding: the affecting sight, for example, of Lear the "poor, infirm, weak, and wretched old man" (3.2.20) ("wretched" was substituted for "despis'd") kneeling and praying in the storm, as he begins to understand that he has taken too little care of the poor, infirm, weak, and wretched. The first great culmination of pathetic feeling is the meeting of the mad Lear and the blind Gloucester, both of whom have endured betrayal of trust and now see the world feelingly. It takes place not, as in Brook's film, on a deserted Dover Beach, but under the branches of a huge oak[19] in a sunlit sylvan glade. In an obvious contrast to the somber stones that form the background for the opening scenes, the technicolor highlights the various shades of green appropriate to Lear's new sense of the natural feelings and relationships that give value to life.[20] The film specifically associates Lear at this point with the druid priests, who venerated the oak.[21] Lear becomes, in A. L. Owen's characterization of the druid, the "sage beneath the spreading oak": "It was under its sway and beneath the consecrated boughs of their oaks that, as [William Mason] says of them . . . 'the holy Druids / Lay rapt in moral musings'" (p. 172).[22] The flowers that encircle Lear's brow and neck substitute for the oak leaves that wreathed the head of the druid as he has sometimes been pictured.[23] Gone are the childish self-centeredness, the need to be catered to, the vain standing on ceremony, the self-pity. Though wandering and disoriented, he is at peace with himself. What anger he possesses he vents on the evils and injustices of the world. With his new-found wisdom he preaches to the suffering, bandaged Gloucester of the "sulphurous pit" of sexual appetite, the hypocrisy of the "rascal beadle," and materialism of man, which breaks "the strong lance of justice" (4.6.167), and he finally kisses the weeping old man, a kiss that forms a contrasting parallel to the Judas-kiss that Edmund planted on Edgar's brow as he urged his brother to escape the supposed wrath of their father. This world is a great stage of fools, but Lear's act partially redeems it, just as Cordelia "redeems nature from the general curse" (4.6.208) that Goneril and Regan have brought upon her. Having eaten the innards of a rabbit, drunk from nature's spring, and put on her garment under the sacred oak, Lear's "special relationship" with nature that is ascribed to the druids (Owen, p. 172) becomes a visual sign of his new understanding of human nature. "Thou must be patient," he tells Gloucester, now second only to Lear in depth of tragic feeling.[24] The oak tree, archetypal symbol of regeneration and immortality,[25] has replaced Stonehenge in the hearts of both Lear and Gloucester.

The most wrenching scenes, those between Lear and Cordelia, quickly follow. They provide the catharsis that Peter Brook avoided. Of Brook's intention in directing *King Lear*, Proudfoot writes, "The pain of change and loss was savagely inflicted and no cathartic consolation was allowed—the purging of pity and terror being curiously spoken of by both Brook and Marowitz not as the *aim* of tragedy, but as a *risk* to be avoided, a problem to be tackled. On no account must the shaken audience be allowed any reassurance before leaving the theatre" (pp. 165–66). No purging of emotions takes place at the end of either Brook's or Miller's film. By contrast, instead of cutting scenes and speeches that would increase the sense of pity, as Brook did, Elliott intensifies the pathos with such additions as Kent's arm encircling Cordelia after Lear's attack on her, Lear hugging the Fool at his first appearance, Gloucester giving the stocked Kent a drink from his flask, Edgar hunted by dogs at Stonehenge and breaking down in tears during his first soliloquy, the Fool shivering alone in the cold after Kent and Gloucester desert him, the mad Lear playing affectionately with a mouse, Cordelia kissing Kent in gratitude upon their reunion in her tent. Such expressions of sentiment prepare for the emotional reconciliation of Lear and Cordelia, he suffering in agony of remorse, she infinitely sympathetic and forgiving. His freshly shaven face suggests his new being. With white robe characteristic of the druid,[26] he has become the High Priest, the Wise Old Man. As she kneels at his bedside, her eyes full of love and tears, his new sense of justice tells him he deserves her cup of poison. The scene ends movingly with their mutual embrace. Grigori Kozintsev might well be describing this point in the film when he wrote that "the most powerful words in the whole tragedy" are Lear's "'Be your tears wet? Yes, faith'": "The tears, slowly running down Cordelia's cheeks, occupy no less a place in the space of tragedy than the darkness and fire of the apocalypse, the black whirlwind of the storm which was hurled down on the earth."[27] The poignant expression of loyalty, love, remorse, and forgiveness—the natural bonds—prepare us for the last scene. Their value is never denied.

Not that the audience is consoled in some simple way at the end of the film. Lear's speech about being God's spies may seem to offer solace, but it is absolutely negated by the fearful vision of the father and daughter lying dead on the altar stone at Stonehenge. The sight communicates what Jaspers calls the truth of tragedy: "the ultimate disharmony of existence."[28] If this scene of pain and suffering is the image of the "promis'd end," the injustice of the Last Judgment will provoke horror, rage, and despair. We have been subjected to the ultimate terror of tragedy; "The abyss," writes Joyce Carol Oates, "will always open for us [in tragedy], though it begins as a pencil mark, the parody of a crack; the shapes of human beasts—centaurs ["though women all above" (4.6.127)] and satyrs and their remarkable companions—will always be returning."[29]

All this is true. At the same time the scene of Lear's death is not nihilistic. Of Olivier leaning over Cordelia's body, Stanley Wells writes, "There is something celebratory about his concern for Cordelia, as if he rejoiced in his love for her even while grieving over her death" (p. 353). And though Lear berates the others as "men of stones," they are not. Kent and Edgar have suffered through their time of disguise, and even the mild Albany has become fully engaged and is strongly affected by what he sees. Lear himself has triumphed over his stony nature, discovering a meaning in a previously meaningless life. Oates' view of tragedy in general is true of this film: "Nihilism is overcome by the breaking down of the dikes between human beings, the flowing forth of passion" (p. 174). Lear dies bestowing a final kiss on Cordelia.

The cathartic effect of this film does its work in various ways. Some may feel that they are no longer quite so determinedly men of stone. Others may sense in themselves a new quality of resilience, a restored ability to cope with life. According to Roy Morrell, "Tragedy's function is to get under control life's most chaotic and difficult parts."[30] A great tragedy, he says, forces us "to live more complexly" (p. 26) by allowing us to overcome our old, lesser, insufficient selves. Our hearts hope, with Lear, that Cordelia lives. He thinks he hears her voice and he draws us in, but the iron calculus of tragedy reasserts itself in his "Thou'lt come no more, / Never, never, never, never, never!" Olivier's lengthening pauses between each "never" communicate the finality of Cordelia's death, reveal Lear's courageous acceptance of mortality, and compel us to let go the fantasy life of happy endings that Nahum Tate pandered to. The knowledge that the world is unjust and that we must die frees us from the bondage of our sentimental selves to live life more courageously, more vigorously. We are more ready.

The film ends as the camera retreats from the bodies of Lear and Cordelia, and we then recognize clearly for the first time that they are lying on the altar stone within the Stonehenge circle. Night closes in, mists blur the moon, and a ring of soldiers surround the stone, kneeling and saluting the pair with votive candles. Lear and Cordelia have become ritual sacrifices in a mystery. The scene answers Northrop Frye's reading of tragedy as "a mimesis of sacrifice."[31] The circle of mourners catches up the sense of communion, for the deaths have brought the survivors into a new unity. At the same time the lonely melancholy of the whistling wind between the great stone pillars (Angel in *Tess of the d'Urbervilles* called it "a very Temple of the Winds") makes one sense the force of the second side of ritual sacrifice: according to Frye, "the other [element] is propitiation, the sense that in spite of the communion the body belongs to another, a greater, a potentially wrathful power." When Lear is captured by the English forces, he tells Cordelia, "Upon such sacrifices . . . the Gods themselves throw incense" (5.3.20–21). He may mean, as Bradley said,[32] that the gods will be pleased with their renunciation of the world, but in his edition Muir states that the phrases seem to carry "an underlying suggestion of human sacrifice, which looks forward to the murder of Cordelia" (p. 200). The culminating shot of the Elliott-Olivier *King Lear* poses the ultimate problem of evil: What kind of gods are they who would throw incense upon such sacrifices as Lear and Cordelia?[33] How are we that are young to understand wrathful powers who would arrange a period so full of dread? If these stones, as Merlin is to have said, possess "a healing virtue against many ailments," the nature of that virtue remains a mystery.

King Lear is "the cruellest play," writes Frank Kermode, because it forces our assent to the proposition "that we can't count on divine or human justice to intervene in the worst moments of life."[34] The Elliott-Olivier film compels our acceptance of this fact, though not our acquiescence in its justice. At the same time this film reveals the transcendent power and value of the natural bonds—loyalty, love, forgiveness—that enable men to face the worst. Horror and sympathy, anger and courage, awe and pity—the film takes us through these emotions to an enlarged understanding of what it means to be in this world.

Notes

1. Charles Marowitz, "Lear Log," *Theatre at Work: Playwrights and Productions in the Modern British Theatre*, eds. Charles Marowitz and Simon Trussler (London, 1967), p. 135.

2. T. R. Henn, *The Harvest of Tragedy* (London, 1956), p. 154.

3. See Jack J. Jorgens, *Shakespeare on Film* (Bloomington, Ind., and London, 1977), pp. 236–37.

4. Maynard Mack, *King Lear in Our Time* (Berkeley and Los Angeles, 1965), pp. 20–21.

5. Mack, p. 30, and n. 76.

6. Benedict Nightingale, "Subtractions," *New Statesman*, 10 June 1983, found the RSC production of *King Lear* in 1982–83 possessed by "the ghost of Nahum Tate" (p. 26): "not for 150 years can the play's true pity and terror have been excised so cleanly" (p. 27).

7. T. D. Kendrick, *The Druids: A Study in Keltic Prehistory* (New York, 1966), p. 151, asserts, "There is one building that may very fairly be called a temple of druidism, and that is Stonehenge itself." Macready, in 1838, and Irving, in 1892, are among those who used Stonehenge, or at least, "druid circles," as the setting of some scenes in their productions of *King Lear* (George C. D. Odell, *Shakespeare from Betterton to Irving* [New York, 1920]), II, 210, 446.

8. Ward Rutherford, *The Druids and Their Heritage* (London and New York, 1978), p. 103, points to the mysterious nature of the Celtic gods during the Stone Age: "[Anne] Ross has drawn attention to the expression of 'withdrawn, inscrutable intensity' which characterizes almost all depictions of [Celtic] deities."

9. Gerald S. Hawkins, *Stonehenge Decoded* (Great Britain, 1966), p. 20.

10. Hawkins, pp. 32, 37. See also A. L. Owen's chapter "The Pomp of Bloody Altars" in *The Famous Druids: A Survey of Three Centuries of English Literature on the Druids* (Oxford, 1962).

11. Richard B. Sewall, *The Vision of Tragedy* (New Haven, 1959), p. 4.

12. Benny Green, "Television," *Punch*, 13 April 1983, p. 66.

13. 1.5.24. The Arden edition of *King Lear* (Cambridge, Mass.) is used throughout. All references are to the revised edition of 1953.

14. Benedict Nightingale, "Closed Circuits," *New Statesman*, 8 April 1983, p. 26.

15. Stanley Wells, "The Sweetness of Age," *TLS*, 8 April 1983, p. 353.

16. Brook's statement is quoted in Richard Proudfoot, "Peter Brook and Shakespeare," *Drama and Mimesis*, ed. James Redmond (Cambridge, London, and New York, 1980), p. 164.

17. This view of Olivier's was described by Michael Elliott at a discussion on the film on 4 May 1983, at the Museum of Broadcasting in New York City. My reference is Marion Perret, "The Making of *King Lear*," *SFNL*, 8, ii (April 1984), 7.

18. H. R. Woudhuysen, "An Interest in Evil," *TLS*, 1 October 1982, p. 1066.

19. Perret, p. 7, reports that "the scenery shopping list" included "a five-ton oak tree."

20. In contrast to Elliott and Olivier's treatment, Kozintsev wrote of his film of *King Lear*, "I refused to shoot the film in colour, as I didn't want to draw unnecessary attention to the environment ("'Hamlet' and 'King Lear': Stage and Film," *Shakespeare 1971*, eds., Clifford Leech and J. M. R. Margeson [Toronto and Buffalo, 1972], p. 195).

21. See T. D. Kendrick, pp. 123–24, 199–201. Kendrick quotes Pliny on the druids of Gaul: "They think that everything that grows on [the oak] has been sent from heaven and is proof that the tree was chosen by the god himself" (p. 89).

22. After the storm scenes and before the reappearance of the mad Lear, that other moral philosopher Edgar is shown lying against the trunk of this same oak, as the Old Man leads the blinded Gloucester towards Dover. All of Edgar's philosophizing here has been cut, the effect of which is to throw emphasis on Lear-as-druid in his later scene with Gloucester.

23. Stuart Piggott, *The Druids* (London, 1968), p. 168. Piggott's reference is to Meyrick and Smith's *Costume of the Original Inhabitants of the British Islands* (1815), plate X.

24. Elliott signals Gloucester's newly developed tragic sense in two ways, first by making him a kind of *memento mori*: at the film's start he is sensual man, but at the end the blood-soaked areas on the bandage around his head give him the aspect of death itself; second by using, for the only time in the film, the technique of superimposition to show the battle scenes taking place in Gloucester's mind. He has reached the point of understanding that ripeness is all.

25. J. E. Cirlot, *A Dictionary of Symbols*, trans. Jack Sage (New York, 1962), p. 328.

26. Piggott, p. 168, and plates 25 and 28.

27. Grigori Kozintsev, *King Lear: The Space of Tragedy: The Diary of a Film Director*, trans. Mary Mackintosh (Berkeley and Los Angeles, 1977), pp. 183–84.

28. Karl Jaspers, *Tragedy Is Not Enough*, trans. Harald A. T. Reich, et al. (London, 1953), p. 45.

29. Joyce Carol Oates, *The Edge of Impossibility: Tragic Forms in Literature* (New York, 1972), p. 8.

30. Roy Morrell, "The Psychology of Tragic Pleasure," *Essays in Criticism*, 6 (January 1956), 24.

31. Northrop Frye, *Anatomy of Criticism: Four Essays* (Princeton, 1957), p. 214.

32. A. C. Bradley, *Shakespearean Tragedy*, 2d ed. (London, 1964), p. 326.

33. Rutherford, p. 121, states that the druids' sacrifices must have been similar to those of the Aztecs: "proud and erect, . . . [those to be sacrificed] stretched out their bodies on the altar-stone to receive the knife's thrust." For the Celts, he says, "ascent to the throne must, therefore, have entailed tacit acceptance of this role as sacrificial offering on behalf of his people." Perhaps, but no sense of pride or acquiescence informs the end of *King Lear*.

34. Frank Kermode, "Why 'King Lear' Is the Cruellest Play," *The Listener*, 16 September 1982, p. 13.

OLIVIER'S *LEAR* AND THE LIMITS OF VIDEO
R. Alan Kimbrough

In the classroom as well as in the critical columns of both scholarly periodicals and the popular press, responsible commentary on a production of a script demands attention to the medium of that production. And to measure a production's success means to recognize the potential and the limitations of its medium. Commentary on Shakespeare productions has—for some time and with much astuteness—insisted on the inherent differences between stage and film. The borders between film and television are somewhat more blurred, and

R. Alan Kimbrough, "Olivier's *Lear* and the Limits of Video," in *Shakespeare on Television: An Anthology of Essays and Reviews*, ed. J. C. Bulman and H. R. Coursen (Hanover: University Press of New England, 1988), pp. 115–21.

the process of defining them often relies heavily on the inferential or inductive conclusions that comparisons between film and television productions of a single text invite. The widely disseminated BBC Shakespeare productions have provided ample material for such comparisons; the 1982–83 Granada Television production of Laurence Olivier's *King Lear* invites similar comparisons even more enticingly for several reasons. First, it follows two very important and highly praised film versions of *Lear*: Grigori Kozintsev's in 1970 and Peter Brook's in 1971. Second, its costs for film and video library acquisition are quite modest. And third, unlike many of the BBC productions, it has elicited considerable acclaim. The recent release of Akira Kurosawa's *Ran* only increases the invitation to compare film and video treatments of *Lear*.

Yet a rather simple test is surely in order. When a Shakespeare production—whether on stage, film, or television—has managed to breathe fresh life into a familiar script, making us aware of possibilities we had forgotten or never realized, making us notice details that had escaped our attention, making us rethink our interpretations of Shakespeare's text, we can usually point to several significant images that have jarred us out of complacency by their thematic or characterizing resonance. With Kozintsev, Brook, and Kurosawa, identifying such images is easy. The same cannot, I think, be said of Olivier's *Lear*. Why? Is the difference a result of the medium? I am very reluctant to answer in the affirmative. Indeed, I think we should resist any rapid conclusions about the difference between film and television as media for dramatic productions, especially of Shakespeare, that would result from contrasting Olivier's *Lear* with Kozintsev's, Brook's, or Kurosawa's.

Some critics' attention to Olivier's *Lear* would foster such comparisons. "Make no mistake about it, this is a 'King Lear' designed carefully for television, not for the theater," wrote John J. O'Connor (C20). Catherine Hughes labelled it "an ideal television adaptation" (112); Bill MacVicar found it "an uncommonly well thought-out and produced play for television" (69). And the reviewer for the *Library Journal* confidently predicted, "This award-winning production will no doubt become the standard against which all future Lears will be measured" (Hagloch 85).

As one might expect, most of the critical focus was on Olivier's performance and interpretation. The context—especially Olivier's age and his history of debilitating illness, not to mention his vast contributions to both theater and film throughout his long career—made the dominant raves predictable. But neither Olivier's acting nor that of his supporting cast is the issue here. Nothing suggests that the choice of medium determined the casting decisions (although a staged *Lear* would surely have been impossible for Olivier by 1982), nor has the choice of medium clearly determined the delivery of particular lines. Olivier himself, commenting on the difficulties he now finds in doing stage work, has said, "I don't see much difference between television and film, except that you do the television work in about a tenth of the time" (Cowie, *NYT* 25).

But one might be pardoned for thinking that the choice of medium is responsible for certain other features of the production. John Simon asked the question directly: "But is TV the right medium for this transcendent tragedy?" (68)[1] Simon's answer begs the question we are addressing, for he faults both film and television as media for *Lear*, insisting that the "living presences of great actors are needed, with just enough framing landscape and architecture, to convey the tremendous, brutal or noble, humanity of these personages, of this play. . . ." Benedict Nightingale goes much farther with two very apposite observations for the issue here, observations specific to this *Lear* but inviting extension to the medium generally:

> For instance, by focusing tight on faces and figures and treating even the lush English countryside as casually as any painted backdrop, [Michael Elliott's production] did much to solve the perennial problem of putting a non-naturalistic play on to a medium with an inbuilt bias toward naturalism. . . . We should have guessed that [Olivier] would score at precisely those points where his talent is supposedly weakest but TV strongest: those demanding contact and inwardness, telepathy and soul. (26)

These two issues deserve separate exploration.

The first—the medium's "inbuilt bias towards naturalism"—may be as true of film as it is of television. For some highly stylized theatrical devices, the distance of a stage is far more sympathetic and convincing than the sharply focussed, detailed clarity of either film or television. But setting aside the question of just how non-naturalistic *Lear* (or any other of Shakespeare's plays) is, we might still question Nightingale's implied prescription for success. He suggests that "a medium with an inbuilt bias towards naturalism" does well to obliterate or deemphasize the setting. The *Lear* films and much of what has succeeded on television strongly suggest otherwise. Kozintsev's rocky terrains and primitive castle interiors and Brook's frozen tundra show that naturalistic photography can work with enormous effect *if* the settings are right for the production. Much of what works well in Franco Zeffirelli's Shakespeare films also derives its impact from Zeffirelli's careful choice or construction of settings whose images will add substantially (in both senses of that word) to his productions. The BBC Shakespeare plays and Olivier's *Lear* alike suggest that the problems for television are not dissimilar. The choice or construction of setting becomes the issue. And the obviously fake—the built-in danger of nearly all non-contemporary settings, especially with limited budget studio sets—becomes only distraction when it is subjected to the clarity of the camera. Paradoxically, the dangers of stylization are less, for audiences can adjust to stylized conventions (witness Kurosawa's success). When the fake pretends to be real, the danger is far greater.

The studio "henge" and the bizarre costuming of Olivier's *Lear* demonstrate the danger all too painfully.[2]

Nightingale's second point—that television is strongest when "contact and inwardness" are demanded—reinforces the standard observations about television's sympathy for very close-range photography. The cause-effect that Marion Perret implies is typical: "Designed as a tv film rather than as a movie, [Olivier's *Lear*] was photographed mainly in closeup" (1). Tucker Orbison's question—"Is the persistent employment of the close-up a necessary concomitant of the television screen? (61)—thus rightly challenges one of the most widely held assumptions about television as a medium. It is true that the smallness of the television screen makes close-ups less intimidating and reduces their potential for the grotesque that can come from the hugely enlarged images of close-ups on a large film screen. But such close focus on faces carries the equal demand that the faces reveal character tellingly. And the close-ups of both Kozintsev and Brook—e.g., the numerous eyes, human and animal, in Kozintsev, the full frame face of Paul Scofield's Lear in Brook—say more than the close-ups in Olivier's *Lear*. The casting decisions become crucial, and filmmakers like Kozintsev and Brook have carefully sought out the faces that their cameras can capture in significant images. The faces are film faces. Despite the extensive film and television experience of many actors in the cast (particularly John Hurt, Leo McKern, and Diana Rigg, in addition to Olivier himself), Olivier's *Lear* gives us the faces of stage actors trained in using broad gesture and vocal inflection for expression, with far less reliance on the nuances of facial expression that theater audiences are too far away to see.

Yet generalization about televised Shakespeare is at best suspect, just as generalization about Shakespeare on film can be very wrongheaded. Nearly a decade ago, Jack Jorgens pointed out the weakness in what had then already become semi-established ways of categorizing Shakespeare on film. Citing Roger Manvell, Donald Skoller, and Peter Woolen, Jorgens noticed that critics "often sort out Shakespeare films by measuring their relative distance from the language and conventions of the theatre." And he labelled the principal categories of these "modes" as the "theatrical," the "realist," and the "filmic." Citing Stanley Wells and Thomas Clayton, he noticed a parallel categorization for "three means of treatment which describe a film's relative distance from the original text—presentation, interpretation, and adaptation." Such categories can be applied to Shakespeare on television with equal ease. And the Olivier *Lear* blends—in Jorgen's terms—theatrical and realist modes in a presentation of Shakespeare's play.

In an interview with Ronn Smith, Roy Stonehouse (the production designer of the Olivier *Lear*) partially confirmed this labelling of the production's mode as intentionally and self-consciously "realistic":

Television traditionally approaches the Bard in one of two ways: either in a very stylized manner . . . or in a very realistic way. The latter, however, is usually shot on location and ends up looking rather ordinary. It's very hard to suggest period on location. . . . Had we filmed *King Lear* on location, the finished product would have been judged as a film. It would also have been compared to other films of Shakespeare's plays. As it is, this production will be judged on whether it succeeds as Shakespeare-in-a-studio. (Smith 12)

Stonehouse repeatedly stresses this *Lear*'s studio aspect, detailing the four composite sets used in the three-and-a-half-week shooting schedule and explaining the difficulties of making anything look old on television:

Television lighting enhances colors, and the high quality camera makes everything look beautiful. . . . We therefore took particular pains to stress and age the *Lear* sets. This, too, gives a certain authenticity to the realism we were after. I say "realism," but what I should say is "stylized realism." It isn't real in the sense that it can be documented. It's more like an impression of what we *think* was real. (Smith 12)

As I have indicated above, the "authenticity" Stonehouse was aiming for proved highly elusive indeed. The clarity of close-range television photography can only subvert such sets, self-consciously "aiming for impression rather than accuracy" (Perret 7). Robert Brustein's assessment was more blunt: "Reputedly the most expensive production ever made for British TV, this *King Lear* looks tacky" (26). But the chief point underlying Stonehouse's comments underscores the need to avoid any broad generalizations about television as a medium for Shakespeare based exclusively on this or similar productions. Televised "Shakespeare-in-a-studio" does not equal all of "Shakespeare on TV."

Peter Cowie points to yet another aspect of Olivier's *Lear* that seems significant. Observing that this production "looks very much a collaborative effort," he expands:

Michael Elliott, the stage director known recently for his brilliant work at Manchester's Royal Exchange, discussed with Olivier and the designer, Roy Stonehouse, an abridged and visually persuasive version of the play that could grip the attention of TV viewers. (*Sight and Sound* 78)[3]

I find Cowie's characterization of the production very telling, for if I read it correctly, it accounts far better than the limitations of the studio for the major disappointments of the production. And I trace those disappointments to what I see as a severely modest—if not indeed patronizing—notion of what could persuade and "grip the attention of TV viewers." The result is simply a literalism that does not warrant inflation as "realism" or "naturalism." And the literalism is patently obvious both visually and verbally.

Visually, the production's camera work fosters stagnation and suggests a directorial vacuum. The shooting is predominantly close range and straight angle, with predictable zooming in for the soliloquies (Edmund's "Thou, nature" directly into the camera). Reaction shots are rare; when the cameras do cut away from the speaker we are hearing, they usually focus on the person being referred to in the speech. The few overhead shots (e.g., the initial establishing of the much-criticized pseudo-Stonehenge setting) are clichés. Imaginative use of cutting is nearly nonexistent. And all too often the entire background is obliterated in the standard shadows of soap opera, depriving speakers (or their speeches) of significant social and dramatic context.

Productions of *Lear* must always wrestle with the tensions between the public-political and the private-domestic tragedies bound together in Lear's fall. It *may* be true that the small screen is inherently more hospitable to a focus on the private, with the vast social panorama of, say, Kozintsev's *Lear* requiring the large screen, even the enlarged large screen of cinemascope. But Peter Brook has shown that film can capture the inner turmoil and psychological disintegration of Lear with striking visual force. In the Olivier *Lear*, the entire burden of such revelation is put on Olivier's shoulders, or, more precisely, on his voice and—to a lesser extent—on his face. In other words, the television viewer's experience is markedly like that of the theater viewer's, except not live and at closer range. The cameras for this production merely record instead of helping to interpret. And one looks in vain for anything beyond the most literally obvious (the 900 gallons of rain, for instance, or the notorious addition of stage business requiring the mad Lear to disembowel a rabbit and eat its viscera raw) that would suggest any affinity with Kozintsev's *sine qua non* for filming Shakespeare:

> The problem is not one of finding means to speak the verse in front of the camera, in realistic circumstances ranging from long-shot to close-up. *The aural has to be made visual.* The poetic texture itself has to be transformed into a visual poetry, into the dynamic organization of film imagery. (Cited by Jorgens, 10 n29; emphasis added.)

In a word, the Olivier *Lear* is simply dated.[4] Part of the evolution of television can be charted by paying attention to the shift from aural to visual, reflected in the ratio between what is thoroughly intelligible to a non-seeing listener and what requires attention to the visual images on the screen. (This evolution reinforces the earlier suggestion that the differences between film and television are becoming fewer and fewer.) For all their differences, both Kozintsev and Brook use frequent and lengthy shots with no dialogue at all. The signifying becomes exclusively visual. The same cannot be said of the Olivier *Lear*.

Despite some abridging, the Olivier script remains almost slavishly faithful to Shakespeare's text. Only three scenes (III.i, IV.iii, and IV.iv) have been cut entirely. On a few occasions (III.iii.36–60; III.vii.1–27; IV.vi.70–80; V.i.38–69; and V.iii.152–75) the sequence of lines and speeches has been modified. Most of the other cuts—some of the Fool's songs, Edgar's asides in IV.i, otherwise without observable pattern—seem to have been motivated principally by a desire to keep the video at about two and a half hours rather than by any coherent or consistent interpretation of character. Olivier himself is on record as saying, "I don't think the medium will hold the interest any longer [than a little over two hours]" (Cowie, *NYT* 25).[5] Teachers looking for a production that students can follow easily in their texts will be pleased, particularly since the visual usually does little more than illustrate or duplicate the verbal and students miss very little by keeping their eyes on their texts. Mindless fidelity and simplistic clarity determine all. The words are relentless, and the acting depends far more on actors' voices than on their faces or bodies. Since the screen usually shows little other than a close shot of the speaker's face, visual attention often becomes superfluous. On only three occasions do the words stop for any significant length of time: at IV.vi.80, for the crudely sensational rabbit-gutting incident and the visual substitute for the description Cordelia gives of the mad Lear in the excised IV.iv (with "Come o'er the bourn, Bessy, to me" reassigned from III.vi to Lear here; cf. Cordelia's "singing aloud" at IV.iv.2); early in V.ii for a tedious overlay curiously allowing us to see both the blind Gloucester and fragments of the battles he can only hear; and in V.iii for the obligatory but dull fight between Edgar and Edmund.

By way of contrast (although still with a largely uncut script in a studio production) I would point to the imaginative use of the medium in the opening of V.v in the BBC *Richard II*. For that soliloquy, director David Giles used his medium to obtain advantages not available in the theater, showing Richard's protracted imprisonment and torture by splitting the speech into segments and indicating the passage of time between segments. The device gives us glimpses of Richard's progressive enlightenment and ennoblement, i.e., his growth in tragic stature. And the very adroit use of the crucifix on the cell wall and the shadows of the prison bars work to pick up and affirm the many religious images elsewhere in the script that encourage serious attention to Richard as martyr and Richard as God's anointed king. In that segment we come far closer to seeing some of television's capacity as a medium for Shakespeare than we ever do in Olivier's *Lear*.

When I try to remember televised productions of other Renaissance plays that have succeeded powerfully, I immediately think of the 1970 BBC telecast of Marlowe's *Edward II* (shown in the U.S. in the fall of 1975 as part of the PBS "Classic Theater" series, originating from Boston's WGBH), a gripping production in a style very different from that of Olivier's *Lear* or the BBC Shakespeare series. Featuring Ian McKellen and the Prospect Theater Company and originally designed for the 1969 Edinburgh Festival, the production was filmed in London's Piccadilly Theater and made no attempt to disguise its "theatrical" mode. Yet director Toby Robertson was able to make Marlowe's tragedy visually compelling and convincing. Such a production reminds us that televised Shakespeare can admit a greater variety than we have seen recently, particularly if we seek to delineate the effects that a medium may have on productions. And it may be fruitful, too, to extend this investigation to telecasts of non-Renaissance plays that have worked well on the small screen.

The history of Shakespeare in the theater would suggest we have seen only the beginnings of television's potential as a medium for creative and illuminating productions of Shakespeare. The limits of video are scarcely to be defined by Olivier's *Lear*, and as we try to answer questions about the different necessities imposed by the media of television and film, the data available today may make inductive answers still exceedingly premature.

Notes

1. One answer to Simon's question appears in Benny Green's 13 April 1983 review of Olivier's *Lear* for *Punch*: "*King Lear* is one of those big plays which will not be squeezed into a small box. Reduced, as it must be by television, to spacial bankruptcy, it cannot meet its emotional commitments. . . " ("Television" 66, quoted by Orbison 68, n12).

2. But see Stephen Urkowitz's persuasive praise for the leather butcher's apron Cornwall puts on to gouge out Gloucester's eyes (3). I would consider that a notable exception to the rule; Urkowitz, by contrast, maintains, "The dress always seems to fit the action."

Tucker Orbison's explication of the Stonehenge setting (particularly its druidical significance, reinforced by the oak tree and its leaves later in the production) is surely among the more elaborate attempts to justify this production's sets.

3. See, too, Lloyd Rose's note—on the authority of David Plowright (Granada Television's managing director and Olivier's brother-in-law)—that Olivier and Elliott "worked out the production's concept together and collaborated in editing the text" (92).

4. Stanley Wells' review suggests that the production, at least its sets "in the pictorial tradition of the nineteenth century," is dated even in terms of the theater: "Irving and Wolfit would have been at home in this setting" (353).

5. See Richard Corliss: "Olivier has pruned the text significantly but fairly" (77). Joseph Sobran, on the other hand, sees a more pointed result—an "ingratiating" Lear—from the omission of "some of Lear's more savage lines" (56). Close examination of the cuts would not suggest such an intention, unlike the deliberate excising of Hal's savagery in Olivier's *Henry V* film.

Bibliographic Note: Articles cited in essays by Cowie, Orbison, Perret, and Ronn Smith are reprinted in Appendix. Reviews are listed in Select Bibliography. For Jorgens, see Shakespeare on Film *(Bloomington: Indiana University Press, 1977).*

"GIVE ME THY HAND": MANUAL GESTURE IN THE ELLIOTT-OLIVIER *KING LEAR*
Frank Occhiogrosso

King Lear is, among other things, a play about taking and giving, and therefore it is not surprising to find it filled with references to the hands. Goneril says, in this context, "I must change names at home and give the distaff / Into my husband's hands" (4.2.17–18).[1] Likewise, Cordelia refers to "that lord whose hand shall take my plight" (1.1.103), and Burgundy, desirous of gaining such a prize and all that goes with it, says "here I take Cordelia by the hand" (1.1.245). But if hands are the medium of exchange for things which are sought (like power, land, blessings, a loving touch), they are also the means whereby things which are definitely not desired (a slap, a murderous blow, a mutilation) are also delivered. In such instances characters are besought to refrain from giving with their hands: "Hold your hand, my lord!" (3.7.73), cries Cornwall's servant as he sees his master putting out Gloucester's eyes; "to let these hands obey my blood" (4.2.64), says Albany as he forcibly restrains himself from laying violent hands upon his treacherous wife, Goneril; "With robber's hands my hospitable favors / You should not ruffle" (3.6.41–42), says Gloucester to Regan after she has rudely plucked his beard; "Thou rascal beadle, hold thy bloody hand!" (4.6.162), says Lear, as he sees in his deranged yet piercing imagination still another image of the violent and unjust laying on of hands that is so frequent an occurrence in this play.

But by far the greatest number of references to the hands in *King Lear* are to hands as a means of making connection, union, a bond, and that is why the single most frequently recurrent line in the play, in one variant form or another, is "Give me thy hand." Characters seek, more than anything else in this play, to be related, attached, linked to one another, though they are as often rebuffed in these attempts as they are accepted. They therefore seek that which is the traditional sign of such connection, namely, each other's hands. "Give me your hand" (3.1.51), says the Gentleman to Kent, seeking a pledge of trust from one with whom he would join in a league to aid the outcast king. And Kent gives him his hand. But on another occasion Gloucester says to Lear, "O, let me kiss that hand!" (4.6.134), only to have the hand snatched away from him as Lear gives the celebrated reply, "Let me wipe it first; it smells of mortality" (4.6.135). "Hold your hand in benediction o'er me" (4.7.58), says Cordelia as she seeks to be reinstated in the good graces of the king her father. (But, "Let go my hand" (4.6.27), says blind Gloucester as, having been led to the brink of the cliff by Edgar, he seeks to break his union with human-

---

Frank Occhiogrosso, "'Give Me Thy Hand': Manual Gesture in the Elliott-Olivier *King Lear*," *Shakespeare Bulletin* 2, no. 9 (May/June 1984): 16–19.

ity.) Lear, when he sees what appears to him to be (and is) a combination created against him by his two ungrateful daughters, says "O, Regan, will you take her by the hand?" (2.4.193). And Goneril, in mock surprise that this sign of a sealed union with her sister should be hateful to him, replies. "Why not by the hand, sir? How have I offended?" (2.4.194). Old Gloucester, deprived of his eyes, seeks to replace them with his hands and thereby to restore the bond with his son Edgar whom he has cast out: "Might I but live to see thee in my touch, / I'd say I had eyes again" (4.1.23–24).

It echoes like a refrain throughout the play: "Give me thy hand" (3.4.41), says Kent to the Fool as he tries to get them both into the hovel and out of the wind and rain; "Give me your hand, I'll lead you to some biding" (4.6.226–227), says Edgar to Gloucester as he seeks to bring him over the heath to Dover and safe haven; "Give me your hand" (4.6.25); "Give me your hand" (4.6.289); "Away, old man; give my thy hand" (5.3.5); "Give me thy hand" (5.3.7). Human beings are, early and often in this play, cast adrift to wander the world's storm-blasted heath; they are, in a variety of senses, in the dark; they are, literally as well as figuratively, out in the cold. They therefore have to grope their way, hands outstretched, towards one another and the warmth of human contact, towards the restoration of those natural bonds of relationship that have been so rudely severed by unnatural and often bloody hands.

In the film of *King Lear* directed by Michael Elliott and starring Laurence Olivier, this symbolic use of the hands in Shakespeare's play is demonstrated through the extensive use and variety of manual gestures interpolated into so many of the film's scenes by the actors. These gestures are the visual presentation of what the film's script—the play's text—is constantly telling us the characters' hands are doing, namely, seeking and making or withholding and denying human contact.

In the film's opening sequence we see, first in long shot and then closer and closer, the Stonehenge-like circle of standing stones outside of which Colin Blakely as Kent, Leo McKern as Gloucester, and Robert Lindsay as Edmund are making political and domestic small talk as they await the king's entrance. Then, as the trumpet sounds announcing Lear's approach, they turn to enter the inner circle. But as they do so, the camera, in middle shot, catches Gloucester turning back to Edmund and holding up his hand in a gesture of arrest. It suggests a forestalling of Edmund's eager advance into the light, into the center of things (which advance he so noticeably desires), a denial of contact or community based perhaps on his father's feeling that Edmund, as a bastard, is an inappropriate figure on the scene. And I find that arresting gesture doubly significant because it will be repeated, by Lear and others, throughout the production.

The court entrance comes next, with special emphasis, in middle and close shot, upon the entrance of Goneril and Albany and then

Regan and Cornwall. Then follows a deep-focus shot in which Olivier, as Lear, enters with his right arm around and appearing to lean upon Anna Calder-Marshall as Cordelia, while with his left hand he gently touches her cheek in a gesture of paternal affection. He then seats himself upon his throne and proposes the love test, at which point Dorothy Tutin as Goneril steps forward upon Lear's command to speak. But before she can speak, Olivier makes a gesture with his hand that stops her: he points downward, to the map of the kingdom which has been spread at their feet. Goneril kneels, kisses the map, makes her speech, and only then does she kiss the hand that Lear now holds out to her. The pattern is repeated when, a moment later, Diana Rigg as Regan steps forth. She reaches for Lear's hand, takes it, moves it to her lips, but then stops, kneels, and kisses the map first; then she raises his outstretched hand to her lips, following her sister's example. The whole sequence suggests Lear's priorities: he'll accept displays of affection from his children only after they have acknowledged his power, authority, and largesse. And perhaps the director, at the same time, makes a larger suggestion to us by means of this series of forestalling gestures, namely, that in both families, Gloucester's and Lear's, affectionate parental contact is withheld from, even denied to, some of the children, and this withholding or denial is at least partial cause of the villainy those children will soon display, once power has been given into their hands.

It is noteworthy, furthermore, that there is no withholding or forestalling of affectionate contact in the case of Cordelia; Olivier's manual gestures towards her, as noted above, seemingly make clear the unqualified closeness of father and favorite daughter. And yet, once she has failed his test, he uses another manual gesture to indicate the breaking of that bond: it is a quick waving of the hand, an evident gesture of dismissal, which Olivier repeats a moment later when he banishes Kent, repeats again when he offers Cordelia to Burgundy (who likewise rejects her), and repeats yet once more when, France having taken her by the hand, Lear seems to include them both in a final gesture of good riddance.

Having established visually through manual gesture a mode of relationship to his favorite daughter (at least until she loses his favor), Olivier's Lear takes up that same mode, and through the same gestures, when the Fool replaces Cordelia in the play. In several sequences we see Olivier with his arm around the shoulders of John Hurt as the Fool, leaning upon the Fool as he did upon Cordelia, and touching him with his free hand. And the Fool, like Cordelia, returns these gestures of affection. He does so in the scene with Kent and Goneril; he does so again as he is leaving Goneril's house with Lear; he does so repeatedly in the several scenes on the heath in the storm. In fact, the Fool's relationship to Lear, made manifest to us through his use of his hands, is such a dependent one, that it is his hands, more than anything else about him, which hold our attention in his (the Fool's) final scene. As Gloucester and Edgar bundle the sleeping king onto the cart that will carry him to Dover, the camera cuts to the Fool still sitting in the straw in the hovel. Though he is silent, his hands are shaking furiously, and they continue to shake as the camera pulls away in a withdrawing dolly shot. The effect of the dolly shot is to show the Fool being left behind; the effect of his constantly trembling hands is to show not only that he is cold but also that the essential connecting tie to his beloved master has been cut and he is now literally out of touch with the one whom he held dearest.

The motif of hands reaching out in supplication, seeking aid in the midst of the disorientation of loss or pain, is of course recurrent throughout the sequence of scenes involving the blinded Gloucester. One of its most notable manifestations occurs when David Threlfall, as Edgar, leads his blind father to a place where they can rest momentarily on their journey to Dover. At this moment it is as if Gloucester recalls his earlier line about Edgar: "Might I but live to see thee in my touch / I'd say I had eyes again" (4.1.23–24), for, as they sit talking, father to as yet unrecognized son, Gloucester reaches forth his hands and touches Edgar's face. As the camera shifts from middle shot to a close-up of Gloucester's face, we read there unmistakably the signs of recognition (although the signs are apparent only for a moment, after which the ensemble is broken up and we see no further sign of recognition on Gloucester's part until Edgar tells us, much later on, of his revelation of himself to his father and its result). Though we may question somewhat the believability of this bit of business— Gloucester develops blind man's hands awfully fast—nevertheless, it has an appropriateness in this particular production, in which repeated use is made of the hands as means of human contact and connection, or in this case, even identification.

This motif, namely of the hands used to identify, to attempt to make contact with one long lost, is repeated shortly thereafter in the scene in which another blind father is reunited with *his* outcast child. As Cordelia leans over her waking father, Lear reaches out his hands toward her face. Then, as consciousness and memory come to him more fully, he holds his hands before him and gazes at them, saying, "I will not swear these are my hands" (4.7.55). And then, in a shot that recalls Gloucester's similar gesture earlier, Lear feels his own face in an effort to recognize and identify himself. Cordelia then kneels, takes her father's face in her hands, and says, "O, look upon me, sir, / And hold your hand in benediction o'er me" (4.7.57–58). There follows a sequence in which Lear tenderly takes Cordelia's face in his hands as he asks her forgiveness. His hands have now gone beyond identification or recognition; instead, they are making clearly visible the restoration of that loving bond broken earlier as lost father reaches out to lost child and finds her even as he finds himself.

The final scene to which I would call attention occurs toward the end of the film. With a superb eye for the symmetry of dramatic design, the director has brought us back to that set with which the production began, that Stonehenge-like circle of standing stones. Into the midst of that circle come the white-robed Lear and Cordelia, prisoners of the triumphant Edmund, who orders his soldiers to take them away to prison. But to prevent them from doing so, Lear holds up his manacled hands in one last defiant (and effective) gesture of forestalling, and then, just as quickly, he drops those hands around the head and shoulders of Cordelia, so that she is literally locked in his embrace. He says:

> Have I caught thee?
> He that parts us shall bring a brand from heaven,
> And fire us hence like foxes.
>
> (5.3.21–23)

As the two go off, Lear hovers over and leans about Cordelia, his arms and hands about her neck and shoulders just as at the beginning. The loving bond between father and favorite daughter is once again as strong as it was initially, and the sign of this renewed relationship is the return of the series of manual gestures just described.

Let me conclude with a couple of disclaimers. This essay does not attempt to make an exaggerated claim for the centrality of hand imagery in *King Lear*. Though there is a definite pattern of such imagery in the play, it is not so obvious as, for example, the much-commented-upon eye and sight pattern. Nor do I attempt to argue there are *more* references to hands in *King Lear* than in any other Shakespearean play. Although there are nearly forty such references in *Lear*, a quick check of the concordance reveals an even higher number in several other plays. Nor do I wish to claim, finally, that there is anything extraordinary about the use of manual gesture in this particular film. Anyone who has any familiarity with drama, on stage or screen, knows how essential to an actor his hands are—What equipment do most actors have besides their voices, eyes, and hands?—to make his character's feelings felt effectively by the audience. What this paper does argue is this: that the pattern of hand imagery in *King Lear* is especially appropriate to the play's concern with human relationships, human bonds, and the making, breaking, and restoring of same, and that the film that Michael Elliott has made with Laurence Olivier demonstrates awareness of this important motif by its careful and original attention to the details of manual gesture in its overall design. So many of the characters in *King Lear* are saying in one way or another, "Give me thy hand"; in the Elliott-Olivier film, hands are given or taken or sought or withheld in accord with this repeated request.

Notes

1. All references are to the Signet edition of *King Lear*, ed. Russell Fraser (New York: New American Library, 1963).

Select Bibliography of Reviews of the BBC and Granada Productions of *King Lear*

Andreae, Christopher. "Laurence Olivier's Lear—A Commanding, Detailed Study." *Christian Science Monitor*, 2 May 1983, p. 14.

Brustein, Robert. "Olivier's Lear." *The New Republic*, 6 June 1983, pp. 26–28.

Church, Michael. "Dare to be Square." *The Times Educational Supplement* (London), 8 April 1983, p. 19.

Corliss, Richard. "Lord Larry's Crowning Triumph." *Time*, 16 May 1983, p. 77.

Cushman, Robert. "Every Inch a King." *The Observer* (London), 10 April 1983, p. 29.

Hackett, Dennis. "Pride and Pathos." *London Times*, 20 September 1982, p. 9.

Hagloch, Susan B. "Audiovisual Reviews: *King Lear*." *Library Journal*, 1 October 1985, p. 85.

Hughes, Catharine. "British Television: As They Like It." *America*, 10 September 1983, p. 112.

Kroll, Jack, with Rita Dallas. "Return of the Prodigal King." *Newsweek*, 8 November 1982, p. 105.

MacVicar, Bill. "Raging at the Dying of the Light." *Maclean's*, 21 November 1983, p. 69.

Nightingale, Benedict. "Closed Circuits." *New Statesman*, 8 April 1983, p. 26.

O'Connor, John J. "TV: A No-Nonsense *King Lear*." *New York Times*, 18 October 1982, Sec. C, p. 13.

Rose, Lloyd. "A Winter's Tale." *Atlantic*, February 1984, pp. 90–92.

Rosenfeld, Megan. "Pride, Betrayal and Wisdom." *Washington Post*, 18 October 1982.

Seebohn, Caroline. "Blood, Frailty and Brilliance." *Wall Street Journal*, 23 January 1984, p. 20.

Shales, Tom. "*King Lear* Without Peer." *Washington Post*, 26 January 1984.

Simon, John. "Is TV Big Enough for Olivier's Lear?" *Vogue*, January 1984, p. 68.

Smith, Cecil. "*Lear:* Miller's Fond Farewell." *Los Angeles Times,* 18 October 1982, p. 8.

Sobran, Joseph. "Lear's Show." *National Review,* 9 March 1984, pp. 55–56.

Urkowitz, Steven. "*King Lear* Without Tears." *Shakespeare on Film Newsletter* 7, no. 2 (April 1983): 2.

————. "Lord Olivier's *King Lear.*" *Shakespeare on Film Newsletter* 8, no. 1 (December 1983): 1, 3.

Wells, Stanley. "The Sweetness of Age." *Times Literary Supplement,* 8 April 1983, p. 353.

Woudhuysen, H. R. "An Interest in Evil." *Times Literary Supplement,* 1 October 1982, p. 1066.

Index

ACTER (Alliance for Creative Theatre, Education, and Research), 62, 108
Adamov, Arthur: *Invasion*, 186
Alexander, Peter, 163 n.47, 172 n
Allen, Michael J. B., 164 n.12
Allen, Sheila, 62
Andrew, Dudley, 205 n.3
Andrews, Harry, 194
Aubrey, John, 216
Ayckbourn, Alan: *Absurd Person Singular*, 209

Barge, Gillian, 76, 167
Barton, John, 106, 123, 124, 125, 144–45, 164n.1, 165nn. 1, 2, and 17
Bateman, Geoffrey, 168
Bazin, André, 199–200, 205nn. 2, 5, and 6
BBC (British Broadcasting Corporation) Television production of *Hamlet*, 16
BBC Television production of *King Lear*, 20, 41, 42–50, 52, 56, 59, 68, 75–84, 86–87, 89, 90, 97–101, 112–16, 118, 119, 121, 122, 128–31, 134, 147–52, 157, 158, 163n.47, 167, 172–85, 190, 205, 206, 207, 208, 209–11, 213, 214nn. 1, 3, 8, 11, and 12, 227, 228, 232
Beckerman, Bernard, 161n.6
Bevington, David, 17, 41, 95, 122, 127, 160n.5, 161nn. 7 and 13, 163n.46, 164n.8
Bhagavad Gita, 183
Bianculli, David, 205, 206
Birch, David C., 214n.4
Bird, John, 129, 148, 167
Blakely, Colin, 102, 168, 189, 192, 219, 235
Blethyn, Brenda, 43, 148, 167

Bloom, Allan, 161n.14
Boose, Linda E., 24–25, 26, 30, 31, 40–41, 59, 158, 161nn. 4–10, 162nn. 27 and 45, 164n.8, 165n.13
Booth, Stephen, 65, 135, 139–40, 143–44, 163nn. 6, 7, and 8, 165nn. 1, 5, 6, 7, 15, and 16
Bradley, A. C., 23, 30, 31, 161nn. 1 and 3, 224, 226n.32
Brien, Alan, 215
Bronson, Bertrand H., 162n.28
Brook, Peter, 18–19, 61, 68, 90, 163n.1, 164n.14, 190, 200, 215, 216, 218, 219, 221, 222, 225n.16, 227, 228, 229, 231
Brooks, Cleanth, 160n.4
Brown, John Russell, 32, 162n.33
Brown, Tim, 167
Brustein, Robert, 230
Bullough, Geoffrey, 28, 29, 161n.18, 162nn. 19, 20, 21, 22, 23, 24, and 25, 163n.2
Bulman, James C., 211, 226n
Burge, Stuart, 204
Burgess, John, 108, 110

Calder-Marshall, Anna, 51, 153, 168, 189, 192, 236
Calderwood, James, 136, 140, 165nn. 2 and 8
Campbell, Norman, 210
Cariou, Len, 210
Cary, Cecile W., 205n.10
Charney, Maurice, 15, 160n.1, 208
Cirlot, J. E., 226n.25
Clayton, Thomas, 229
Cleese, John, 208
Cobb, Lee J., 142
Coleridge, Samuel Taylor, 23
Cook, Hardy M., 197–205

Cooke, Alistair, 207
Corliss, Richard, 233n.5
Coursen, H. R., 205, 205n.10, 226n
Cowie, Peter, 163n.50, 187–93, 228, 230, 232
Cox, Brian, 168
Crosse, Gordon, 167, 196
Culler, Jonathan, 160n.4
Curry, Julian, 167
Cushman, Robert, 190

Davenport, Nigel, 209
Dean, John, 176
Dessen, Alan C., 16, 17, 109, 160nn. 3 and 5, 162n.44, 164n.2
Dews, Peter, 210
Dickens, Charles: *Bleak House*, 206; *Hard Times*, 186; *Nicholas Nickleby*, 209
Dieterle, William, 204
Donne, John, 39
Dove, John Roland, 23, 26, 27, 30, 31, 38, 161nn. 2, 11, and 12, 162nn. 26 and 41, 163n.49
Druids, 131, 152, 215, 216, 221–22, 225nn. 7, 8, 10, and 21, 226nn. 23 and 33, 233n.2. *See also* Stonehenge
Dunaway, Faye, 189
Durbach, Errol, 166n.1
Dyer, Christine, et al.: *Coronation Street*, 188

Edinburgh Festival (1969), 232
Egan, Robert, 93, 94, 95, 111, 141, 164nn. 1, 3, 5, 6, and 10, 165n.9
Elizabeth I, 26
Elliott, Michael, 20, 50, 60, 101, 116, 119, 120–21, 131, 152, 167, 185, 188, 191, 192, 194–205, 211, 213, 215–16, 219, 221, 222, 224, 225n.20, 226n.24, 230, 233n.3, 234–39
Euripedes: *Hippolytus*, 216

Fabyan, Robert, 161n.18
Fenwick, Henry, 163n.47, 172–85
Flett, Sharry, 210
Folio (1623), 19, 37, 40, 41, 67, 72, 75, 91, 101, 112, 127, 138, 142–43, 145, 146, 162n.31, 163nn. 4, 5, and 48, 164n.2. *See also* Quarto (1608)

Foreman, Walter C., Jr., 142, 165n.10
Fraser, Russell, 239n.1
Frost, William, 164n.3
Frye, Northrop, 224, 226n.31
Furness, H. H., 164n.11

Gamble, Peter, 23, 26, 27, 30, 31, 38, 161nn. 2, 11, and 12, 162nn. 26 and 41, 163n.49
Gardner, Helen, 162n.28
Gendel, Morgan, 214n.2
Geoffrey of Monmouth, 28, 161n.18, 216
Gielgud, John, 142
Giles, David, 211, 232
Goldman, Michael, 15, 160n.2
Goldring, Beth, 163n.48
Gorrie, John, 211
Granada Television production of *King Lear*, 20, 41, 50–60, 68, 84–90, 101–4, 112, 116–21, 122, 128, 131–34, 147, 152–57, 158, 167–68, 172, 185–98, 211, 213–14, 227, 233n.3
Grant, Lee, 206
Granville-Barker, Harley, 31, 91, 92–93, 162n.29, 164nn. 1 and 4
Gray, Hugh, 205n.2
Green, Benny, 225n.12, 233n.1
Greenhalgh, Ron, 185
Greer, Germaine, 31, 162n.28
Grey, Charles, 208
Grillo, John, 167
Grosse, Gordon, 193
Guard, Pippa, 62
Guinness, Alec, 194

Hagloch, Susan B., 227
Hallett, Charles, 160n.6
Hallett, Elaine, 160n.6
Hardy, Thomas: *Tess of the d'Urbervilles*, 224
Hawkes, Terence, 33, 161n.35
Hawkins, Gerald S., 216, 225nn. 9 and 10
Henn, T. R., 215, 224n.2
Hinman, Charlton, 163n.12
Homan, Sidney, 160n.1
Hordern, Michael, 20, 76, 98, 148, 167, 173, 175, 176, 185, 190, 197, 198, 208
Hoskins, Bob, 208

Hughes, Catherine, 227
Hughes, Raymond, 167, 178, 179, 180, 181
Hunter, G. K., 36, 143, 162n.38, 165n.14
Hurt, John, 102, 168, 189, 191, 219, 229, 236

Ibsen, Henrik: *Hedda Gabler*, 166n.1
Inge, William: *Bus Stop*, 209; *Come Back, Little Sheba*, 188, 193
International Shakespeare Congress, Berlin (1986), 36
Ionesco, Eugene, 71
Irving, Henry, 193, 215, 225n.7, 233n.4
Isenberg, Si, 194–96

Jacobi, Derek, 16
Jaffa, Harry V., 27–28, 59, 161nn. 14, 15, 16, and 17, 163n.51
Jaspers, Karl, 223, 226n.28
Javachef, Christo, 177
Johnson, Samuel, 31, 97, 162n.28
Jones, Emrys, 161n.6
Jorgens, Jack J., 224n.3, 229, 231

Kean, Charles, 162n.31
Kemp, Jeremy, 168, 188, 192, 220
Kendrick, T. D., 225nn. 7 and 21
Kermode, Frank, 162n.35, 224, 226n.34
Kimbrough, R. Alan, 226–33
Kitchen, Michael, 129, 167
Kott, Jan, 71
Kozintsev, Grigori, 190, 215, 222, 225n.20, 226n.27, 227, 228, 229, 231
Krauss, Werner, 142
Kurosawa, Akira: *Ran*, 227–28

Lang, Robert, 168
Lapotaire, Jane, 144
Laughton, Charles, 142, 215
Leech, Clifford, 164n.3, 165n.19, 225n.20
Leighton, Margaret, 194
Lesser, Anton, 98, 113, 148, 167, 182–83
Limouze, Henry S., 205n.10
Lindsay, Robert, 132, 168, 192, 218, 220, 235

Lowrey, Colin, 167, 176–78

McGuire, Philip C., 146–47, 150, 165nn. 18 and 21, 166nn. 22, 23, and 24
Mack, Maynard, 215, 224n.4, 225n.5
McKellen, Ian, 232
McKern, Leo, 117, 168, 191, 217, 229, 235
Mackintosh, Mary, 226n.27
McLeod, Randall, 163nn. 4, 5, and 10, 164n.12
McLuhan, Marshall, 33, 162n.34
Macready, William Charles, 215, 225n.7
MacVicar, Bill, 227
Malone, Edmond, 127
Mantzius, Karl, 142
Manvell, Roger, 200, 205nn. 7 and 8, 229
Margeson, J. M. R., 165n.19, 225n.20
Marlowe, Christopher: *Edward II*, 232–33
Marowitz, Charles, 200, 215, 222, 224n.1
Mary Tudor (Queen Mary I), 26, 28
Mason, William, 221
Matthau, Walter, 210
Meagher, John C., 146, 165nn. 19 and 20
Mercator, Gerardus, 33
Messina, Cedric, 207
Meyrick, Samuel Rush, 226n.23
Middlemass, Frank, 43, 98, 167, 173, 174, 175, 176, 219
Millard, Barbara, 205–14
Miller, Jonathan, 20, 42, 46, 49, 60, 79, 100, 112, 114–16, 121, 128, 147, 163n.48, 167, 172–85, 194, 197–205, 215–16, 219, 221, 222
Miller-Timmins, Derek, 167
Moiseiwitsch, Tanya, 167, 185, 188, 196
Morrell, Roy, 223, 226n.30
Muir, Kenneth, 161n.7, 163n.10, 164n.12, 224
Mullen, Michael, 214nn. 1 and 12
Myerscough-Jones, David, 178

Nero, 96
Niall, Ian: *Country Matters*, 186

Nightingale, Benedict, 225nn. 6 and 14, 228
Nunn, Trevor, 145

Oates, Joyce Carol, 223, 226n.29
Occhiogrosso, Frank, 234–39
O'Connor, John J., 227
Odell, George C. D., 225n.7
Olivier, Laurence, 20, 59, 102, 153, 156, 168, 185, 187–204, 209, 211–12, 213, 215–39
O'Meara, Jean M., 162n.28
Orbison, Tucker, 215–26, 229, 233n.2
Oregon Shakespearean Festival (1985), 16, 145
Osborne, John: *The Entertainer*, 193; *Look Back in Anger*, 193
Owen, A. L., 221, 222, 225n.10

Papp, Joseph, 209
Pasternak, Boris, 190
Penn, Irving, 177
Perret, Marion, 196–97, 225nn. 17 and 19, 229
Perrett, Wilfred, 32, 40, 161n.18, 162nn. 32, 39, and 43
Petherbridge, Edward, 168
Philip of Spain, 26
Piggott, Stuart, 226nn. 23 and 26
Pinter, Harold: *The Collection*, 188
Pliny the Younger, 225n.21
Plowright, David, 167, 185, 187–88, 192, 194–95, 198, 233n.3
Plowright, Joan, 192, 194
Proudfoot, Richard, 221, 222, 225n.16

Quarto (1608), 19, 36, 37, 40, 41, 67, 75, 83, 101, 122, 126, 127, 138, 141, 142–43, 145, 146, 149, 150, 156, 161n.13, 162n.31, 163nn. 4, 5, and 10, 164n.12, 165n.13. See also Folio (1623)
Quayle, Anthony, 211

Reagan, Nancy, 190
Reagan, Ronald, 190
Redgrave, Michael, 142
Redmond, James, 225n.16
Reinhardt, Max, 204
Ressover, Fredric, 214n.4
Ribman, Ronald: *The Ceremony of Innocence*, 186–87

Richardson, Lois, 185
Rigg, Diana, 85, 168, 188, 189, 192, 217, 229, 236
Rintoul, David, 108, 110
Roberts, Tony, 210
Robertson, Toby, 232–33
Rodway, Norman, 113, 167, 183
Rose, Lloyd, 233n.3
Rosenberg, Marvin, 37, 62, 69, 72, 142, 162nn. 31 and 40, 163nn. 3 and 11, 164n.13, 165nn. 11 and 12
Rowe, Nicholas, 162n.31
Royal Shakespeare Company, 122, 145, 215, 225n.6
Ruskin, Ian, 168
Rutherford, Ward, 225n.8, 226n.33

Sardee, Lou, 539n
Scofield, Paul, 190, 215, 218, 221, 229
Scott, Paul: *The Jewel in the Crown*, 188
Sewall, Richard, 216, 219, 225n.11
Shakespeare, William, *King Lear*, scenes in: *1.1*, 18, 23–60, 61, 62, 63, 64, 66, 68, 69, 70, 73, 75, 77–78, 78–79, 86, 87, 90, 92, 151, 152, 158, 162n.31, 165n.13, 202–3; *1.2*, 30, 49–50, 70, 92, 93; *1.3*, 64, 69, 75, 77, 84, 163n.5; *1.4*, 18, 19, 61–90, 93, 109; *2.1*, 69, 75, 80, 87, 92; *2.2*, 69, 75, 80, 87, 92; *2.3*, 93; *2.4*, 19, 61–90, 92; *3.4*, 110, 126; *3.5*, 92; *3.6*, 19, 91–104, 146; *3.7*, 61, 62, 69, 74, 75, 82, 88, 89, 92; *4.1*, 83, 105, 107, 108; *4.2*, 61, 106, 136; *4.3*, 106; *4.4*, 106; *4.5*, 106; *4.6*, 19, 93, 96, 105–21, 136, 139; *4.7*, 73, 92; *5.1*, 61, 126; *5.3*, 16, 19, 55, 61, 89, 92, 112, 122–34, 135–57, 238
Shakespeare, William, other works by: *Antony and Cleopatra*, 177; *As You Like It*, 211, 214nn. 3 and 7; *Coriolanus*, 162n.38; *Cymbeline*, 162n.29; *Hamlet*, 15, 16, 41, 109, 190, 204, 225n.20; *1 Henry IV*, 33, 211; *Henry V*, 162n.37, 190, 197, 204; *Henry VIII*, 36; *Julius Caesar*, 36, 162n.28; *Love's Labor's Lost*, 172; *Macbeth*, 139, 160n.6, 163n.6, 165n.1, 190, 194, 211; *Measure for Measure*, 208; *The Merchant of Venice*, 194, 209; *A Mid-*

summer *Night's Dream*, 178, 204, 208–9; *Othello*, 177, 178, 179, 189, 204; *Richard II*, 176, 208, 232; *Richard III*, 190; *The Taming of the Shrew*, 177, 178, 209, 210, 214, 214n.7; *The Tempest*, 162n.37, 164n.1; *Troilus and Cressida*, 177, 178; *The Winter's Tale*, 20–21, 164n.1
Shand, G. B., 31, 36, 38–39, 40, 162nn. 30, 39, and 42
Shaw, George Bernard, 142; *Heartbreak House*, 193
Shaw, Glen Byam, 164n.2
Shaw, John, 137–38, 165nn. 3 and 4
Shrapnel, John, 98, 148, 167, 173, 178, 181–82
Silverman, Fred, 188
Simon, John, 228, 233n.1
Skoller, Donald, 229
Sly, Christopher, 210
Smith, Charles Hamilton, 226n.33
Smith, Ronn, 185–87, 226n.23, 229
Sobran, Joseph, 233n.5
Stewart, Patrick, 122, 123
Stonehenge, 131, 152, 156, 179, 186, 189, 191, 194–95, 197, 198–99, 201, 211–13, 215–16, 217, 221–22 223, 224, 225nn. 7 and 9, 229, 231, 233n.2, 235, 238. *See also* Druids
Stonehouse, Roy, 53, 167, 185, 186–87, 188, 191, 192, 194–97, 211–12, 229–30
Stratford [Shakespeare] Festival (Ontario), 15, 209, 210
Stratford-upon-Avon, 164n.2
Styan, J. L., 164n.1
Sulik, Boleslaw: *Three Days in Szczecin*, 186
Sutton, Shaun, 167, 205n.1, 207
Suzman, Janet, 158, 166n.1

Tate, Nahum, 225n.6

Taylor, Gary, 161nn. 7 and 13, 163nn. 4 and 48, 164n.2
Tchaikovsky, Peter Ilich: *Swan Lake*, 206
Teague, Frances, 36, 162n.38
Threlfall, David, 102, 117, 168, 192, 237
Treays, John, 167, 178, 179
True Chronicle Historie of King Leir (1605), 29, 39–40, 61
Trussler, Simon, 224n.1
Turner, Victor, 94–95, 164n.7
Tutin, Dorothy, 85, 168, 189, 191–92, 217, 236

Urkowitz, Steven, 67, 161n.7, 163nn. 9 and 10, 164n.12, 233n.2

Verdi, Giuseppe: *La Traviata*, 206

Warren, Michael, 161nn. 7 and 13, 163nn. 4 and 48, 164n.2
Warren, Roger, 164n.2
Watergate, 176
Waters, Harry, 167
Waugh, Evelyn: *Brideshead Revisited*, 188
Wells, Stanley, 161n.7, 209, 219, 223, 225n.15, 229, 233n.4
Weston, David, 167
White, Chris, 185
Williams, Tennessee: *Cat on a Hot Tin Roof*, 188, 193
Wilton, Penelope, 76, 167, 173, 180
Winner, Michael, 189
Wolfit, Donald, 233n.4
Woolen, Peter, 229
Worth, Charles Frederick, 180
Woudhuysen, H. R., 225n.18

Zeffirelli, Franco, 206, 228
Zitner, Sheldon P., 201, 205n.9